His life set the pattern . . .
of Kennedy greatness
. . . and Kennedy tragedy.

Loved by women, admired by men, he was the natural heir to his father's driving ambition, the acknowledged figure to be the first Kennedy to assume the presidency.

He lived a dazzling life, he died a hero's death, he left a legacy of excellence for future Kennedys to aspire to.

YOUNG JOE, THE FORGOTTEN KENNEDY

"It explains as much about this dynastic and incredible family as any book—and does the job with dash, style, romance and action."
—*Chicago Sunday Tribune*

"A HAUNTING BOOK . . . one which captures the spirit of the family as well if not better than anyone who has written about these extraordinary individuals."
—Mrs. Ethel Kennedy, in a letter to the author

THE LOST PRINCE:
Young Joe, The Forgotten Kennedy

Hank Searls

BALLANTINE BOOKS • NEW YORK

*The author wishes to thank the following individuals
and organizations for their permission to use the
photographs appearing in this book:*

Senator Edward M. Kennedy
Mrs. Arthur H. Bastien
Thomas Killefer
James Simpson
Mark Soden
Wide World Photos
Brown Brothers
Underwood & Underwood
U.S. Department of the Interior (National Park Service)
United Press International
Bradford Bachrach
Boston Herald-Traveler
Keystone Press Agency Inc.
Alfred Eisenstaedt Life Magazine © Time Inc.
U.S. Government Photos
Department of the Navy
Fox Photos
Imperial War Museum
Pictorial Parade

*The author also gratefully acknowledges the help in
research of Catherine Greene, Bill Adler, and Captain
E. V. Crangle, U.S.N.*

Library of Congress Catalog Card Number: 73-93468

ISBN 0-345-27395-8

Manufactured in the United States of America

First Ballantine Books Edition: October 1977

DEDICATED TO
those of Joe Kennedy's
squadron mates—
Grumbles, Parish, Ryan, Barton, Moore,
Byrnes, Williams, and their crews—
who died less spectacularly than he, far
from help under Luftwaffe guns over the
English Channel or the Bay of Biscay or
in Irish fog against Great Skellig Rock,
where no one was at all.

ACKNOWLEDGMENTS

THIS book owes much to many: to the late Senator Robert Kennedy, who speculated for a few moments, swallowed his doubts, and arranged to open his brother Joe's files; to Ethel Kennedy, who took time that sad and harried summer at Hyannis to show me Joe's favorite home; to Mrs. Rose Kennedy and Joe's sisters, who searched their memories in what must have been a painful quest; to Senator Edward Kennedy, who did that too and helped in other ways as well. And the book owes thanks to teachers and governesses and schoolmates and friends and men who flew with Joe, to those who liked him and those who didn't. It owes even a debt to the naval establishment, which after twenty-five years bared top-secret documents of a mission tarnished with human error, so that the truth of his death might be known.

No one asked the slightest personal favor in the writing, neither the woman he finally loved, who for that, among other reasons, shall be nameless, nor those who might be blamed for his death. No one asked favors for Joe Kennedy, Jr., either. Neither brothers, sisters, nor mother asked to see the manuscript, apparently trusting his virtues to outweigh his faults if the picture was true. So it is no one's fault but my own if it is not.

HANK SEARLS

CONTENTS

Someday I'll be President.

JOSEPH P. KENNEDY, JR.

*I'm only trying to fill his
shoes. . . . If anything happened
to me tomorrow, Bobby would run
for my seat in the Senate. And
if Bobby died, our younger
brother Teddy would take over
for him.*

SENATOR JOHN F. KENNEDY

ONE

SILVER SPOON

1

THE evening was warm for England, even England in August. Despite the secrecy veiling their mission, the weather was judged hot enough to leave the door of the briefing hut open, so the big, blue-eyed Navy flier and his copilot in the first row could glance past the weather officer and see their doomed bomber squatting distantly across the vast Suffolk airdrome. She sagged huge, white, and clumsy in the late-setting summer sun, already so crammed with explosives that she seemed about to squash flat her ridiculous tires. Two broomsticks, painted black to fool attacking Messerschmitts, poked from what had once been her tail turret. Odd clusters of antennae stuck askew from her back, as if she had been overcome by pigmy archers. The Negro U.S. Army detachment loading her had finished and gone to chow. An armed Air Corps private sauntering near her and a red-haired Navy mechanic checking her tie-down lines seemed at this safe distance Lilliputians entrusted with a tethered giant. Packed carefully into her gut was the largest explosive charge ever assembled by man.

The pilot in the briefing hut was on temporary duty from a U.S. antisubmarine squadron to the south, in Devon. He was almost too handsome: just under six feet and broad-shouldered, with dark chestnut hair and the sapphire eyes of his family and a curving patrician nose and teeth straightened at Choate School. He had a remarkable lopsided grin, devastating to women. He was barely twenty-nine, unmarried, and a millionaire. He was well traveled: he had seen Moscow under Stalin and Berlin under Hitler and had faced death before Communist rifles against a wall in Madrid. He radiated energy and seemed always in motion. He could be arrogant, warm, abrasive, charming. His humor was dry and sometimes biting. He had met the King of England and knew Roosevelt well, but he seldom talked of these things, which would have built walls between himself and his fellows. In important matters he was honest, but he often embellished the truth for the sake of a story. In an archaic way, he was devout as Lancelot: he knelt every night to pray, and if roommates smiled at this, the hell with them. He was Harvard *cum laude;* he liked Santayana and Somerset Maugham and claimed to have met them; he had studied under Laski.

His voice was strident Boston, quite often in these last few days raised in irritation. For almost a year he had hazarded English weather, fog-shrouded barrage balloons, and fake German radio beacons to fly unescorted wavetop patrols off a hostile continent, with no protection from Messerschmitts out of Brest or Saint-Nazaire but his own gunners and sometimes the clouds under which he flew. He had been recently attacked, and a few weeks ago, against orders, had strayed close enough to German-held Guernsey to draw flak. Now he was flight-weary and tortured with a personal problem.

He was afraid that he was falling in love. Since adolescence he had maneuvered humorously and with growing skill through a minefield of golden girls from Back Bay, café society, show business, and the British aristocracy. He intended some day to be the first Catholic President of the United States, admitted it freely, and preferred for a while to travel swiftly and alone. But neither experience nor ambition had conferred immunity against a girl he had met last year in London's chaos, and in a few months he had grown so close to her that some of his squadron mates thought that if he survived this last mission he would be married within the week. They thought wrong: the woman was already married.

He had been invited this weekend to a country home in Yorkshire, and the girl would be there. Despite the overwhelming shadow of his strange mission—of the first six Army pilots to try it during the past ten days, one had been killed, one had lost an arm, one had broken his back, and only three had escaped with minor injuries—his yearning to be with her plagued him and made him impatient and jumpy.

His name was Joseph Patrick Kennedy, Jr. He was known to the better informed of the men in the briefing hut as the oldest son of the former ambassador to England. He was a lieutenant. So was Wilford Willy, the copilot beside him, but Willy was regular Navy, from a different world: his home base was in the States, or wherever his special talents took him, and he had been in England less than a month. Willy was thirty-five, a wiry, cheerful ex-enlisted man who liked to party; he had a moustache, a large hook nose, a fox smile, and crooked teeth. He had been married for almost ten years to a sweet and gutty girl in Fort Worth; they had two sons and a tiny daughter. He had only a high-school education. He had found his home in the Navy at seventeen and expected, when the war was over, to revert to chief petty officer.

Pilot and copilot waited while the meteorologist wrapped up his forecast: a calm Channel and good weather by sunset tomorrow at the target, which was a V-1 launching pad in the Calais area, exact location secret for now even to them. An Air Corps intelligence officer took the lectern to address Kennedy, Willy, and those who would act as their escort, including the President's second son Elliott, who would fly wing on them in a Mosquito photo plane. Colonel Roosevelt's detachment had today sneaked some fast infrared shots of the target, said to be a huge concrete bunker with steel doors thirty feet high from which led short railroad tracks aligned on London. Prints would be ready tomorrow at the final briefing if the weather was right, at which time location of the top-secret target would be divulged.

The intelligence officer gave a short, dry recap of the toll of flying bombs on London: of almost ten thousand buzz bombs launched in the eight weeks since the night when the first had come popping and snorting across the Channel like a runaway truck on a downgrade, one thousand had slammed into the city. The rest had gone astray by themselves or been shot down or tumbled by pursuing fighters, which would dive on them at 350 miles per hour, join up in formation, and tap their tiny ailerons with their own wingtips. London casualties were already twenty thousand; five thousand had been killed. Worse seemed to be in store. Buzz bombs were simply jet-powered gyro-stabilized aircraft without pilots, launched with a prayer and carrying a standard German one-ton bomb, but a pure German test rocket named the "V-2," Buck Rogers from nose to tail, had recently crashed into Sweden. Allied intelligence, suspecting that it was radio-controlled, predicted an attack by an unstoppable, ultimate weapon if some way were not designed to jam its guidance electronically or to knock out the launching sites.

Those who launched the V-1's from their invulnerable bunkers seemed far more culpable than the German bomber pilots who had bombed the city in the Battle of Britain. The Luftwaffe fliers had after all been risking their own lives; the madmen in the launching sites were invulnerable so far, and the Allies intended to show them how it felt to be the target of automated fate.

As a pep talk, the rundown of casualties was wasted on Joe Kennedy. With the girl he cherished and with William Randolph Hearst, Jr., he had already seen the damage a V-1 could do near her home. No one had been hurt in that particular explosion, but the potential was obvious. He needed no incentive anyway, only good weather at the target, wherever it was. His main worry was that the Army Air Corps would try again and sneak in a successful attack before he scored first for the Navy. His copilot, Willy, and the rest of their little unit wanted the Navy first out of simple service loyalty, but Joe had a family reason, besides.

When the session was over, he climbed on his Raleigh English racing bike and whirred across the concrete to gaze as he often did at dusk on his own country's first answer to the age of rocket warfare. The sun had dropped to the gentle East Anglian hills and for a few moments his plane was etched in gold. Someone running up a distant engine throttled it back, and it coughed and died and left rare silence; the scent of summer hay drifted from drowsy fields beyond the chain link fence. A guard dog barked. Joe spoke to Red Bradfield, the little mechanic he had brought with him from his home base. Bradfield mentioned a faulty magneto on the number-three engine; Joe nodded and changed the subject. He had been lending Red his bike to visit a local pub and had fixed a flat just before the briefing session so that it would be available tonight. Bradfield thanked him, but did not think he would go.

Together they studied the aircraft. From her bulbous

Plexiglas nose, instead of bow guns, stared a primitive TV camera, so that, head on, she was a popeyed cyclops with a lens for a pupil. The six ill-fated Army pilots who had taken off on similar missions during the last ten days had been flying "Weary-Willies"; like Joe Kennedy, their Fortresses were tired and on their second tour. But this plane was only five months old and a virgin to combat and had come all the way from Philadelphia for her hour of glory, perhaps a measure of the superior concern of the naval establishment for the men who flew its aircraft. She was otherwise, like the planes of his own squadron, an Army Liberator modified in San Diego for Navy patrol, and the Navy called her type the PB4Y-1 patrol plane. An Army pilot would have named her *Petunia*, maybe, or *Bucket of Blood*, or *Kennedy's Crock*. No such heroics for a naval aviator, though: the Navy had given her a bureau number, 32271, and painted on her fuselage a massive side number, T-11; these sufficed. Only seagoing naval vessels deserved a name. An aircraft, although she might be referred to as "old four-boat" or "that frigging eight-boat," was depersonalized by edict and tradition.

Cheated of a name and even the Air Corps Petty-girl which rode the breast of so many Army aircraft, the guarded plane was further victimized. Luftwaffe pressure had already eased on her sisters patrolling the Channel and the Bay of Biscay, for Eisenhower was taking back the airfields in southern France. Arriving so late in the combat zone, she should have lived to end her days baking in a line of lucky veterans at Litchfield Park on the Arizona desert. But her chance of survival was precisely zero.

After her transatlantic flight she had been gutted at Kennedy's base in Devon, robbed of all but minimum radio and radar, and stripped of guns and even her copilot's seat: tomorrow Willy would have to stand behind Joe Kennedy for takeoff. There would be room for only two. Filling her belly, stacked neatly on oak-strengthened plywood decks in her sealed bomb bay, stowed on the flight deck where the radioman and navigator normally sat, lashed even in the tunnel leading to the disarmed bow turret, were boxes of explosives: twelve tons of Torpex, a charge almost twice as powerful per pound as TNT: 374 crates of it, now that the Negro troops had finished. The Torpex was fused intricately and cleverly to explode on contact. Tomorrow, if weather finally permitted, Joe Kennedy would gentle her four throttles forward. With the first movement of his hand her death would be assured. She would jounce faster and faster down the runway; once airborne, no matter what, it would have taken a kamikaze to try to land her again.

Joe Kennedy was no kamikaze and had no intention of trying to land her again. He was bigger than Willy and, wearing two chutes, it would be a tight squeeze past the nose wheel, but he was scheduled, once certain operations were concluded, to crawl forward and follow his copilot out of the bow.

Bradfield felt a responsibility to protect him from possible Army incompetence: that was why he was here. Except for one incident during the loading last night he had seen no foul-ups so far, but he was depressed. The number-three engine had shown an excessive drop-off in rpm during the magneto check at morning runup; he had dried out the mag with carbon dioxide, as the Air Corps did often in this damp corner of England, but he was dissatisfied. Last week's attrition on the Air Corps pilots launched from this same field bothered him: one dead and two maimed out of six made a fifty-percent casualty rate that was not reassuring.

The light southwesterly breeze was rich with the smell of damp manure from the farms behind the fence. They watched the big Army Fortresses from Knettishall Airdrome lumber back across the Suffolk coast from the afternoon work over France, saw them drop into the setting sun like planes in a grade-B movie. It was 8 P.M. and still light enough to read. When the summer twilight finally deepened and turned the plane from gold to tin, Joe squeezed Bradfield's arm, perhaps to cheer him. He pedaled back past the gray concrete operations building and stopped at the weather desk. The forecast for tomorrow along the French coast had suddenly deteriorated.

Depressed, he cycled back to his Quonset. There was a phone in the hut and eight officers living there and the room partitions were thin. He had been calling the girl so often that, if everyone in the Quonset had not thought he was planning a wedding, he would have been embarrassed. He got through to Sledmere, the country home of her hostess, Lady Virginia Sykes, near the village bearing the astonishing name—and telephone exchange—of Wetwang. He spoke to Lady Sykes, herself a prewar flame of his, and confirmed his expected arrival on Sunday: today was Friday. He did not of course mention that it all

depended on his finishing his secret mission. Then the girl
came to the phone and he talked to her very quietly and
when he was through he went to his room, where he had a
stock of immensely valuable eggs, lying gloriously in a box
shaped like a treasure chest which went with him everywhere. He had a bucket of coal, too, filched from a
guarded coal pile. He began to scramble some eggs.

Eating them with his roommate, an owlish, hard-rock
Baptist named Jim Simpson, he heard from B.B.C. that
Third Army troops were crossing the Loire at Nantes and
heading south toward the Breton naval base at Rochelle.
Anything heading south was good news, but incredibly
Patton's tanks had wheeled and were simultaneously
sweeping counterclockwise from Le Mans toward the
north, too. Two months after the Utah and Omaha beach-
heads, Eisenhower seemed tonight to be breaking from his
Normandy cul-de-sac and to be pocketing von Kluge's 7th
Army and Panzer Group West in the process. This morn-
ing the B.B.C. had talked of 100,000 Germans in the
snare: tonight it upped the estimate to half a million if
Patton could smash seventy-five miles northward to
Bradley or to the Canadians at Falaise.

Joe switched off the radio. Now he had not only the Air
Corps to race, but the dog-faced U.S. infantry as well.
Summer fog might drift in to his target and hang for
weeks; if he didn't get on with his mission quickly, the
Army would gobble up Le Havre, Boulogne, Calais—the
whole Channel coast—and there would be no buzz-bomb
sites to hit.

When the eggs were finished he strolled a few yards
through the blackout to the "ablution" hut, washed, and
returned to his room. He knelt and prayed and then he
climbed into his bunk and apparently slept.

2

Squeezed into a row of identical brick-faced flats, the
apartment at 151 Meridian Street in East Boston stands
above a haberdashery and on Friday reeks of frying fish.
Gusts of wind swirl tiny cyclones in the entrance; the
stairway is dark and gloomy but the lace curtains above
the busy street are kept strenuously clean. Joe Junior's
father, someday to be the first Irish-American ambassador

to the Court of St. James's, was born here in 1888. The "Founding Father" was the son of Patrick Kennedy, whose own father, landing in 1848 when East Boston was Noddles Island, had become a cooper, planted his seed in a new and hostile world, and died in poverty of cholera when Patrick was one year old. Patrick in his early teens had worked as a stevedore on the docks while his widowed mother scratched a living in a notions store within sound of the wharves. By his twenty-eighth year he had fought his way two blocks east of the waterfront. He had saved his wages and moved up a step: he had married a pretty girl named Mary Hickey, one of whose brothers was a police captain and another a doctor. By the time the future ambassador arrived, his father owned a cheap tavern across the water on Haymarket Square.

Patrick was a big, blue-eyed practical man who wore rimless glasses and a handlebar moustache. He did not drink behind his bar, he listened. He did not merely sympathize with a man fresh from Cork whose wife was sick, he lent money. He did not suggest a job for a widow, he found her one. He laughed at other people's jokes, telling few himself. His customers repaid him with their loyalty and finally their votes. He won a seat in the Massachusetts House of Representatives; by the time the future ambassador was four, his father was a state senator and a power in Boston politics. He accepted appointive office when it was offered, both from Yankee and Irish mayors. He was fire commissioner, wire commissioner, election commissioner—the last a touchy job in a neighborhood where men often voted from their graves, usually for Patrick Kennedy's candidates.

He wanted no elective office higher than the one he held; he had found that he spoke poorly in public, so he disliked campaigning and was content to let others wear the trappings—Lomasney, Honeyfitz Fitzgerald of the North End, Smiling Jim Donovan of the South End, and Joe Corbett of Charleston. But Patrick Kennedy was in the inner circle—the "Board of Strategy"—and when he talked the "Board" listened, because he could deliver the East Boston votes. He had, like most Irish politicians of the day, considerable elasticity in matters electoral. His son Joe once overheard two ward heelers reporting to his father that "we voted one hundred and twenty-eight times today," and he saw no sign of displeasure on his father's face. The Irishman's vote was his only weapon in his assault on the Yankee holding the high ground; who could blame him for firing it more than once?

Patrick ruled his family as he ruled his political diocese: compassionately but firmly. He prospered, bought a liquor-distributing business with an office on High Street in central Boston, invested in a coal-mining company, and helped organize two banks in East Boston, one of them called Columbia Trust. He saw no reason why Yankee bankers should have the use of his Irish neighbors' miniscule savings when Patrick Kennedy's family could profit from them equally. He moved the household from the clatter of Meridian Street to 165 Webster a few blocks away. There was a park nearby for Joe and his sisters Loretta and Margaret; the street was tree-shaded and the house halfway up a hill. Now the future ambassador, lanky and redheaded in his teens, could look down from his back-bedroom window past the outhouses to the wharves. Tall-masted down easters such as the *Sovereign of the Seas,* built in the sixties at the same East Boston docks, were still fighting for lumber, grain, and nitrate trade against steam competition; they nestled below, reeking of tar and hemp, Horn-battered and 120 days out of San Francisco. The big Cunarders from Liverpool berthed there too: County Wexford, which Joe's grandfather had left at twenty-five and which his father had never seen, seemed not so far beyond Deer Island, ten miles east. But Joe had little time to look back on his roots; he was too bright and active, and he was the subject of great expectations.

His father disliked ostentation. To flaunt his relative wealth among his poorer neighbors would at best have provoked their snickers—being Irish they professed nothing but amusement for the feats of other Irish. At worst it would have cost him friendships he valued. He conformed to most of the Irish-Catholic mores: early Mass, big Sunday dinner, fraternal meetings; he would even sip whiskey at a wake. But on one matter he would not follow the herd: early years in a Catholic grammar school were all right—he had gone to one himself for what little formal education he had—but Joe would go to prep school where the best prep school was, parochial or not, and Patrick would take his chances with the disapproval of the community.

The oldest, best, and toughest prep school in the city was Boston Latin, founded in 1635. It was a one-cent

ferry ride across the Ship Canal. If Joe could graduate
from it, even Harvard might not be too bright a goal.
Patrick had the money if Joe had the brains.

The future wolf of Wall Street had the brains, but used
them in only one field, mathematics. He was weak in
Latin, English, and history. But he was a charmer, cap-
tivating teachers and his Yankee fellow students. With his
warm smile and vibrant energy he became colonel of the
Cadet Regiment and marched it to victory in the city drill
competition; he was tall enough for basketball and played
three years; he managed the football team. He was captain of the Boston Latin baseball team for two years. He
was a poor loser, fighting out every adverse decision with
the umpire, but this trait was no fault at all in the eyes of
East Boston, where he became a minor hero. He batted
an incredible .667 his senior year and won the Mayor's
Cup, which was presented by his father's occasional
friend, Mayor Honeyfitz Fitzgerald. He was elected sen-
ior-class president. He graduated a year late because of
academic difficulties.

Joe had another interest, money. His family obviously
needed no contribution from him, but most of his friends
had to work, and he refused to be excluded from the
game. Besides, money was demonstrably useful; without
his father's moderate success at accumulating it, they
would still be living over the men's store.

He hawked newspapers. He clerked in a clothing store.
At the bank he thought of as his father's—Columbia
Trust—he ran errands. For tips, he overcame enough of
his Boston-Irish distrust of Jews to light stoves for the
Orthodox on holy days. He made his first reconnaissance
of show business at twelve when he put to sea on the
sight-seeing boat *Excelsior,* selling tickets to rubbernecks
for a cruise through Dewey's triumphant Great White
Fleet, anchored in Boston Harbor after the Battle of
Manila Bay.

At fifteen he organized a baseball team, the Assump-
tions, named for his local church. He dunned the congre-
gation for uniforms; when the team began to draw
crowds, Joe Kennedy hired a ball park and they left the
sandlots. They showed a profit their first year. The entertainment business was almost too easy; he branched into
food. Roast squab was a popular East Boston Sunday
dish. Joe had a pigeon-raising friend, and an idea. He
went into the first of his rare partnerships. They smuggled

his friend's birds into the flocks on Boston Common and rode back home across the Ship Canal to find their original birds had returned with guests. Their investment had flown back with one- or two-hundred-percent interest. No one could tell a municipal squab from a private one; the venture was as low a risk as any Joe Kennedy was later to undertake, and the leverage remarkable.

The prestige of Boston Latin outweighed his mediocre grades and he was admitted to Harvard. He refused to commute with the "untouchables," as day students were called; he lived in the Yard. His personality and quick smile almost outbalanced his unfashionable forebears. He could never make the better "final" clubs, Porcellian or Fly, but he made Hasty Pudding and in his senior year roomed with Bob Potter, a good athlete from an old Philadelphia family. Joe did not snub the rare Irishmen in his class, though; he cultivated them, more at ease with them and with their sisters than with his Back Bay classmates and the Boston debs.

He grew to love music, even the classics at the Friday symphonies. He was popular with those he esteemed and became competent academically. He learned to channel his acquisitive drive toward acceptable undergraduate ends until a crisis arose; then his stubborn will took over.

More than anything else, he wanted a letter in baseball. He hurt his arm against Navy, and had somehow lost his batting eye. Charles "Chick" McLaughlin, a year ahead of him, beat him out for first baseman and then changed to pitcher and became captain of the team. In 1911, Joe's junior year, Joe failed even to make the squad. He raged, and some of the disappointment colored his feelings toward McLaughlin, who seemed to reciprocate. But in the Yale game of McLaughlin's senior year, to the surprise of those who noticed, Joe appeared for the first time that spring and sat in uniform on the Harvard bench. In the ninth inning the game was on ice with two out and Harvard leading four to one. McLaughlin inexplicably stopped the play and asked the coach to put in Kennedy at first base. The coach complied. The batter hit a grounder and was thrown out to Joe at first. Joe pocketed the ball. Leaving the field, McLaughlin asked for it. Joe shook his head. He was jovial enough, but adamant: he had made the putout, he deserved the trophy. He never gave it up and no one forgot. Harvard legend explains McLaughlin's strange magnanimity and even perhaps Joe's ingratitude: some of Pat Kennedy's political friends, knowing that McLaughlin intended to apply for a Boston theater license after graduation, had bluntly pressured him to let the pride of East Boston get his Harvard "H."

Joe had always been popular with girls, but only the best would do. She was Rose Fitzgerald, blue-eyed daughter of Honeyfitz, Mayor of Boston, from whom Joe had received the baseball cup five years before. They had met as children. When he was in high school, they had dated quietly, sensing that her father would disapprove. She was the youngest graduate of Dorchester High in the school's history. Her mother was a retiring woman and shy, so Rose acted often as her father's political hostess. She had met President McKinley, was a fine pianist, had traveled with her father to South America and Europe, and had considerable poise. When Sir Thomas Lipton, sixty-year-old self-made millionaire, had dropped a bombshell at a Copley Plaza Hotel party by naming her as the future Lady Lipton, she said pleasantly: "I won't accept you, Sir Thomas. I think you are altogether too fickle."

If Sir Thomas was too fickle or too old for Rose, Joe Kennedy was too young and poorly born for her father. Despite their occasional political enmity, Honeyfitz had not minded handing Patrick Kennedy's son the batting prize, but the hand of his beautiful daughter was another matter. He packed Rose off to a Prussian convent. Joe, whose family had moved up another notch, to Winthrop on the outskirts of Boston, simply worked harder. In his senior year he landed a paying job at Harvard as an assistant freshman football coach. With a partner, he bought a sight-seeing bus for six hundred dollars and went back into the rubberneck business, picking up tourists at South Station and yammering a fast routine through a megaphone as his partner drove the bus through the historic sites of Boston, Lexington, and Concord.

He graduated from Harvard in 1912. He had decided to try banking, but chose an indirect approach, since the Yankee banking chambers hardly welcomed Irish latecomers, Harvard graduates or not. As a senior he had had to drop accounting rather than flunk it, but this did not deter him: he took a qualifying examination and, with his father's influence behind him, became a state bank examiner at a starvation salary of $1,500 a year. The chance to inspect the books of the financial empires of Boston was, to a budding financier, recompense enough.

With his savings from the sight-seeing bus operation he bought one third of a real-estate investment company. This sideline prospered, but a crisis threatened elsewhere. A larger bank wanted Columbia Trust, and his father's voice in management was endangered by the threatened merger. Patrick had pried what cash he could from friends and relatives; he put the rest up to Joe. Joe charmed $45,000 out of Harvard friends, talked to stockholders, and girded for battle behind his proxies. The bigger bank, realizing that it would be defeated, gave up without a fight. Joe Kennedy, who had quietly vowed to make his first million by thirty-five, claimed his prize from the directors, who dutifully voted him his reward. This time it was not the game ball, but the whole ball game.

At twenty-five, trim, handsome, and clear-eyed, having vaulted years of struggle and executive intrigue, the future ambassador became the youngest bank president in the United States. The institution was tiny, there was nothing impressive about his cluttered office or rolltop desk, the salary was small, but the prestige in Irish Boston was enormous. Mayor Fitzgerald observed his daughter's suitor, marveled, and dropped his objections. His assent was probably academic anyway; Rose had returned from Prussia more independent than ever, organized an Irish counterpart of the Junior League, and at twenty had taken a seat on the Boston Public Library Examining Committee. She was perfectly capable of wedding whom she pleased, and he was Joe Kennedy.

They were married by Cardinal O'Connell in his private chapel on October 14, 1914. After a honeymoon at White Sulphur Springs they moved to a gray frame house on Beals Street in the quiet Boston suburb of Brookline. Joe paid $6,500 for the place. Still in debt from the stock battle, he had to go further into the red to finance the two-thousand-dollar down payment.

Rose's father had owned a stately Tudor summer home on a knoll commanding the beach at Hull, Nantasket, with a neat stucco guesthouse by the seawall in which Rose and her sisters had played. Honeyfitz would have owned it still, had he been able to stay out of Nantasket politics, but Hull was run by a tight political oligarchy, the Republican "Old Ring." It was an organization that for unabashed perfidy made his own Boston "Board of Strategy" look like a sewing circle. Honeyfitz, daring one summer as mayor of Boston to blast the "Ring" at a Hull town meeting, met frigid silence from the "ins," who then ordered a ditch five feet wide and seven deep dug around his mansion for an alleged municipal project. They left it there all summer. After years on the South Shore, the Fitzgeralds read the message accurately and sold out.

But Rose, who was already expecting by spring, was used to summers at the beach, and Hull was only a two-hour side-wheeler journey via the Nantasket line from Boston, or a trolley ride by land, if there was trouble at the bank. Dr. Frederick Goode, the chosen obstetrician, spent his summers at the beach anyway. Joe leased a big, airy gray house at 201 Beach Avenue on the strand of Kenburma and they settled down to wait.

They were not bored. There was the clean, breeze-cooled sand by day, and in the evenings there were always the great resort hotels a few blocks south. Across the Atlantic, British and Canadian troops were writhing under the first chlorine-gas attacks, the Kaiser was cutting the Russian lines in two, and the casualties had suddenly reached a million; but Nastasket in 1915 was a blend of Monte Carlo and Coney Island. Lorry wheels spun in the mud of Flanders; in Nantasket roulette wheels turned. In the paneled game rooms of the Atlantic House, where rooms were twenty dollars a day at a time when boat fare from New York to Boston was $2.50, dice rattled. The beach had the only liquor licenses from Boston to Provincetown.

Joe Kennedy seldom gambled, except when he could dictate the odds; he almost never drank. But he and Rose listened to John McCormack and George M. Cohan in the magnificent wooden Pacific House Hotel, watched the parade of sweeping skirts and straw boaters drift past the wide front porch of Villa Napoli. Joe, in plus fours, played the local courses. Their entertainment as Rose's time approached became still more domestic: family evenings with her sister Agnes at the piano, and summer friends singing the old songs and the new ones: "I Didn't Raise My Boy to Be a Soldier," "Has Anyone Here Seen Kelly?," "By the Light of the Silvery Moon." June and early July passed, and on July 25, 1915, a boy was born in an upstairs room of the boxy gray house. A month later he was christened at St. Ann's, a neat tile-roofed church a few blocks south. His godmother was his aunt Agnes and his godfather Joseph E. O'Connell, a prominent Boston "Board of Strategy" friend of Honeyfitz.

He was christened Joseph Patrick Kennedy, Jr. He was sturdy and healthy. All the rest of the summer the surf on Kenburma beach rumbled and swished in baby ears. His grandmother Hickey's father had come from Clonakilty Bay on the southern shore of Ireland; Joe would become a fair football player, a good student, a minor diplomat, an embryo politician, and a competent airman, but his real love would remain the sea.

2

EVERYONE in Palm Beach parks double, as in New York, but here the taxis are seven-passenger Cadillacs.

North Ocean Boulevard skirts the water. You glimpse one jungle-plagued mansion behind a broken stucco wall, but the vast, sparkling Palm Beach Country Club, equally old, proves by its beautiful maintenance that some property close to the waterfront is just too rich to be allowed to age. The golf course crosses the main street; a caddy holds up a club to stop traffic as an ancient foursome creaks across in electric carts.

The neighborhood around the country club is what Saratoga must have been in happier times, or, if you are a Californian, Pasadena in the thirties. The old man walking his mastiff should be in blazer and boater instead of Bermuda shorts. The palm-shadowed cars in the driveways should be LaSalle convertibles or Stutz Bearcats; T-Birds and the chauffeured Lincolns of today look out of place along the sleeping street.

The home on North Ocean Boulevard is 1923 Spanish, designed by Addison Mizner for Rodman Wanamaker of Philadelphia. It cost Joe Kennedy, Sr., $100,000 during the Depression. It is a long way from Meridian Street in East Boston or even Beach Avenue in Nantasket. Nevertheless it is elbow to elbow with its neighbors. It seems modest by comparison with most of them, though it embraces a swimming pool and a tennis court in its narrow boundaries. A Plymouth sits in its garage and only a

Chrysler lends a touch of affluence. Except for a green-and-white sign warning trespassers that the Palm Beach Police Department will not tolerate loitering here, the house is not distinguished from its mates. Fifteen hundred miles north, the Kennedy Hyannis compound squats behind a twenty-four-hour uniformed guard, complete with sentry box; here in Palm Beach a Negro gardener simply points his clippers at a pink door leading to a patio and you pass in and ring the house bell.

A cheerful gray-haired maid leads you across an airy red-tiled living room, which opens onto the beach and swimming pool, to a tiny study. The little den is crammed with Kennedy memorabilia: the President, Bobby and his children. The sire, in a silver frame, is a whispy Kodacolor ghost in a wheelchair clutching a grandchild. On the couch lies a mustard-colored pillow inscribed with an ode to friendship, kept perhaps as a reminder of lacier-curtained days.

Rose Kennedy arrives instantly. She is fragile but tanned from golf. It is almost impossible to believe that she is actually seventy-six. She wears a white sharkskin dress and a single strand of pearls. She is reserved and shy at first, avoiding your eye. The den is Joe Senior's province and Rose does not want him disturbed with memories of her oldest son; she is nervous and it is only when she checks with the burly young collegian who is his bodyguard and companion to make sure that Joe Senior will not come down that she decides finally to stay and use the room.

She sits on the couch with the mustard pillow, back straight—perhaps the convent school in Prussia—and talks of her first son. "He had a wonderful smile and a fine physique. He was always popular with the girls. He was a hard worker and would tackle things that he didn't like, whereas the President—John—was more interested in things that pleased him."

The voice, which a Brookline neighbor from before the days of affluence has told you was whiny (it is not) and professionally trained away from the Boston twang (it apparently is) becomes stronger after a drink of water. "The younger children worshiped Joe. He had everything. He didn't smoke or drink until he was twenty-one, and they saw that he didn't suffer from this. And it must have been embarrassing, in British homes, where he would be offered

a spot to drink, before the days of Coca-Cola and lemon-
ade; and cold, too, before central heating."

She remembers Joe as a child being a loner like herself.
"Kathleen—he called her 'Kick'—was closest to Joe, because our oldest daughter was retarded." John, she says,
always had a pal with him. Joe at first seldom did, and yet
Joe in later years was more outgoing than John. "John, I
always thought, would have ended on a foreign commission of some sort, or in an embassy. Because both boys,
you know, were trained in diplomacy. Or John thought at
one time that he might run a boys' school." A certain
cautious friendliness seeps through the reserve. "Joe liked
dogs. He had one named Satyr and he had to throw him
off the pier at Hyannis in a dogfight and had to dive in
after him. Joe's puppies were a problem."

She speaks more easily now, but after a while, as she
talks of her oldest son, her eyes seem to tire and to water
and it is time to go. Leaving, you hear her rebound and
call to the young man: "How does it look for a swim?"
She means not the pool but the surf, for the boy answers
from somewhere: "No, Mrs. Kennedy. Too many jellyfish,
too rough today."

She is strong-willed and possibly very stubborn, but she
defers.

2

Joe Junior's first real childhood home still stands at 83
Beals Street in Brookline. It is a three-story gray frame
house with wooden shutters and white trim. A memorial
to his next-younger brother, whose bronze profile on a
granite marker attests it to be his birthplace, squats outside. The late President seems amused and a little impatient at being here.

The hedges are carefully trimmed, the tiny lawn in back
is mowed. Similar houses face the street for blocks in
either direction; elms wave over them but nothing else
stirs as far as the eye can see. A view down the street is a
stereopticon look at World War I America. If North Ocean
Boulevard in Palm Beach longs for the return of the
Stutz, Beals Street listens for the clop of the milk wagon.

Joe arrived from Nantasket eight weeks old, in a travel-
ing basket and in style: his father had bought a new

Model T, arousing quiet envy and some comment on Irish
pushiness in a neighborhood of Anglo-Saxon Protestants.
Prejudice remains: "Bicycle Irish—give you a pain in the
ass."

On the second floor of the house were three bedrooms:
the back one, smallest, had been prepared as a nursery. In
it Joe was installed and in the adjoining bedroom his
ample, warm-hearted nurse, Katherine Conboy, an Old
Country woman who spoke with a brogue and believed in
leprechauns and elves and whom he was soon to christen
Kico. Off the master bedroom on the second floor was a
sewing room. Rose had a desk placed there. In it she
started her famous card file of family inoculations, dental
work, and doctors' appointments. Above, on the third
floor, were two more bedrooms; in one of them slept a
live-in seven-dollar-a-week maid. There was only one
bathroom in the house, but in another leap of affluence
Joe Senior had a partial bathroom installed downstairs.

The furniture below was relatively impervious to attack
by Joe, except for a piano given Rose by her brother. The
furnishings were sturdy, mostly covered in velvet brocade.
Rose scorned the "parlor for company" concept: the living room was for living, with no conversation pieces and
not a lace antimacassar in sight. When Joe could crawl, he
explored the patterns of the Oriental rug without risk of
scolding; there was little he could hurt even when he
pulled himself erect to inspect the soaring bulk of the
silver cabinet in the dining room.

But the front porch and backyard were even better
places for him to crawl, and Rose installed a swinging gate
on the former and fenced the latter so that he could be
outdoors every waking moment in good weather. Even the
second-floor veranda was safe enough for a while, with a
white wooden fence unscalable for months to come.

Joe Junior had Rose, Kico, and assorted laundry girls to
play with. He was not neglected by his father either. Joe
Senior, still president of his bank, was under hot political
attack in a municipal position handed him by his father-in-
law and he was trying for a seat on the board of trustees
of Massachusetts Electric and driving hard to pay off his
debts, so he rarely came home early, but when he did, the
boy was his. One often-repeated story of his father's
preoccupation with financial matters proves that Joe
Junior knew himself loved: Joe Senior, strolling one winter morning with his father-in-law's secretary, Eddie

Moore, towed two-year-old Joe in a sled. He fell off, and when the father left discount rates and land values long enough to notice that he was tugging an empty sled, they retraced their steps, expecting to find him bawling. Instead they discovered him confident of rescue and smiling sweetly in the snow.

Three months before Joe's second birthday the United States declared war on Germany. Joe Senior had anticipated it; early in the year he had handed the helm of Columbia Trust to his father and become assistant manager of Bethlehem's Fore River Shipyard. He was assigned to find housing for the swelling work force. He erected a company town. To feed it he built a cafeteria, which he retained for himself. His salary was $20,000 a year. The cafeteria profits were his, and he lashed himself furiously to earn the bonuses that Bethlehem Steel paid its executives. Fore River launched thirty-six destroyers in twenty-seven months; it finished one, keel to commissioning, in less than six weeks. Joe Senior's moments with his oldest son became rare, but John had been born a month after America entered the war and soon Joe had a roommate in the nursery. The father spent what time he had with them, naturally favoring the elder as a more interesting companion, and Joe accepted his younger brother without trauma.

Their sister Rosemary arrived just before the armistice, and Kathleen the following year. The boys were moved upstairs, but the house was bulging. Joe Senior took a job after the war as a stockbroker at $10,000 a year, as training for what he hoped would be a Wall Street career. Obviously they could not wait for the first mansion: they had to move now. He bought a corner house a few blocks away on Naples Road and Abbottsford. The new place was also gray and white, also frame with turreted windows on the second floor, but it had twelve rooms, two chimneys, and a magnificent front porch, which Rose partitioned with folding wooden gates into individual plots to prevent territorial squabbles. Eunice was born here, and Pat and Robert.

The children were at first central in Rose's life. Though the nurses would put them to bed and the youngest ones ate at a separate table, she would leave a party early to be home for Joe's bedtime or Jack's. Joe Junior, sturdily pushing a carriage with the latest arrival, began to become useful as the tiny army issued forth on walks. His mother and father did not mix much with the neighbors. Joe Senior was too busy for the self-conscious neighborhood parties in which the middle class flaunted Prohibition. Rose spoke German and French, two too many languages for the Yankee wives of contractors, minor city officials, and bank managers who peopled the neat gray streets. She already had more domestic help than most. The family had accumulated a Locomobile and was rising too fast; besides, the Kennedys constituted a Catholic island in a sea of Protestants, and seemed overly content, self-sufficient, and a little aloof behind their white-trimmed turrets.

Rose went to Mass every day and quite often took Joe. She wanted the children to make religion a part of their daily lives, not something to be reserved for Sundays, and she tried to mold the eldest brother into an example they might follow. She was gentle and playful with them all, but she used her famous ruler, too, to keep the troops in line, feeling that when they were young this was the only admonition they could understand.

When young Joe was five, with his religious training in his mother's hands, his father began to investigate the educational facilities of Brookline. Joe Senior had gone to Catholic grammar schools but thought he still felt the chill of anti-Catholicism in downtown Boston. Years before he had endured months of uncertainty and several rebuffs while he fought for the thankless seat on the Yankee-dominated board of the Massachusetts Electric Company with its opportunity to "meet people like the Saltonstalls." He had finally won, but if a Catholic background had slowed him down in business, his eldest son must go to a nonparochial institution. A few blocks away from Naples Road was Devotion School. It sounded religious, but it was not. It was a public school and so named only because it was located where one Edward Devotion, town constable, "perambulator," and tithing man, had built his home in 1680, when Brookline was "Muddy River."

Joe Senior asked questions. He found that the school, though public, had high academic standards—even W. Barton Leach, a famous intellect and an authority on property at Harvard Law, had found the going tough at Devotion when his own family moved to Naples Road in 1909. Graduates remembered the faculty with affection. The classes were large but the methods advanced. Joe would start there in kindergarten.

3

Edward Devotion's original big brick house stood under an oak on the school's front lawn, protected from undergraduate enthusiasm by a gleaming picket barrier that would have brought joy to the owner's heart, for he had also been "fence viewer" of Muddy River Township. The fence was hardly necessary; Joe Kennedy at five and the rest of the neat, neck-tied youngsters at the grammar school in the fall of 1921 were unlikely vandals. The school, like the Colonial dwelling in front, was brick with a gray slate roof. It crouched massively behind Devotion's home, faintly foreboding. Joe had walked the few blocks from Naples Road with his mother. Now, with a squeeze of the hand, she was gone and he entered.

The children were met at the door, assembled, and marched hand in hand to class. Joe started badly. For weeks his attention wandered. He felt that he was not doing as well as expected. He wanted help, but though there were two teachers, Betsy Beau and Cornelia Gould, and a young assistant-in-training, there were sixty-two boys and girls in the class. After the warm household on Naples Road, where his mother or Kico or one of the maids were always glad to aid on a project, Miss Gould and Miss Beau seemed remote. The games they had the children play in class were all right, but drawing and painting defeated him; he was a husky, healthy boy, but he became nervous now and sometimes he cried in frustration.

The young teacher-in-training, Helen Gallagher, noticed his struggles with the crayons. He had an Irish name, after all, and so he made his first conquest, noted with disapproval by the Misses Gould and Beau. Helen helped Joe with his art-work. Just out of school herself at twenty, she was lectured on the prevailing theories: a child should learn independently. But she sneaked encouragement to him anyway: his smile was so charming after the tears of frustration that she had no choice. His mother had noticed his distress from the first few days; she packed him animal crackers for recess and had a maid pick him up at noon when kindergarten was over. Joe teetered through the crisis of confidence; he was promoted to the first grade and earned a "Good" for the year.

For the next four years he did well, getting *B*'s. Jack had entered Devotion a year behind him. Rosemary was affectionate and lovable, but she had been slower to crawl than they and slower to walk and talk. Her mother had taken her to doctors, who assured her that she would be all right, so she was entered in Devotion kindergarten in 1923. Margaret McQuaid, who taught there, thought her a charming child with beautiful manners, but charm and manners were not enough. This time the problem was deeper than Joe's temporary insecurity. The Misses Beau and Gould could not recommend her for the first grade. She tried again next year and finished kindergarten with a *C*. While the Kennedys would not publicly admit her retardation for almost forty years, it was the last of her normal schooling.

Joe Kennedy Junior at nine shared his parents' hidden grief. He always treated Rosemary, who seemed sometimes the prettiest of his sisters, with special warmth. But Kathleen, his father's darling, became his favorite sister. At six, she was already eager to learn to throw a ball and field a punt. Eunice was fun, but still too young, and Jack failed to defer properly to his greater strength and wisdom.

Joe and Jack were compatible, but they were brothers more than friends in their early childhood. Jack used impishness to even the odds between them: Joe, much stronger and heavier, used more direct methods to keep the odds properly weighted. He was gentle with his sisters as he was with most younger children, but Jack was an exception. He would lob a football to Rosemary or Eunice; he would slam one at Jack and grin when the younger boy missed it or doubled up, winded, on the sidewalk. Racing around the block on their bicycles in opposite directions, each refused to veer and they collided on Abbottsford Road through sheer stubbornness; Jack required twenty-eight stitches; Joe was unscathed.

Joe had learned early to handle adults. He had inherited from his father the magic smile. When he was too old for the ruler treatment, his allowance might be docked if he were bad. Then he would grin at Kico and con her out of a loan for a movie. His mother had to warn Margaret, the huge Irish cook, that when Joe was banished on bread and water to his room it did not mean that he could raid the icebox for cake and milk.

Joe's father was raiding a bigger kitchen, Wall Street. He had learned the techniques in his apprenticeship in the Boston brokerage of Galen and Stone. His reputation for cunning grew. Newspaperman Walter Howey, prototype for Ben Hecht's city editor in *The Front Page,* was a friend of Kennedy's who had invested in Yellow Cab of Chicago. He came to him one evening in April, 1924, with a plea for help. He and John D. Hertz, a newspaperman himself who had gone on to manage boxers, breed horses, and finally to found Yellow Cab, needed help. Yellow had slid from eighty dollars a share on the New York Stock Exchange to fifty dollars in six weeks; in the ungoverned market of the day, there was only one explanation: a raid by bears, selling now to drive down the stock in order to pick it up cheaply later. The New York brokerage of Block, Maloney, and Company was suspected, but who the bears were didn't really matter; if the stock dipped below fifty, Howey and Hertz faced ruin.

Joe Senior heard the call of friendship, and perhaps something else. He had neuritis and Rose was expecting her sixth child, but he phoned Eddie Moore and the two entrained for New York that night. He met Hertz, stated his terms for taking command, and sent the cab man back to Chicago to raise five million dollars if he could. Then he ordered a ticker tape and extra telephones moved into a suite at the Waldorf. While Eddie Moore stood by for errands, Kennedy began to inject Hertz's borrowed millions into the market to buoy up Yellow stock. The five million was hardly enough, and to sow confusion he began to flood the market with illogical buy and sell orders, keeping track in longhand on a pad of paper. All through April and May he stayed in the suite, buying shares, selling, buying again, through brokerages in San Francisco, New Orleans, Chicago, Baltimore. The stock jumped and sagged, leaped and fell, while the unknown bears, perplexed, fought back. On May 9, Kennedy and his secret antagonists traded a million dollars' worth of Yellow. When it was all over, his new daughter, Jean, was a month old and he had not yet seen her. But Hertz's borrowed five million was intact, Yellow Cab was rock-steady where Joe had found it, at fifty dollars; his friend Howey was saved, and Kennedy was paid off.

He had earned Hertz's respect, but not his trust.

Months later, when the solid floor he had apparently erected under Yellow Cab collapsed, the founder decided that Kennedy, the only man who really understood his own wild tinkering, had suddenly sawed through the supports he himself had erected and sold Yellow short. The cab man, livid, stated publicly that he would punch Kennedy in the nose next time they met. Whether or not Kennedy had actually kicked out the props for private gain, most of his friends thought him capable of it, and the legend of another marketplace freebooter like Boston's Jesse Livermore "the Boy Plunger," Frank Bliss "the Silver Fox," or Bill Danforth was born.

"It's easy to make money in this market," he told an associate, when they once discussed the idea of setting up their own brokerage in New York. "We'd better get in before they pass a law against it." Piratical or not, his operations began to earn him the million he had promised himself by thirty-five. He accumulated the trappings swiftly: he hired the first of the Kennedy chauffeurs, Harry Patison, whom Rose had to warn, like Margaret the cook, not to spoil Joe Junior. He bought a Rolls-Royce. He lent it immediately to Burton K. Wheeler, La Follette's running mate on the Progressive ticket, for the presidential campaign of 1924, although it was thought that Kennedy preferred Coolidge. Wheeler wrote years afterward: "I denounced Wall Street often from the back seat of a Rolls-Royce owned by a Wall Street operator. It occurred to me later on that Kennedy actually might have been trying to undermine me in this fashion."

If the time had come for the Rolls, it had come also for a private school for Joe Junior and Jack: Edward Devotion was all right academically, but had no organized sports and besides it was time for the boys to meet some of the sons of Beacon Hill. A short distance from Naples Road, on St. Paul Street, stood the lower branch of Noble and Greenough School. It had had a good reputation at Harvard since its founding in 1866 by an overseer of the university. The principal of its Brookline branch was a dedicated, brilliant woman named Myra Fiske. Not suspecting imminent trouble, Joe Senior entered his two sons in 1924.

The school was small, but its roster read like a Back Bay social register. The "Junior" tacked proudly on Joe's name had seemed a little pretentious at Devotion among the Finebergs, Gustavsons, Walinskeys, and Cerussis. Here there were so many III's and IV's that Junior looked plebeian. Kennedy was the only Irish name on the rolls. To Joseph Randolph Coolidge IV, to George Saltonstall West, Jr., to the Bundy brothers, to Edward Filene Little, and to James Jackson Storrow III, grandson of the millionaire Yankee investment banker against whom Joe Junior's grandfather had rallied the Irish bosses to defeat for mayor in 1910, young Joe was a new breed of cat, reeking faintly of the alley.

Like Joe, the students at Noble and Greenough were the product of considerable care at home. They were polite to outsiders, if a little reserved, but they were, after all, boys at a combative stage. In the face of Joe's size and a certain dignity about him, they were individually cautious in their approach. But he was Irish, Catholic, and a loner, and he lived in nearby Brookline and was delivered daily by private car, or walked, while most of them commuted by school bus from gold-plated neighborhoods downtown. Besides, his mother, who looked so young that classmate John Clark Jones III at first thought she was a sister, often picked him up after school. He clearly required testing.

One afternoon he was cornered by a group of shoving, shirttail-tugging schoolmates. There were simply too many to handle, and one, John Clark Jones III, was even bigger than he. Joe took it as long as he could, then spun and sprinted across the street. He loped up the steps of a Catholic church, whirled in the doorway to face his pursuers, fists cocked in case all else failed. "This is a shrine! You can't touch me here!"

Jones and his cohorts skidded to a stop. For a moment they pondered the new concept of sanctuary, which seemed suddenly reasonable in view of the fists. They retreated. Joe was not troubled again, and Jones became one of his best friends in the school.

He went to summer camp at Wyanoke, in New Hampshire, and his postcards home show none of the traditional homesickness of a boy set adrift from his parents. He liked his counselor and won every swimming meet in sight—or at least those he reported; he came home more self-assured than ever. From infancy, when his father had made time to play catch with him and teach him to field a baseball, Joe Junior had liked athletics. He was not exceptionally well coordinated, but he worked hard, was fast, and he was very aggressive. In the scrambling, fully uniformed grammar-school football games with the surrounding private schools he became a fair backfield man, tough and hard-hitting in comparison with his more highly refined classmates. In baseball he pitched, and here he really shone. He was a fastball artist. His part-time coach Dick Flood, himself a student at Harvard, found him more mature and competitive than his teammates, who were inclined to gather daisies in the outfield. He had an unfortunate tendency to bicker with the umpire, less acceptable in the private-school league than in his father's day in East Boston; he had a bad habit, too, of shoving infielders aside to go for every fly within reach. But Flood played him whenever he could. Jack Kennedy, despite his slight build, was the only catcher who could come close to holding him behind the plate. Jack hung on, mitt stinging and tears in his eyes, sometimes knocked down by the whiplash delivery and often, to Joe's disgust, dropping the ball. Joe took aim at batters from nearby Parks and River schools and simply pitched harder.

Joe had one regret: his father was seldom at the games to see him play. Joe Senior, working frantically in a boom market, was home less and less and Rose was temporarily occupied with Robert, born on Naples Road in the winter of 1925. Young Joe developed a bond with his gentle grandfather, Honeyfitz, who came to games and became more important to him perhaps than if his father had been continually home. Joe was always at ease with older people, and Honeyfitz would take him to the zoo at Franklin Park or to Braves Field nearby; Joe began to eat dinner after Mass in his grandparents' third-floor suite at the dowdy old Bellevue Hotel downtown. One Sunday, dining there with his aunt Agnes and her friends Marie and Ben Greene, he asked his aunt why she didn't marry: didn't she want any children? Agnes shrugged toward Marie and her husband and said: "Look at Marie and Ben. They're married and God didn't send them any children."

Joe sensed an opening: a maiden aunt and a large audience. "Aunt Agnes! That isn't the way you get children. Do you want me to tell you how?" And when his aunt tried to change the subject, he bored in straight-faced with the facts of life gleaned from a text issued at school —until she begged for mercy.

Ward politics and history were more likely subjects than sex at the Fitzgerald table. Joe began to absorb them with the food he ate. Across Bowdoin Street rose the golden dome of the State House; there were long walks in Boston Common with his grandfather, who had a rich collection of stories of Boston Irish and U.S. history. Studying the American Revolution at school, Joe decided that he wanted to see its nearby sites. He knew the Common well, but asked Miss Fiske if she would take him and Jack to Concord if they provided the car: in a burst of optimism, he promised the Rolls-Royce. The Kennedys had never flaunted the Rolls and it had never before appeared at school. Even to wealthy Beacon Hill boys the prospect of seeing it was exciting. Crowds awaited its arrival, but when Patison drove up the curving gravel driveway, he was in a Ford; the Rolls was in the garage. Amid gibes at Joe, the three embarked. At Concord Joe was interested in the headstones of the patriots, but after a while Miss Fiske sensed boredom and they did not stay long.

Suddenly, with Joe making friends in class and on the athletic field, the whole school, Miss Fiske included, seemed about to disappear. Just after Christmas of 1925, as he and Jack were getting ready to start a new semester, their father found in the mail a form letter from the school's board of trustees advising that it planned to accept a favorable offer for the purchase of the property. The letter spoke of the "disappointment that the parents would feel."

Disappointment was an understatement: rage, at least so far as Joe Senior was concerned, was more the word. He had never been informed that the school might close its Brookline branch; investigation proved that the trustee delegated to write the parents had forgotten to mail the letters in the excitement of the Christmas season. Joe Kennedy and eight other parents conferred stormily. Then they simply bought the school for $188,000. They kept the beloved Miss Fiske as principal, renamed the institution Dexter, after the original owner of the field on which it was placed, and re-opened without a break.

Joe's prestige as the son of one of the school's saviours increased further when he and Jack arrived one morning in sombreros, courtesy of their far-ranging father, direct from Old Mexico via Olivera Street in Los Angeles. It soared higher at Joe's eleventh birthday party, when his classmates, after pinning the tail on the donkey on the big Kennedy porch, were herded inside to find, incredibly for the Twenties, a movie projector set up. The shades were drawn and they saw *Felix the Cat* and Charlie Chaplin's *Gold Rush*, just as if they had gone to the Rex and paid. When they left they were convinced that Joe had a pipeline to Heaven.

It was not Heaven, but Hollywood. His father was easing in, attracted by quick profits and the financial innocence of the "pants-pressers," as he characterized the studio heads. He had been sewing up American rights to British pictures, and the previous summer he had gone to London to try to buy a British corporation, Film Booking Office. There, on the slimmest of foundations, he passed himself off as a friend of the Prince of Wales. The deal went through, and he was suddenly Boston's only motion-picture magnate, president of his own film company. With the acquisition came an ulcer and more long trips to Hollywood, New York, and London. Rose sometimes accompanied him, and both missed young Joe's confirmation. "The most important thing I have to tell you," he wrote them, "is that I was confirmed yesterday by Cardinal O'Connell." The event did not pass entirely unnoticed: Grandpa Patrick Kennedy had to go to a funeral instead, but gave him a five dollar gold piece; the rest of the family, as well as Eddie Moore and his wife, went to the services; his aunt Agnes and Grandma each gave him rosary beads, and Grandpa Fitzgerald a signet ring.

Joe missed his father. When he selected a card for his thirty-eighth birthday that year, it was an expensive, gilded one, but showed the vacuum. The verse was tender doggerel: "No father was ever so dandy before / They just don't make them and don't anymore / For there's only one you and there hasn't been since / A dad who could touch you because you're a prince." The picture was the back of an armchair with a pipe protruding; the man was invisible.

Invisible or not, Joe Senior's presence hovered over his son on Naples Road. His expectations were so great and his confidence so evident that he did not have to be physically in Brookline to motivate young Joe. When home, his father treated him as an adult: he never demanded but suggested, quietly, man to man. He gave so few orders that those he gave Joe obeyed instantly. He seldom scolded; together they simply cut cleanly and surgically to the root of errors, in what turned out often to be an interesting search for the truth. Honesty and loyalty were the two main virtues, winning was the prime value.

Young Joe agreed. He had been taken to see Meridian Street in East Boston and now the family had millions and he went to the best school in Brookline. Anyway, winning made sense; the loser worked almost as hard and got none of the prizes.

Young Joe, who knew his father much better than any of his younger siblings, saw with every glance between them that he would not lose his father's love if he were a slob in class or a bumbler on the gridiron; so far as he knew, all fathers imperishably loved their sons. But love and respect were different, and the way to hold his respect was rockier: that took work. It was easy on the playing field, but not so easy in class. Miss Fiske's precept— "Today our Best, Tomorrow Better"—was regarded with rare seriousness by her pupils. Competition was tough, but Joe did good work and stood near the top of the class.

His father was delighted, but it was time for the family to move on. His Film Booking Office was turning out fifty profitable B pictures a year, but he could not properly run a motion-picture company from Boston, or touch Wall Street's racing pulse. About to leave anyway and angry at what he considered a lifetime of Protestant bias, he characteristically killed two birds with one stone and brought his family into the act. The family had been renting for the summer a great gray house overlooking Massachusetts Bay at Cohasset on the South Shore. There, despite Joe Senior's Harvard degree, personal charm, beautiful wife, and new wealth, he had been blackballed when he applied for membership to the Cohasset Country Club; he was a bartender's son, and that was that. Joe Junior had brushed prejudice and stood it off on the steps of his church; his close friend of later years, William Randolph Hearst Junior's ex-wife Lorelle, says, "I don't think he gave a damn about it." But Joe Senior was leaving town for young Joe, he claimed in a blast at all who would listen: he would relocate in New York for the sake of his family: "Boston is no place to bring up Catholic children." Thus relieved, he moved Rose, Joe Junior, Jack, Rosemary, Kathleen, Eunice, Pat, Robert, Jean, Kico the nurse, Patison the chauffeur, and Margaret the cook south to a leased mansion in Riverdale, a few miles up the Hudson from the Big City.

Joe Junior had bounced into Boston by Model T Ford in a basket; he glided out by rail in a private car.

3

JOE JUNIOR'S new home in New York was opulent, smelling of fresh paint and floor wax. It was a slate-roofed manor on a curving driveway, and from its grounds, he could glimpse the Hudson River past "Wave's Hill," a bluffside estate across the street in which Mark Twain and Theodore Roosevelt had once lived. Joe and Jack shared a room on the third floor. The wooded areas beyond their own property smelled of the wilderness and demanded exploration: they were forbidden to Rosemary and the younger children unless escorted, but he and Jack were turned loose to climb the mossy walls, splash through the creeks, and slog along the Hudson shore.

His father was gone almost as often in New York as in Boston, and Joe's role as the presiding male sometimes got too large for him. He was anxious to project his father's image—a man with respect for the dollar. Kathleen decided at breakfast one morning that she needed a new schoolbag.

"She doesn't need a new schoolbag," he told his mother, knifing his favorite sister neatly in the back. "Her schoolbag is plenty good."

Kathleen, shocked at his perfidy, fought back. Rose withstood the ensuing argument as long as she could. "Joe," she said finally, "you go upstairs, and—"

"Mind my own business?" he suggested, to forestall worse.

45

"Go upstairs and write it down," commanded his mother. "A hundred times: 'I must mind my own business.' "

Joe might needle Jack and Kathleen; younger children he still treated more kindly, and they liked him. Marie Greene, whose childlessness had given him the excuse at his grandfather's table for the lecture to his aunt Agnes on the facts of life, arrived for a visit. God had by now presented her with a son, Skipper, who was two; before school Joe would drop into the boy's room to tousle his hair and play with him. He taught Eunice to catch a pass and Pat to somersault, and spent long dull hours on a nearby tennis court easing careful lobs to Rosemary, who returned them as best she could.

The town of Riverdale was more rural than suburban, peopled with middle-class Dutch and Irish, but there was great wealth in the surrounding estates. Riverdale Country Day School was just as expensive, athletic, and progressive as the school he had left in Brookline, and as full of the great-great-grandsons of patroons as Dexter had been of the descendants of Yankee shipowners. The student body was solid—Charles Evans Hughes' grandsons were schoolmates of Joe's and Jack's—but there was none of the baiting Joe had endured—or refused to endure—at the Brookline private school.

He was chunky and sturdy at twelve. Harold Klue, a twenty-two-year-old social-studies teacher and coach, found him a spirited competitor on the athletic field. His grades were excellent and he was neat on the campus, but he was usually late for the gleaming Reo school bus. Herb Corirossi, who drove it, had often to wait outside the Kennedy home for Joe, who would appear stuffing down the last of his breakfast and kissing his mother good-bye before he scrambled aboard. Herb was a great fan of Joe Kennedy on the baseball diamond. When he would make an error, he would threaten not to drive him home, but only once did he throw him out. He caught Joe wrestling in the back of the bus, made a quick call to the school for permission, and dumped him far from home near a local racetrack.

The same Hollywood magic that had made a party at Naples Road attractive to classmates worked at Riverdale; Joe was a source of films for his playmates and he was not beyond dropping an occasional name. He and Jack were able to report one day that their father had asked their advice on hiring Red Grange, the Galloping Ghost of

Illinois, to act in a football movie. Their enthusiasm got Grange the job, but the real proof of their connection with the mighty was a telegram sent them when they measled, from no less than Tom Mix: I HAD THEM MYSELF ONCE AND KNOW HOW YOU FEEL.... VISIT ME IN CALIF AND I WILL GIVE YOU A GOOD HORSE AND A COMPLETE OUTFIT TO USE.... YOUR PAL TOM.

Joe's father was uncomfortable paying off someone else's equity by renting a house. He began to look for a permanent New York home, through a real-estate agent who complained to Eddie Moore—now Kennedy's own secretary—that the Kennedys didn't want a house, they wanted a hotel. They found it in nearby Bronxville. It was a red-brick Colonial mansion with towering white columns and a huge garage on six acres of elm trees and manicured lawn off Pondfield Road. It had twenty rooms, a gardener's and chauffeur's cottage for Frank Deane, their handsome, good-natured new driver. It had been built for Anheuser-Busch, and Joe Senior bought it for a quarter of a million dollars. Joe, Jack, and Kathleen had rooms on the third floor, where there was a huge playroom and a room for a governess. Pat, Eunice, Bobby, and Jean had rooms on the second floor between the nursery and their parents' bedroom. Rose quickly changed the master bedroom to childproof modern, so that Pat, Robert, and Jean could play with her without wrecking the decor. She had a natural desire as a housewife to keep a neat establishment, but there were more important things for children to do than help with housekeeping and discipline was light. They would be better occupied, she thought, playing outside than picking up their rooms.

Joe Junior, the model for the younger ones in all things, agreed. His pants stayed where he stepped out from them for the night; his bed remained unmade until someone else made it; his aunt Agnes hated to follow him into a bathroom until someone had cleaned it up. Jack fell into line enthusiastically, with original twists: he would start the tub, move to the hall phone to call a friend, forget the water until plaster dripped from the ceiling of his parents' bedroom below. Joe, despite his own carelessness, would help around the house if necessary and was popular with the servants; not so Jack. In later years, when the boys went away to school, it was Jack's vacation time that the maids tried to predict and to match, to be away from the house when he was home.

The elegance of the garden, so impressive to business acquaintances, was not permitted to interfere with the touch-football games Joe organized for his classmates; teachers from Riverdale enjoyed the informal movies in the basement projection room and Joe Senior's bootleg Scotch. They were pleased with the parents' interest in the school: Joe Senior was particularly anxious that his boys study Current Events.

He tried to stay as close to their lives as he could, despite his hectic schedule. Saturday was a half-work day even for the boss in his FBO office at 1560 Broadway, but Saturday afternoon was for the children, who would, with a governess, join him for lunch at Longchamps or Reuben's and then go with him to the circus or a rodeo in Madison Square Garden or to a movie. Lunching at 21, he introduced them to Gary Cooper, and for months afterward Kathleen and Eunice collected movie magazines.

One afternoon, standing in a Manhattan oyster bar, Joe Senior shook hands on a half-million-dollar deal with David Sarnoff which brought RCA into his Film Booking Office. He then decided to give his family, at least for the summers, New England roots again. He may have had more than sentimental reasons. He had noticed during the freewheeling dinner discussions, from which Joe had not been excluded since he was an infant, that no matter how lengthy and intricate the conversation or exalted the diners—Arthur Krock, Bernard Baruch, or William Randolph Hearst—Joe listened intently to the talk of politics; his questions made sense; he seemed able to swamp his elders, when he pleased, with boyish charm. Jack was indifferent, but Joe cared. If Joe Senior privately asked his political opinion—and the elder's own charm lay in his habit of doing this to everyone he liked—Joe's answers seemed, for an adolescent, quite solid.

Joe Junior might want a future in politics. If he ever ran for office, it should be in Massachusetts, powered by built-in-loyalty to Pat Kennedy in East Boston or Fitzgerald allegiance on the North End. New Yorker or not, a residence in Massachusetts might someday save him from charges of carpetbagging. Perhaps at Hyannis on Nantucket Sound, fifty miles south of Cohasset, they would be safe from the Yankee chill.

2

Downtown Hyannis and nearby Craigville Beach have a
tourist smell of hamburgers and cotton candy; the Hyannis
Port waterfront reeks of fish and tar. Toward the sound,
the streets begin to curve affluently and shade trees swing
low; the scent here is of freshly cut lawn and burning
leaves; along the Kennedy road to the water, the smell is
of salt water and scrubby Great Island bushes across
Lewis Bay.

The house stands on a quiet road leading to a sandy
marsh and beach. It is the closest to the water of any of
its neighbors. It is bigger than it looks, built in the early
1900's in Cape Cod style. It is white and square, with
fifteen rooms and nine baths, a private theater, Swedish
sauna, and a pool. Two acres of lawn slope to the beach;
a breakwater stretches toward Great Island, which is
really a low-lying sandy spit across sheltered waters, good
for sailing picnics and to furnish a lee for small boats and
not much else.

Joe Junior, arriving in 1929, was not really a stranger in
town: many of his Brookline playmates summered there
too. Whitney Wright, a schoolmate from Dexter, was
there, and Bert Ellis and Bobby Fogan. They started a
four-man club, called BoBeWiJo from their first names.
They decked the floor of a boathouse that Wright's father
owned on the Hyannis Port waterfront. All were in training for athletics at school and worked out on the Kennedy
grounds. Kennedy hospitality after the workouts was aus-
tere—Joe Junior served water rather than ginger ale after
a workout because soft drinks, he explained, were expensive and cut one's wind anyway. But despite Spartan
refreshments the home on the point was fine for digging
holes in the sand, calisthenics, and touch football on the
lawn. The big white house was always jammed with local
adolescents.

Kico was still the nurse for the younger Kennedys, but
Rose felt some tutoring necessary for the middle of the
family. She hired Alice Cahill, a perky, brown-eyed graduate of Framingham State Teachers' College, to act as
governess. Miss Cahill arrived on her first day at the big
house before lunch to find that Mr. Kennedy was out of

town and Rose planned to eat elsewhere. Rose asked her if she minded being "thrown to the lions." She claimed that she didn't, but Joe, thirteen, took charge anyway to ease her introduction to the small army. The noon meal was the main one for the household. Joe sat at the head of the table, carving the roast and dispensing meat, compliments, and barbed remarks about dirty fingernails. Thereafter he was Miss Cahill's ally. Rose went abroad seventeen times in the next seven years, and if Jack or Pat or Robert thought some ruling diverged from family policy, Joe Junior's word was final: even Jack accepted it, sometimes reluctantly.

Joe and Miss Cahill got along very well. With her trust he earned certain political and financial advantages. She doled out the allowances: five cents a week for Pat to fifty cents for himself, the birth of each new child having meant a nickel raise for everyone. Sometimes she could be prevailed upon for an advance. Until he was old enough for a driver's license, he represented transportation to the Wianno Yacht Club. And sometimes, when Rose gave her unused season tickets to the Cape Playhouse, she might take him along to a play.

He liked to go to the theater or a movie, but he preferred friends for a buffet supper at home to lolling in front of Hyannis drugstores. He loved music and had a record collection: Fred Waring, Vincent Lopez, Rudy Vallee. His idea of entertainment was a film in the basement projection room or a songfest with the family around his mother at the piano: he had, for a Kennedy, a good voice.

His daily life was by choice rigorously organized. Like his father and mother, Joe went to bed early and arose early; his brothers and sisters conformed. There was simply too much to do to sleep late. He was due on the lawn at seven, along with Jack, for a session of calisthenics with Mr. Swinerton, a gravel-voiced physical-education instructor who, it was said, could be heard on a quiet morning from Nantucket Sound to Cape Cod Bay. Breakfast was a raucous family affair; there might be a morning swim, and when a decent breeze came up, there were the sparkling sailing waters of New Harbor and Wianno.

It was just as well that Joe preferred his family to the local teen-age crowd. The same forces that had barred his father from the Cohasset Golf Club were soon to rise against the family here. The arrival of one more household beautifully staffed with Irish servants in the midst of the old Cape Cod summer community was not remarkable, though in 1929 it was several decades too late to be socially acceptable. What was really unusual, besides the vitality and easiness of the children, was the fact that not only were the gardeners, chauffeur, and governesses Irish Catholics—everyone's were—but the master and mistress as well.

Cape Cod had private beach clubs: sooner or later, the family would want to get into one; they already belonged to the Wianno Yacht Club, an unobtrusive, modest frame structure at the base of a crooked pier. The Boston Brahmins and their offspring were too polite to openly snub anyone, but the young Kennedys were bound to overstep their social limitations and the oldest brother was the first. It was inevitable but a girl caused it all.

At thirteen, Joe fell in love. The girl was not a Bostonian, except by descent: she was the daughter of a California Unitarian minister, visiting an old Cape Cod family with her mother. She was fourteen, a tiny nut-brown creature with sparkling dark-blue eyes. She was full of western laughter and gave not a damn for the white-flannel set. Her host's son, it had been assumed, would be her escort for the summer. Her name was Eleanor Leavens, and Joe came upon her peering wildly into the waters off the yacht-club pier. She had just dropped her Navaho ring into the water. Her tubby escort flapped his arms and made sounds of distress, but Joe, fully dressed, began to unbutton his shirt: "Go sailing with him," he ordered her. "I'll dive for it." As she tacked away with her proper partner, she peered over the side to see Joe's untanned bottom flashing far below. His search was unsuccessful, but the next day when she went sailing it was with Joe.

Local ice began to form around Eleanor in Hyannis. It was all right to discard one's host, but to pick the nouveau-riche son of an Irish Catholic speculator put her beyond the pale. A generation removed from Boston prejudice, she could hardly believe the reaction; neither could her mother. Life became chilly even in the home of their hosts, but Eleanor, happy with Joe and intrigued at his more venturesome sailing, had chosen her summer beau and she stayed with him. They sang and splashed each other; she talked of new records and California; he spoke of football, Lindbergh, and Latin. In the late afternoon, returning, their eyes would hold and neither would speak. At night, for Eleanor and her mother, the frost thickened. And Joe, floating home to parents, sisters, and brothers, never knew what his sweetheart faced.

Four brief sailing dates finished it. The Hyannis mood was glacial: mother and daughter talked it over and left for California. Joe, shattered and still kept from the truth, saw them off. There had to be a memento: Eleanor gave Joe one of a pair of prized and garish gloves. In a few months he would write: "I have been thinking about you ever since you went away. I was going to kiss you good-bye but you didn't give me any encouragement when I see you I will if you don't mind. Really I love you a lot." She was his first love and he moped the beaches for a few days, but like his father when Rose was sent to Europe as a girl, he refused to sulk. Instead he began to win sail-boat races.

He had learned to sail at Cohasset. In 1927 he and Jack, relaxing after winning a race in the family star boat *Rose Elizabeth*, had charged back from their front porch to rescue one Ralph Russell, who was clinging to his own swamped craft. "He was taken aboard the *Rose Elizabeth* in an exhausted condition," reported the Boston *Post*, describing the rescue as "daring" and Joe Senior as a "motion-picture magnate."

At Hyannis were even better sailing waters. Joe Junior, who would rather sail than eat, assumed that others would rather sail than walk. When his aunt Agnes and her friend Marie Greene innocently mentioned a stroll to Craigville Beach, he enticed them onto the *Rose Elizabeth* and sailed them there. A hundred feet off the surf he informed them that this was the end of the trip; no one would expect an experienced skipper to risk hull scratches on the sand. They dived out bravely at five knots. Marie ripped a lifelong rigging scar in her leg and Joe sailed home, his good deed done.

Joe Senior, a powerboat owner, deferred to his son's superior knowledge of sail. Young Joe campaigned for new boats to buy and a professional boat keeper to tend them. As Jack, Kathleen, and Eunice became more profi-cient—Eunice was a natural sailor—Joe Senior added to the fleet. The Wianno Junior class of rugged little sixteen-foot sloops was a local favorite: the family soon had two swinging at anchor: first the *Tenovus* and then, after Teddy was born, the *One More*. They bought another star, *Flash II*, and Joe found, secondhand, a Wianno senior, a beamy gaff-rigged twenty-five-footer with a little cuddy for overnight trips. He let Jack name her. Jack decided on *Victura:* "Something to do with winning." Ted Kennedy still sails her.

The name was appropriate, for Joe was beginning to collect all the silver in sight. To Eric, a handsome, hard-drinking Viking who had skippered transatlantic races and who now tended the Kennedy fleet, Joe was a lad after his own heart. Joe scorned polished binnacles, glittering varnish, and white yachting clothes; boats were to sail, as fast as possible; they gave cups for winning, not painting. At haul-out, Joe would scrape barnacles; he would slosh on Eric's own brew of bottom paint—laced with beer—at Crosby's Yard because boats raced on their bottoms and sailed fastest clean; but he wouldn't touch a brush for topside work. To his mother's despair he and Eric would drag dripping Egyptian-cotton sails across the living-room floor and hang them from the balconies to dry for tomorrow's race, but to Joe, furling them neatly at anchor was a waste of time. Kennedy boat-keeping became as much a horror to the neat local yachting set as did the ceaseless Kennedy victories.

Joe set the standard for Jack's and Kathleen's sailing; Eunice needed no example: she was as aggressive at the tiller as he. The goal was victory, the style wild: split-second timing at the start, recklessness at the windward buoy, disregard for the risk of a tiny misjudgment. Joe carried full canvas when others reefed; he had a gut sense for the touch of the breeze in light winds and a special feel on the tiller; he was last to head up for safety in a squall and first to ease off again. Alice Cahill, driving the family station wagon to collect Joe and his silver cups from the Wianno Yacht Club, found herself interrogated by parents about the Kennedy plans for next weekend's races: if Joe or Jack or Eunice were going to compete, it seemed futile to send their own children out to get beaten.

Joe Senior followed the important races in the family powerboat *Davilis.* He was no rag sailor and knew little about sailing, but he had an analytical mind. When Joe finally lost, it seemed to his father that he was racing with too small a sail, and luffing; Joe, white with anger at losing, explained that the sail sagged because it was three years old. Eric was commissioned to order another. In a few weeks, under a glistening new main, Joe picked up his winning streak again. Then the blow fell: sharp yachting eyes had noticed that the throat of the new sail seemed to ride too high; too little mast showed above the straining gaff.

It was no trivial matter. Sailing is a sport so deeply rooted in honor that yachtsmen finishing a race when the committee boat is absent are trusted to take their own official times; to carry more canvas than your class allows is, in certain New England clubs, tantamount to voting Democratic. The mainsail of the great-grandson of the first Patrick Kennedy, immigrant cooper, was quietly measured by tight-lipped descendants of Yankee skipper-merchants; it was found nine inches too high along the mast. Despite the family's contention that Eric, after all, was a professional and had personally ordered the sail, the Kennedy name came under a cloud in Cape Cod waters from which it has never quite emerged.

Joe had trained Jack into a good crewman who would move swiftly to shift ballast in a jibe or to harden a sheet. The two could work together when the object was to win, but while in their teens they often fought in earnest, and it was still hopeless for Jack. Behind his flashing smile and easy laugh Joe was steel and his status was always at stake. Robert recalled to the author thirty-five years later that he and Pat and Jean would gape from the stairway, or hide, as the two struggled on the living-room floor; the style of the family was to let Jack fight it out on his own.

He never quit trying, and he struck at Joe's weakness: food. Joe's appetite was enormous; he liked roast beef and Margaret's orange meringue, but most of all he liked chocolate pie; when that was served for dinner, he would flash the grin at a maid and ask for his piece early, just to look at. It would be placed on display by his plate. One noon Jack snatched it, stuffed it into his mouth, and took off at a dead run. With Joe in pursuit, he dived off the breakwater into Lewis Bay. Joe waited in implacable anger until his brother finally emerged, shivering with cold, and then there was a free-swinging brawl, for keeps. The lesson was clear to Jack: to embarrass Joe Kennedy before an audience was a dangerous affair.

Salvation for Jack was just over the horizon. He could be top dog in Bronxville. Joe, on the strength of his good work at Riverdale, was going to prep school in the fall.

4

THE school lay north of New Haven, in the town of Wallingford, Connecticut. Its name was Choate—pronounced somewhat as in piglet—and it was a place of sweeping lawns and white-columned halls of brick. The shingled, tree-shaded residence halls were homes, not dormitories. A student lived in one of the scattered houses with a master and his wife; Joe Junior's house, under Housemaster Tobey, was on the fringe of the little community. A Choate boy had to be well dressed in class or lab; tweed sport jackets and wide school ties were the mode in the fall of 1929. Standards were high and an Ivy League college was the assured goal of almost everyone. A few students had to leave after the Crash, but those who remained were insulated from the cloud of despair that covered the country. The school's goals were so ascetic that it frowned on any allowance of more than two dollars a week, but it was so isolated that there was no place to spend money anyway. Jack Kennedy, finding himself next year in a similar vacuum at nearby Catholic Canterbury School, asked his father for a subscription to *Literary Digest* because he hadn't heard about the "market slump until a long time after."

Joe was called "Rat Face" at Choate, perhaps because of the Kennedy protruding teeth, corrected by Dr. Cloney, who occasionally visited him there to check his progress. But he was self-contained and not depressed by schoolboy epithets or new surroundings. He was a raw

55

diamond by Choate standards of discipline, but happy
enough to be there. He wrote Eleanor in California that
he liked the school, adding that after she left the Cape he
had found it necessary to take a swing at her ex-host's
son. He flailed at suitors unknown, too: Eleanor had
written him of a West Coast boyfriend whom, she confessed, she allowed to read her mail, and he warned her
not to let him read *his* letters: "If he wants to, tell him to
go to H–LL. Love and kisses, Joe Kennedy."

His combativeness had not been much discouraged at
home. He had learned arrogance as the commander of a
group of seven brothers and sisters, but at Choate he was
fair game for any sixth former trying to prove his man-
hood. Joe was good-natured under hazing, but he was
boisterous and not ready to change. On his first trip home
to Bronxville his younger brother Jack reported gleeefully
to his father, who was out of town: "He was roughhousing
in the hall a sixth former caught him he led him in and all
the sixth formers had a swat or two. Did the sixth formers
lick him. O Man he was all blisters, they almost paddled
the life out of him. What I wouldn't have given to be a
sixth former. They have some pretty strong fellows up
there if blisters have anything to do with it." Jack also
commented that the "first thing he did to show me how
tough he was was to get sick so he could not have any
thanksgiving dinner. Manly youth. He was then going to
show me how to Indian wrestle. I then through him over
on his neck."

To top it off, Joe showed up late to school after his first
Thanksgiving. "Dear Mother," he wrote, "I got up here at
8:30 last night and found out I was suppose to be back at
5:30." He went on to ask for a football forgotten at
home, signed by the Notre Dame team, and then: "I
showed Mr. Tobey this letter and he said I would have to
write a longer letter. I had a wonderful time at the game
yesterday, didn't you think it was a good game. It sure
was cold."

The padded letter presumably satisfied Mr. Tobey, but
there was plenty else that did not. He complained that
Joe was the one boy on his corridor whose room was
generally out of order, that he made trouble for the sixth
formers, and that he started roughhouses with his roommate, Covell, on the slightest provocation. Sunday-evening
study periods, he had noted, were seldom used to good

advantage. "Some of these matters are trivial," he admitted, "but they show his spirit."

At Choate you followed rules, even if your father contributed to the Foundation, which Mr. Kennedy did. Young Joe had been AWOL Thanksgiving and that was that: he would be held over at Christmastime. Rose had been to school in Prussia; she agreed that there was no excuse for him. But she was a mother, too: "I feel it was more carelessness than disobedience or indifference to rules. Though many faults, he has always been truthful."

The school held him over anyway and went on to build more character. Joe did poorly in Latin, a little better in English, barely passed French, and broke eighty only in algebra. The next semester he improved despite a *D* in public speaking; and the headmaster wrote: "Joe is bright enough to finish quickly his day's assignment. . . . But he is too easily satisfied and does not go that second mile that would make him a real student. Joe is still somewhat superficially childish. We like Joe so much that we want his best and Joe himself really wants to give it to us."

He was right. Joe, at sixteen, suddenly realized that he was in a race, and his marks became important to him. Term reports bypassed the students and were sent directly to the parents; Joe demanded them from home, to keep his own score. Mr. Tobey changed his evaluation and decided that a great change had come over him and that now he was doing his work well without pressure from the outside. And Headmaster St. John wrote that Joe had gone from the fourth scholastic group to the third, and that it did his heart good to see it.

Joe was happy, but not well known around the school at first: he was simply an insignificant guard on the junior varsity. That was unthinkable, so he took long, lonely jogs through the rolling Connecticut countryside to build up his stamina. On one of them he met another runner, a sturdy, prematurely balding student with a Scandinavian look. His name was Jack Hopwood. He had been rooming with Tom Schriber, chairman of the Student Council, until the two had caused so much trouble on their corridor that the headmaster had split them up. Hopwood, who did push-ups for fun and took cold showers at 7 A.M., sensed in Joe a kindred stoic. He introduced him to the dominant clique at Choate. Joe moved in as his roommate. Later, as sixth formers responsible for helping the housemaster keep order on their floor, Joe refused to haze underclassmen:

instead, he and Hopwood would pour sand into the house-master's shoes, short-sheet his bed, and then meet with him in long, serious conferences to plan how best to uncover the mysterious saboteurs. Joe and Hopwood took weekends together: at a white-tie-and-tails party at the Kennedy Bronxville estate they successfully tied the coat-tails of Jimmy Roosevelt, the President's oldest son, to those of his flankers on either side in the stag line, and Roosevelt never knew who had done it. Hopwood had an aunt with a home in Berlin, Connecticut, and when she was away for the winter, they clambered in through a basement window, slept under furniture covers, and some-times culminated the weekend with a stealthy party for friends. The two roommates sometimes had quarrels—Hopwood used Joe's Vitalis until Joe poured bleach into it, turning Hopwood's remaining hair white overnight and almost causing a permanent rift between them—but despite a few arguments, Hopwood made Joe's life at Choate even happier.

Joe, accepted by the ruling set, became a campus pow-er. But he never immersed himself in school so far that he lost sight of his first interest, the family. Sometimes he prodded his mother for not visiting him, tongue in cheek: "I can easily understand how busy you must be buying antiques and clothes." Usually he bared his sins to her, reporting that he and Hopwood drew two weeks of study hall for throwing snowballs out the window. But some-times he tried to protect her from the Awful Truth, and of course, she found out, and he had to explain:

"There was no secret about my getting a ticket. I was hurrying along a wide cement road with no car in sight near New Haven, a town called Orange, when a cop came alongside and told me to pull in to the curb. . . . I got in touch with a policeman up there I know and he went down and talked to the Captain of the Wallingford Police force who went to Orange and talked to the judge, but he couldn't do a thing, you know the judges in small towns." He had to borrow twenty-five dollars to post bail. "The Captain knew a certain judge in town that knew the judge in Orange very well, he got the case off the list and had it annulled for the cost which amounted to $15. I am going downtown sometime this week to get my $10 back."

While he was at Choate Teddy was born at Bronxville. When the baby was less than a month old, the Lindbergh child was kidnapped from his home on Sourland Mountain in New Jersey. Joe Junior and the rest of the family were shaken; twenty-four-hour-a-day guards were hired in Bronxville, photographers were avoided, and Rose expressed concern to Henry Luce about the publicity the Kennedy name was getting.

Teddy became Joe's favorite brother; for years he would go first to the nursery to play with him when he returned from Choate on a vacation. He did not neglect the others: he would ride a train a hundred miles east to Providence to escort Rosemary to a dance at her special school; his mother would help by writing for permission to Choate, describing her daughter as suffering from an inferiority complex. When Eunice, at twelve, was in a New York hospital with a stomach ailment, Joe somehow visited her "about four days out of seven," cleaning up a fast ten dollars when he bet her that she couldn't lie still for ten minutes at a time.

He was concerned even about Jack and visited him at Canterbury School twenty-five miles away. He reported home that Jack seemed to be doing pretty well, although he had no roommate. But Jack was not really doing well. His spelling was poor, his Latin worse than Joe's had been.

Joe tried to follow his father's career in the papers—Joe Senior had just settled on him and on each of his brothers and sisters a million-dollar trust, so set up that while grandchildren would benefit, future wives or husbands would find it impossible to pry loose any capital—and Joe Junior was grateful and awed by the incredible financial adventures that had made it possible. Pathé Films, of which his father was now chairman, was going broke; his father merely sold its production facilities to RKO, hurriedly unloaded the stock which he had been given as an incentive, and got out from under. "I read about the Pathé deal," Joe Junior wrote his mother. "Has Dad gone to Florida yet? What is Dad's address south?"

Joe's interest in higher finance was more mature than that of his classmates, but otherwise he was typical. He had a shabby, dirty trench coat, so tattered that a matron who picked him up hitchhiking home on holiday offered to send the young millionaire her husband's old coat if he would give her his address. He was more religious than most of his contemporaries and more communicative to his parents: he reported to Rose almost every time he went to church or received communion, and even when he got a card from a Catholic magazine thanking him for a subscription. He reported to his dad, when he had an address, the score of every football game.

He still professed love for Eleanor and wrote her that he was "all in a sweat" about her mail-reading boyfriend. He begged for a picture. "You don't know how much I miss you. My brother is probably going out west this summer and maybe I will. Dad is out there now making a picture with Gloria Swanson." But he had decided, like his father in the stock market, to diversify. He sent his mother a picture of a girl at a dance: "What did you think of Caroline? Maybe you didn't notice her, she was the blonde. I'm going to have her up for Festivities, so you'll have a chance to meet her then."

Joe's speedy maturation at Choate had so impressed his father that he decided to send Jack there too. Rose wrote Choate Headmaster St. John that Jack, while he hated routine work, loved English and history and that he had a very attractive personality, though quite different from Joe's, for whom the school had done so much.

Joe's scholastic problems were by this time over; he was editor of "Briefs"—the yearbook—and he was playing first-string football. Jack was too light for varsity football, although the coach admitted that he made up for what he lacked in size with his fight. Faced at Choate with his brother's growing reputation as an athlete-scholar, Jack could not compete and tried to show that he didn't care. His housemaster was soon reporting that he studied only at the last moment, kept appointments late, and could seldom locate his possessions. Headmaster St. John, apparently forgetting Joe's early years at Choate, asked his father to school for a conference, unable to see how two boys from the same family could be so different.

While Jack digested the grim facts of Choate life, Joe widened the gap further. In Joe's last year, Mr. St. John wrote his father that he had established habits of thoroughness that would be a permanent help to him, thanking him for contributions in a postscript: "for all my life for all you are doing for our school."

Joe graduated in front of Grandfather and Grandmother Fitzgerald as well as his peripatetic parents. He won the Harvard Trophy, a small bronze statue of a football player donated by the Crimson team when it stayed at Choate on the eve of the 1931 Yale Game. It was awarded to the graduating sixth former who best combined scholarship and sportsmanship. Jack, temporarily out of Joe's shadow, was to become cheerleader at Choate, bringing a surprised comment from Headmaster St. John to Joe Senior that he would be willing to bet that within two years they would be as proud of Jack as of Joe, and that Jack had a clever, individualistic mind, simply harder to put in harness than Joe's.

Joe Kennedy Senior had no intention of further harnessing either son's mind. He had scholastic plans for Joe's next year that would probably have flabbergasted Mr. St. John and his whole establishment, but November of 1933 was a poor time to expect a reply from the elder Kennedy, and his answer to the headmaster, if any, is not preserved.

The autumn of that year had been a busy one for him on the market. Prohibition was ending in a few months. He had joined a stock-market pool which deliberately took advantage of the similarity between the names of Libby-Owens-Ford Glass Company, a plate-glass concern, and Owens-Illinois Glass, a bottle manufacturer; obviously, with Repeal, a bottle company's stocks would soar. The pool bought, on a monthly payment basis, options on Libby-Owens-Ford stock held by the company, which needed cash. Walter Chrysler was one of his partners, and they hired the "Silver Fox" of Wall Street, Frank Bliss, to encourage rumors on the floor that the company was in the bottle business. Before the stock dropped, Kennedy cleared $60,000 on no investment and headed for Europe with James Roosevelt to set up a less artificial and more permanent tap on the anticipated flood of legal alcohol. He returned with the U.S. franchise for Haig & Haig, John Dewar & Sons, King William Scotch, and Gordon's Dry Gin. To beat the gun on the eve of Repeal he imported liquor, as did others, under medicinal licenses. He filled warehouses with Dewar and Pinch bottles until his stock became so huge that his permits were reduced. Ready at last for the Great Day, he rested in Palm Beach with the President's eldest son, who soon found that if he had considered himself partner in the venture, he was wrong. Kennedy simply convinced him that any partnership he envisioned would embarrass his father, and James did not even, as later alleged, write the insurance on Kennedy's liquor shipments.

Kennedy's support of Roosevelt in the campaign of 1932 had earned him the distrust of Wall Street, but he had had reasons—family reasons—and now he basked in the light of political favor. In its warmth, and awaiting an inevitable rain of wealth after Repeal, another man might have felt secure, but not Kennedy. He had emerged from the '29 Crash unscathed; perhaps even richer for selling short. Nevertheless it had shaken him and the undertow of Depression scared him more. Despite the million-dollar trusts for his children, he was uncomfortable. Fear of outright revolution, should a safety valve not be provided, had impelled him to campaign for Roosevelt as early as 1930, when, as he said, "I was the first man with more than $12 in the bank who openly supported him." If socialism was coming, he preferred Roosevelt's brand to that of Norman Thomas or the late Eugene Debs. "I wanted [Roosevelt] in the White House for my own security and for the security of our kids and I was ready to do anything to elect him."

Now the country had the New Deal, but Joe was graduating from Choate into a world in which Hoovervilles sprouted by railroad tracks and breadlines had formed from San Francisco's Embarcadero to Boston's grimy docks. Even Roosevelt might not divert the socialist tide. Rose Kennedy had suggested that Joe go to Oxford or Cambridge for a year, but her husband, as always, consulted others too—Justices Frankfurter and Holmes among them—on how best to train the first of his young millionaires to deal with a share-the-wealth society.

In London there was a brilliant little Jewish socialist with a mousy moustache. His name was Harold Laski. Joe Senior hated his politics and had already called him "a nut and a crank." Later, when Joe Senior was to say that democracy was dead in England, the two would really break, but now Joe Junior, before he went to Harvard, would travel there to study under him.

5

A MILE toward the Thames from the University of London, across an alley called New Inn Passage from Dickens' original Old Curiosity Shop, a hideous gray building nudges smaller and equally sooty structures. It is the University's London School of Economics. From there Professor Harold Laski twanged socialistic arrows at the right. Joe Kennedy, Jr., was eighteen when they met; Laski, a Manchester Jew, who had broken with his own prosperous family before he was twenty, was still only forty. Joe went to seven lectures a week under Laski, who had taught at Harvard until his support of the Boston Police Strike in 1919 made his tenure uncomfortable. The Professor thought Joe "adorably young and still more adorably unsophisticated."

Joe, through his father's British friends, found digs at 20 Courtfield Gardens in Earl's Court. The flat was excellent: his bedroom looked out on the gardens, but the place was too big; he was lonesome. He had taken to Rugby quite naturally and on the field one day he met Aubrey Whitelaw, now a Connecticut executive. "Whitey," then simply another young American studying under Laski, wanted to write the story of Laski's life. Joe said, "Come on over and share my place." Whitey went home with him to see it. When he saw that there were two bedrooms and a living room he knew that it was beyond his finances. Joe asked him what he was paying where he was and then said, "Come on over and you won't have to pay any more than that for this place."

Whitelaw, who had never heard of the Kennedys or their wealth, wrote home that he had moved in with a Boston Irishman he liked. He was soon to become as familiar by proxy with the family as if he knew them in the flesh. Joe Senior would phone at a set time every week; while waiting, Joe's mind would wander. He worshiped his mother, Whitelaw recalls, and he would point out his brothers and sisters on a family portrait placed like a shrine in the living room, explaining what Jack and Bobby and Teddy, or Kathleen and Eunice and Pat were going to do in life; he had already decided their futures for them. Sometimes to Whitelaw it seemed that he was talking to the photo.

The two would travel London together, seeing people Joe's father had asked him to meet. Whitelaw recalls that "We saw Felix Frankfurter. Now Felix was a good friend of Hal Laski. And I thought this Felix Frankfurter is a hell of an important guy, which he was, and asking for my opinion, what the hell is going on? But he was sort of drilling. He was drilling Joe to see how effective Laski's teaching was with him. I really felt Laski was a hell of an important teacher, but Joe took him, I think, with a grain of salt because the Old Man said just check in with him. Joe, he was pretty much of a church guy and was pretty conservative."

Whitelaw's London life began to change. Joe recruited him into his own physical-education program: up before breakfast for a jog around the garden walks—fifteen times for a mile. He dragged Whitelaw to Rotten Row for riding, somehow finding him riding clothes, for the U.S. image was at stake; everything had to be right. Joe had letters of introduction to movie people from his father, and he did not let his good looks go to waste. The apartment filled at teatime with starlets from the British studios; one, a beautiful brunette, appeared more often than the rest. Whitelaw began dutifully to disappear, but she never spent the night. There were, apparently, obligations and pitfalls for Joe that went with wealth and his growing ambition. He treated the starlets with caution and the London debutantes with a teasing air.

He was amused by pretense. If he saw pomposity at a dinner party, Joe's face would get red, and if his eyes met Whitelaw's, the two would burst out laughing, so they would have to invent something innocent to explain their amusement. They traveled in society richer than any Whitelaw had known. They visited distiller John Dewar's estate. With him they toured his grounds, cutting at high speed in his Rolls across moors that could better have been traveled by mule; the forty-three-year-old Dewar drove and his new wife, Kathleen, beside him explained the lineage of scores of fine-blooded horses—"Old Angel by First Earl out of Magpie One"—while the two Yankee students bounced on the edge of hilarity in leathered luxury in back.

Between terms Joe bought a Chrysler convertible in London for a trip to Rome "to see the Pope." Joe and Whitelaw would share gas and expenses. On the eve of departure they discovered that Joe had forgotten to insure the car. He had made plans to leave the next morning; his plans were always immutable. He called the knighted head of a large insurance company and asked him to stay overtime. He raced downtown and discovered that he was too young for foreign insurance. He talked the Britisher into making an exception, and the two students left next morning as scheduled.

Whitelaw, forced to bring white tie and tails for the Vatican, had not figured on Joe's determination, or his father's connections, and still thought the Pope was a pipe dream. But they saw the Pope, kissed the ring, and visited U.S. Ambassador Long. Joe reported to his mother that he "met a German girl, grand-daughter of Schumann the composer, very good looking, and speaks four languages," and that finding no lodging in Rome they were taken in by an Italian family for ninety cents a day including breakfast. Whitelaw, more interested in socialism than history, was bored with sightseeing, but Joe dragged him along anyway, checking off the sites his mother had asked him to see: Catacombs, Forum, Colosseum, St. Paul's, San Pietro in Vincoli, Santa Maria Maggiore, St. Peter's, where, he wrote home, he had "climbed the holy stairs on my knees."

Joe was alert to modern history too. One afternoon Whitelaw, guiding the Chrysler top-down through Milanese traffic past a billboard from which Il Duce glowered, glanced in the rear-view mirror and noticed in horror that his roommate had climbed into the back seat and was braced at attention, thumb to nose. No Black Shirts apparently noticed, and they left Italy to tour Austria, Germany, and France.

"We had some wild rides," Joe reported to his mother when he got back to London, "as the brakes on the car weren't very good. An Italian smashed into us outside of Rome, he was going about sixty around a curve, and we about twenty. School begins next Monday."

Back in London the two devoted part of their time to showing the British how to pass a Rugby ball. Given a free throw for out of bounds, Whitey would heave it in with a long American spiral, Joe would snag it far down the field and be on his way for a goal. The British would rebel—"I say, you can't do that"—but they never could find a rule against it. The two would wait for an opportunity to rough it up with crashing, head-on American tackles; in one game in London the opposing team lost five injured players to their tactics.

But London was not all mayhem, fun, and games. Joe took a course in elementary economics under Lionel Robbins and another in literature, on which he worked enthusiastically. Whitelaw, in London for Laski alone, noticed with surprise that Joe would actually spend time on other courses than Laski's *Social and Political Theory,* which was the core of their lives and the reason both were there.

The famous socialist had been teaching for two decades. He illuminated his lectures with an inexhaustible stream of anecdotes, often quite true; stories of his own dialogues with the political figures of the thirties. He was no grubby, narrow grind: he could flabbergast his more athletic students by reciting from memory the batting and bowling averages of every great English cricketeer from 1880 on. "Certainly one reason that his lecture room was always packed," recalls a student, "was that no other professor provided comparable entertainment." Laski would mount the rostrum, small, shy-looking, take off his wristwatch, lay it on the lectern, and begin to speak without notes in a dry monotone. "In five or ten minutes," remembers Whitelaw, "you'd forget the insignificance of the man in what he was saying. He was a terrific teacher."

"I am a socialist," Laski would say, "though from time to time I shall prescribe other books as an antidote to my poison. If you disagree, come along to my study and tell me where I am wrong." He loved his audiences because they were young, alive, eager. He attracted graduate students from all over the world. Joe Junior, who had not yet been to college, found himself stranded in the bleak gray halls, straining to keep up with men years older and minds better trained. But he had a goal, a more ambitious one than any possible for the older Chinese, Indian, and English scholars cramming the dingy lecture rooms.

The motive was no longer a good report for the folks at home. His dream was perhaps unrealistic, but he did not hide it: he admitted it to Laski, to Whitelaw, to anyone anywhere, frankly and unselfconsciously. He was going to be the first Catholic President of the United States.

"Joe loved to—he sort of loved to spoof and, you know, aggravate enough to challenge, dare people to come out and say this or that," Whitelaw says. "He had a helluva good sense of humor. When people were suffering from any amount of affectation, he loved to mimic them. He could take them off. And it was in his old Boston Irish way. He tried to imitate a British accent. It was pretty pathetic, but he tried to."

Joe was a great kidder. He kidded others and he kidded himself, smiling the lopsided smile. His eyes smiled, too, so that few, except sometimes his brother Jack, took offense. He smiled the same smile when he said he would be President, but Whitelaw noticed then that his eyes did not smile at all.

2

The flat at 5 Addison Bridge Place faces a grimy delta of London railroad tracks. Harold Laski called the place "Devon Lodge." It is a row house and its bricks are sooty and its marble steps, though clean, are worn. For twenty years, until Harold Laski died in 1950, hundreds of students, politicians, educators, and at least two U.S. Supreme Court Justices climbed the steps to knock at the door. One night during the London Blitz, while the professor and his wife, Frida, slept in its basement, a German bomb blew a forty-foot crater in the tracks a hundred feet away. British Tories and U.S. Republicans would have said that it was a hundred feet too far, but the next morning Laski wrote to Felix Frankfurter: "We are alive; the house stands up proudly. . . . So we are well content."

An ancient housekeeper lets you into a small study overlooking a tiny garden which has learned to live with the grime from the railroad yard. Nehru smiles down from the wall and the late professor gazes down too, with quizzical, kindly eyes. He would have been seventy-five now, and with a shock you realize that Frida Laski, who married him amid parental hysteria when he was eighteen and she twenty-five, must be eighty-two.

She is solid, brisk, and very sharp. She wears a plain cardigan sweater and her eyes snap aggressively. In the twenties she was a suffragette and she supported Marie Stopes and the birth-control movement of the thirties. She has great disdain for the Kennedy wealth and a smoldering rancor against journalists, fueled over the years in which her husband was painted red by the Fleet Street brush. Her distrust has just been fanned by a newspaperman who twisted a quote of hers to his own ends. She smiles dryly: "We have a saying: 'Never try to bribe an honest British journalist; he will twist what you say anyway.'"

Harold Laski's jammed lectures in the halls of Houghton Street were not really the heart of his course. Laski's real teaching took place here, in the little room above the garden, at the famed "Laski Sunday teas," where the students would sprawl on the rugs and the air would grow heavy with pipe smoke and dreams of a world in which all men owned all things. Of Joe's presence at the teas, Laski wrote: "He has often sat in my study and submitted with that smile that was pure magic to relentless teasing about his determination to be nothing less than President of the United States."

"Joe would always come to the teas," Frida Laski remembers. "He was tall and very good-looking. And argumentative, and very bright, but of course he was at a disadvantage. My husband would finish discussing some point and then he would turn to Joe, sitting on the floor, and say, 'Now Joe, what will you do about this when you are President?'"

Joe's roommate, Whitelaw, has described the usual answer: "In a room full of experts . . . dead silence for only a second, and then Joe would tackle the problem in a completely logical manner and struggle through it until he had answered—not batting an eye or retreating from established positions either." Whitelaw recalled all of the answers as simple and some of them as naïve, and remembered that Laski would deflate him humorously afterward. Whitelaw remembers that Joe, though open-minded, always took the conservative viewpoint, but Mrs. Laski thinks Joe at the time was politically to the left of John, who studied for a few weeks under her husband the following year.

Joe went to Russia with the Laskis at the end of the term. Whitelaw went down to see them off at the boat: Frida Laski remembers that he was carrying a tennis racket. Whitelaw had wanted to go, but couldn't afford it. "Whitelaw was going to write a book about my husband, but he didn't have the money to stay here and do the research." The clear old eyes glint. "If you have a rich daddy," she says, thinking of John Kennedy's *Why England Slept,* "you can get a book published."

For a moment Laski's gently sardonic ghost hovers over the worn rug and the tired furniture. His widow remembers that they went by boat to Germany and by train to Moscow and Leningrad. Joe was impressed with a man they met on the train who said that the Russians, who prior to the Revolution had four meals of meat per year, now had meat every night. Her husband spoke at the Soviet Academy of Science. His message was anti-Marxist, plugging British socialism. He was well received, but when they came back, they were told by the London School of Economics that he shouldn't have done it. "Joe," she says, eyes twinkling, "got a headache when we visited the Anti-Religious Museum and he said he didn't want to argue."

For Joe, who loved to argue, the headache must have been real and the lost opportunity must have seemed a defeat. The professor, in one of his weekly letters to Justice Oliver Wendell Holmes, had once written that "It is impossible to make peace with the Roman Catholic Church. It is one of the permanent enemies of all that is decent in human spirit." In another letter he mentioned telling an Arkansas minister who inquired of the religious beliefs of Laski's London students that "(I) I had never had the curiosity to inquire and (II) I hoped sincerely that they had none."

Nobody was budging Rose Kennedy's son on religion. Rose recalls proudly that she had heard that when Laski pressed him too closely, he would say, "I don't know, but Catholicism is the right religion for me." Neither did Harold Laski's views on birth control—"if mankind learns to control population the event might be more important than any since the discovery of fire"—shake Joe a bit, but

the teas at the Laskis' helped broaden politically an inquis-
itive mind that had so far only known the horizons of the
mayor of Boston, a few judges and New Deal politicians,
and some successful businessmen.

When Joe returned to Hyannis from London he was
changed. Rose Kennedy recalls that "he put on a good
show of having absorbed Laski's teaching, and some of us
asked him whether he'd be willing to give up his boat if he
had to share the wealth. He decided that just his boat
wouldn't make that much difference."

John sided with Joe's new liberalism, hinting that his
brother understood the situation better than their father.
Irked that they would question her husband's wisdom,
Rose suggested to Kennedy that they were presumptuous.
Remembering his two sons' childhood conflict, he said,
"As long as they stick together, I can take care of my-
self." Rose was not adamant by nature either; when Joe
Junior suggested that she and Kathleen go to Russia to see
the Anti-Religious Museum for themselves, she agreed and
the next year they did.

Cold facts and lucid reason were the keys to victory in
a Kennedy debate, and Joe's new independence might
have actually pleased his father, but both were short-
tempered. Once Joe Junior left the table; at another meal
it was his father who stalked away in disgust. To Lorelle
Hearst Joe Junior later described the arguments as "terrible fights."

Laski's influence on Joe's politics was not as transitory
as his father hoped. All his collegiate life he provoked
argument by citing the need to look at both sides, to "see
things through the eyes of Laski." Just as important had
been his eye-opening contact with Laski's pupils. He met
young men he would never have met elsewhere, from a
background he would never see again. Professor Laski
wrote: "He was with me during a year when the three
outstanding students in my department all happened to be
at once Socialists and poor Jews from the East End of
London. Nothing was more admirable than Joe's attitude
to them, a deep respect for their ability, an ardent promise that one day he would know enough to argue with
them on equal terms, and his keen satisfaction and obvious affection for them. . . . His mind was only just beginning to discover the enchantment of thought."

3

Dusk falls on the snowfields around Whitelaw's home,
"Tar Barrel Hill," in Connecticut. Embers pop in the huge
fireplace of his second-story study; the eyes of a stuffed
hawk glow amber. Whitelaw is gray now, but with white
teeth that slightly protrude to give him an air of youthful
eagerness. He is articulate and has to hide his enthusiasm
behind gruffness. His mind drifts back to Rome, incredulously, as if he cannot believe his own recollections:
"When I remember this moonlight night when we were in
the middle of the Colosseum and him with Diana Something and me with Barbara Hoyt and . . . not a soul
around, you know, and the moon beaming down and this
beautiful blonde . . . and the Colosseum. . . ." He sighs.
"And then he wanted to see the museums and things. . . .
He had a regular check-off list. He accumulated this
Italian guide—crooked little bastard—stole his watch
when he left."

His eyes brighten. "We went to Germany. In Munich we
watched this brown-shirt parade, and everybody was 'Heil
Hitlering' except Joe and me, and some guy nudged him
on the other side to get his hand up. Joe didn't pay any
attention and the guy nudged him again. I saw Joe's fist
come back and I grabbed it or they probably would have
kicked the hell out of us. He hated the Nazis as much as I
did. He'd jump into anything, both feet. As soon as we
arrived in France, he'd want to speak French. Insisted.
Even if they spoke better English than he did, he spoke
French. Very annoying and his friends there used to tell
him, but it improved rapidly. Italian border, same thing;
Austria he wanted to speak German."

Whitelaw saw Joe one more time after he said good-bye
at the London dock before the Russian trip: at the Polo
Grounds in New York when Joe, a Harvard student, was
playing Rugby for the All Eastern Team. Whitelaw introduced him to a professional boxer he was backing, hoping
Joe would back him too. Joe sparred with him in Whitelaw's father's apartment. "They busted up a couple of
chairs. It was typical of Joe to test the man out before he
put any money on him. He didn't back him, but when he

was through, he admitted this two-hundred-and-twenty-pound guy was pretty rugged all right."

Whitelaw's bourbon is low in your glass. His massive dog, Sam, stretches. It is time to go, for the country roads are growing slick and the Connecticut Turnpike is a long way off. Whitey Whitelaw has what he calls a "mundane job" as a division head in General Dynamics now, but he was once a liberal student in London and he seems reluctant to leave Courtland Gardens and the little flat on Addison Bridge Place. Suddenly he shows you a picture of President Kennedy. It is inscribed, "To Whitey, who has been for a Kennedy for President since 1933."

You leave him in his big house on the hill, sorry that he never got to write the book on Laski.

But Joe Kennedy never got to be President, either.

6

JOE KENNEDY, Jr., scrambling in the shadow of the stadium by the Charles for an end spot on the Harvard frosh, had been a minor star at Choate. It must have felt good to be back from English Rugby to the smash and the shock of the sport he liked, next to sailing, better than any, for there is a feel in the slim taut hide of an American football that a Rugby ball never has.

He was highly motivated. His father had made him a millionaire, sent him to England, sent him here: now he must prove that he was not simply a rich man's soft son. He wanted a letter in football. There was only one way to get one—sometime between his sophomore and senior years he must get into a Yale game. His father had not played football at Harvard, but had after all won his "H"; if some old classmates still questioned the means, it was beside the point.

Joe was aggressive and hit hard, but perhaps not jarringly. By the standards of the day he was big enough— almost six feet and around 175—but certainly not tremendous. He was fast but not blinding. The odds were against him. Tom Bilodeau, a rugged, hawk-nosed athlete who, though a year ahead of Joe, was one of his best friends and a star halfback himself, found Kennedy a little green and uncoordinated by college standards. "But the kind of guy, though, who would spark a team, a guy you could depend on for the *big* play, if you let him in." Worst of all, Joe tended to come apart in joint and muscle, and

competition was rugged. The Ivy League was not the Big
Ten, but it was not the Eastern Prep School League either. Harvard competition was of another order: the
university was never too proud to hire a coal-miner's son
or the odd South Boston high-school star who might
qualify academically. The jocks were there by the score;
they might never make the Hasty Pudding Club, but they
were all over the greens, slamming the blocking sleds and
rocking the dummies.

Joe survived the initial cuts and made the freshman
squad. Frosh coach Henry Lamar thought him full of
fight, with a fine pair of hands, and highly motivated, but
he was not first string, or even second, and he actually
began to carry a football around the Yard to keep the
feel of it. He noticed a bantam-cock quarterback with a
good arm and asked him to stay after practice and toss
him passes. The quarterback's name was Timothy J.
Reardon—"Ted" to most, "T. J." to Joe. T. J. became
Joe's closest college friend, and one day he would become
President John Kennedy's trusted aide. In 1934, a "yard-
ling" like Joe, Reardon was just a poor boy from Somer-
ville, near Cambridge, and knowing Joe changed his life
even more than it had Whitelaw's. Forced by finances to
commute to school, he sometimes slept in Joe's room at
the freshman Soule Hall, and when he did they would toss
a coin for the only bed; Joe, if he lost, slept on the floor.
Joe invited him to the Cape for the summer; they conferred before they left on who else would be *simpático*.
Joe decided on Bob Downes, a tall gray-eyed guard from
Oshkosh, Wisconsin. In his dry teasing way Joe came to
call him "Chubby-Bubby." Downes accepted. Sophomore
year, when Joe was eligible for one of the graduate
houses, he chose Winthrop and offered to pay two-thirds
of T. J.'s board and room. T. J. refused, so Bob Downes
roomed with Joe instead, and T. J. gradually moved in too,
unofficially, braving Joe's icy window-open-at-night policy
and sleeping on the couch in their living room.

Reardon is a nervous, high-strung Irishman with lively
brown eyes. Today, as an executive of the Federal Deposit
Insurance Corporation, he can still hardly speak of Joe
without emotion. "I remember once, when he tore up his
knee in football and he was in the hospital from the
operation—I went to see him and told him I couldn't
continue, I'd have to leave school—and he wrote me out a
check for a year's tuition."

Reardon finally ripped up the check and got a loan

through the Student Council. Joe recovered from the knee operation and broke his arm in a scrimmage. Reardon remembers him at the wheel of his yellow Ford with a plastered arm, whizzing his grandfather Honeyfitz through a police cordon at the Boston Marathon, a big Irish cop trying to stop them, and Honeyfitz, the injured politician, squawking in wrath from the rear seat.

Reardon made a mistake once: from it he learned never to joke about anyone close to Joe. Discussing graft, he said, "Sure, these city officials are all the same. Now, you even take John Fitzgerald—" Joe's sense of humor, which Reardon remembers as among the most acute he had ever known, suddenly failed: Joe ordered him out of the room and took a kick as he scrambled out which had "direction and force but luckily lacked speed."

Reardon was lucky. One night another Harvard student, not so close to Joe and probably unaware that he was Honeyfitz's grandson, made a patronizing crack at the ex-mayor, ex-congressman, and unsuccessful gubernatorial candidate, and Joe leaped from his chair and decked him. His loyalty extended past his own relatives to the relatives of his friends. Years later in law school when a Jewish classmate derided Joe's friend Bob Taft's father, the senator, Joe barked, "If Bob were here you wouldn't say that," and then, having by that time substituted a caustic tongue for a flashing fist, proceeded to cut the young man to pieces verbally in his most acid, biting way.

2

Winthrop House is brick, as are all of the undergraduate residence halls. It snuggles against the wall of the Yard on the Charles River, shaded by trees. Its components— formerly Standish and Gore Halls—are old, combined a few years before Joe arrived to form a complex which includes a dining hall, library, commons rooms, and masters house. It is quite beautiful outside; inside, though suites are Oxford-like in their dimensions—bedrooms, baths, living rooms, and maid service—it has still the smell of any college fraternity or dormitory: tobacco too highly flavored with rum, stale beer, shaving lotion, and bedding changed not often enough. On the river side of the house the Charles slithers under low stone bridges, framed from the upper windows of Winthrop by the boughs of ancient oaks.

Harvard undergraduate houses are named after the most revered of Harvard presidents: Leverett House, Winthrop House, Hollis House—President Leonard Hoar was venerated, but for obvious reasons lost out. The houses change in character, from generation to generation. Joe's father had roomed in Hollis, which was the athletic house when he was at Cambridge. Joe Junior's charm and obvious abilities could have got him into any one he wanted: intellectual Adams, scholastic Eliot, Leverett or Hollis. Eliot was socially desirable, but he picked Winthrop because by now it had become the athletic house and he felt more at home with football players than with Cabots, Lodges, or Lowells. Though John Roosevelt— a good-natured target for designing females with plots to embarrass his father—lived there and gave the place some minor social prestige, it was the "jock" house of the day. Joe, Bob Downes, and T. J. Reardon had a corner room near a stairwell, convenient for spiriting girls up to cocktail parties. The suite swarmed after Pi Eta theatricals and football games. Joe did not drink, but he liked to watch the results when he spiked the Purple Passion in the bathtub with extra gin, and Downes wonders today how they got through four years.

Joe, having made the frosh, fought hard for an end spot on the Harvard varsity. Harvard used the Notre Dame system depending on ends to turn plays inward on defense. It was the age of limited substitution and sixty-minute football; coaches seldom changed their minds; if you were not named Friday to start a game, you were lucky if you got in at all. Joe was inexperienced and still prone to injuries. Massachusetts Congressman Torbert MacDonald, a fast Harvard back who later roomed with Jack and kept Kathleen's picture close on his desk, says, "If he was injured he'd never let you know until afterwards." But a more important obstacle to Joe than any injury was his own dislike for Head Coach Dick Harlow. Harlow had come from Western Maryland, where tackles were Neanderthal and backs were purchased by the lot. He was a complicated, many-faceted man: he had instructed in ornithology at Penn State and was an expert in the field. He was fat, bald, with bright-blue eyes, high blood pressure, and an enormous appetite: at a Boston restaurant he once wolfed a dozen oysters, followed by steamed crabs, three broiled lobsters, potatoes, and onion rings. He then ingested two more lobsters, dabbed his lips, and announced, "Now *that* was a nice dinner."

He was an intelligent and original coach. He invented the mousetrap and the looping line. He put winning on Saturday above everything; he once wanted to freeze with Novocaine the injured ankle of Torb MacDonald. Torb's cousin Frank Ryan, Harvard's publicity director, objected and lost his job.

When Harlow felt like it, he could charm strangers. He had a resonant voice and was a good public speaker. He appeared in the reception line of his first Harvard Athletic Association dinner with the record of every Harvard letterman since 1922 committed to memory; as he met each potbellied alumnus, he recited his accomplishments as if he had been following the man's career for life.

Such gimmicks, and his success with football material traditionally regarded as initially weak, at first endeared him to alumni. He made good copy, had a sympathetic press, and tried to keep it; he had a quick mind for printable epithets like "The Magnificent Faker" for halfback Vernon Struck. He would throw a huge arm around a player's shoulder on Friday and announce to photographers that he wished he had "more fighting Irishmen like this one," but Joe Kennedy, Jr., was unimpressed.

MacDonald says, "Joe was very good, actually. But it came hard for him to just subordinate his own personality to some guy like that." "Gentleman Dick," who demanded total loyalty, sensed Joe's animosity, which he might have overlooked in a finer player—MacDonald and Tom Bilodeau shared his dislike for Harlow without suffering on Saturdays. But Joe's position was always marginal anyway, and there were plenty of ends to draw on. Joe and those who refused to become "robots for Harlow" began to coalesce around a backfield coach named Howie O'Dell, who still feels that Joe was a fine football player.

Joe finished his sophomore season without success. He went out for Rugby and here the long hours on the fields of London University paid off. At New Haven he scored the winning try against Yale: the *Harvard Tribune* headlined JOE KENNEDY RUNS 30 YARDS FOR CRIMSON'S TRY and the *New York Times* called him "outstanding in the Crimson attack." To his dad he reported: "It was a pretty tough game as they had nearly all football players and we were missing two of our regulars. I got a pass in the first ten minutes and managed to get over for the only score of the game which gave me quite a kick." Of his healing football knee he said; "The doctors weren't too enthusiastic about the idea of playing, but I got it well wrapped and it stood up very well."

He was sent to Bermuda on the Harvard Rugby team and shot a postcard back to Jack: "Plenty of good girls here," and one to Bobby: "There is plenty of sailing and bicycling". He returned to find more bills than he could pay. He wrote Paul Murphy, his father's wispy, diminutive aide, whose zeal in the Kennedy cause would eventually drive him to drink. And then he wrote his father: "Am writing Paul today to advance me a month's allowance and it looks like I'll have to pay you back July 26. If this is not okay I guess I'll have to write back or go over to your bank in East Boston and get a loan." He diplomatically mentioned making the Dean's List and the Tercentenary Celebration Committee, and then pointed out that the blame for his financial condition rested squarely on Harvard and his father: "The big reason for my finances being in such a state is my trip to Bermuda. I bought clothes and with other incidentals it about finished a month's allowance. You gave Jack and myself quite a tongue-lashing about doing what the college demands rather than what you yourself want to do. Had I gone to Florida it would have cost you another $120 at least for a plane trip so I should think the sporting thing to do would be to pay me the difference for carrying the name of Kennedy and Harvard to foreign lands."

Joe Senior congratulated him on his prospects of making Dean's List: "Besides doing a good job it means additional prestige and that all helps in the long run." He was happy that he was on the Tercentenary Celebration Committee: "It may bring you into touch with a great many interesting people." But he attacked his son's excuse for bankruptcy: "As I see it I am afraid discussions of general policy between us must in the future be limited to each particular occasion so that there can be no misunderstanding. However, I am glad you went to Bermuda and I shall have Paul send you a check for $120 which I hope will ease your financial difficulty." And then, more seriously: "All I want you to do is to look at the total amount spent one way or another and I'll trust your good judgement to keep it in line."

Joe would have preferred less parasitic methods of raising funds than simply asking the Old Man, and he was alert to passing financial opportunity. As chairman of the freshman smoker, he had made theatrical contacts. It was a day in which success of a dance committee lay in how big and expensive a band it could get, and Joe decided to become an agent. "As I know a lot of the fellows in charge," he wrote his father, "they would book the bands through me providing I could give them as good a price as the other agencies. . . . I would do it through the R.K.O. where I know Doc Breed."

But he lacked his father's touch and the idea died. In the press he watched his father play Midas again: David Sarnoff asked him to unsnarl RCA's finances and Joe read of his $125,000 fee. He made a proposal: "I feel that I am ready to offer myself as one of your business partners. Would you employ me as one of those accountants to whom you paid $30,000 and it would save you trouble on your income tax?"

Joe Senior replied that his fee had been widely misquoted and he had actually only netted $120,000. "The government will get 70% of that. As you are still un-. qualified as an expert, I am very much afraid I cannot get you on the payroll. If you will hurry up and get through while I am still able to do any work, maybe we can work out something for you."

In the meanwhile Joe, for a nominal millionaire, stayed broke. The income from his trust would begin this summer, but that, once tuition and board were paid, would merely replace his allowance: his real need was cash, and he sweated out a reward promised him for not smoking or drinking until his twenty-first birthday. "That two thousand smackers," he wrote his father to remind him, "is going to save me." His problems were not all athletic or financial. He was failing a course in fine arts that his mother had suggested. Rather than face a *D* and banishment from the Dean's List, he wrote his father that he had decided to take tutoring in it and to "send the bill to Mother with my kindest regards."

After Jack Kennedy's term with Laski had been cut short by illness, Jack had decided to follow his Choate friends to Princeton rather than compete with Joe again. His father had not tried to change his mind; he had a motto on his desk: "Once you've done everything you can, the hell with it." Joe had not tried to influence him either; he was too busy trying to batter his way onto the Harvard varsity to worry about family turncoats. As spring training commenced again, Joe wrote his father: "I would say there are about four ends ahead of me. I am not looking like any ball of fire, but I think I can give them a fight." His father suggested that, with his usual determination to get what he wanted, some intensive work that summer might whip him into shape to get at least within the first four—"which would probably get you into the games." Then he consulted Arthur Krock, who submitted that a few months on an Arizona ranch might toughen Joe up for the next season, and improve Jack's health too. Krock wrote John G. F. Speiden, an old New Jersey friend who had moved west to Benson, Arizona, to run a thousand head of cattle on a ranch he had purchased in the early thirties. "Work hell out of them," Krock suggested. Speiden agreed and the two arrived ready for manual labor at the beginning of the summer.

They were to be paid ranch hands, but they logged into the guest book when they arrived. Jack signed, naturally enough, "Bronxville, New York," but it was not so simple for Joe, the embryo Massachusetts politician. He might legitimately be said to reside in Cambridge, but perhaps a college address would someday be vulnerable to charges of carpetbagging. The same might be said of a summer colony like Hyannis. Stretching a point, he scrawled: "Joseph P. Kennedy, Junior, Brookline, Massachusetts."

3

The Jay Six Ranch reclined along a great watershed between the San Pedro and Santa Cruz rivers, halfway between Tucson and Naco on the Mexican border. It sprawled over forty-three thousand acres on the topographical map on the wall of the main house, but maps are bird's-eye views and a great many of the actual acres, being straight up and down, were not accounted for on the wall. Visible or not, the whole spread had to be contained in barbed wire, and in the maintenance of the wire even the vertical planes had often to be traversed, usually by horse but sometimes in the last resort by foot. Tending the wire Joe and Jack found that actual life as ranch hands in the Old West bore little relation to that portrayed on the screen by their old friend Tom Mix.

There was plenty of riding—out to fences and back— and Speiden's ambiguous verdict on the boys' horsemanship was that it was "completely adequate." There were a thousand head of cattle clinging to the mountains, most of whom Joe would meet socially by the time he left, but there was no time to savor the excitement of a roundup or the romance of beef on the move. There was not a lariat in sight: Speiden, like most cattlemen, viewed the roping of good beef on the hoof as a new-car salesman regards a stock-car race. There were no six-guns; any heat Joe or Jack might have chosen to strap to their legs would have interfered with their secondary purpose in life, which was, when not riding fence, to transport by wheelbarrow one part of the forty-five thousand acres to another.

They had arrived at a propitious time—for Mr. Speiden. He intended to carry out the suggestions of his old newspaper friend to the letter. He was building permanent ranch offices, and he was building them in the old way, of indigenous adobe mud and strong backs, a method which, when employed by the Spanish priests, had effectively wiped out the more devout of the aborigines of Arizona, New Mexico, and California.

John Speiden, a quiet man given to understatement in a deep gravelly voice, found them "philosophical." They lived in the bunkhouse with the other ranch hands, who never knew of their wealth. They ate enormously. They were hauling adobe each day before the sun was baking the eastern flanks of the Galiuros, broke for midday dinner, and worked until it sank behind Apache peak to the west. With a Mexican, an alcoholic Scotsman named Mac, and Speiden himself, they erected an adobe complex to house the ranch offices. They worked six days a week. On Saturday nights they would bump in a ranch truck to the border town of Nogales; after his twenty-first birthday, Joe was free of his promise to his father and could sample the local tequila, which may have accounted for a relatively abstemious life thereafter. He made one dollar a day, the only money he would ever earn through physical labor, and when he left after almost four months, they had finished the ranch offices, which stand today.

He returned east bronzed, lean, and according to Speiden, "like leather." Jack was similarly toughened. He decided to transfer to Harvard and to go out for football.

4

Joe's social life in college was active but simple. Only one in three Harvard undergraduates ever saw the inside of a

Harvard Club, but Joe was elected to Hasty Pudding—
during hazing he had to carry a fragrant Boston haddock
strapped to his belt for a week—and to the Spee Club
without effort, though, like his father, his religion and
background barred him from the best final clubs like
Porcellian or Fly. He didn't care. Ted Reardon recalls
that his idea of a big night out was to go to Reardon's
father's house for a home-cooked meal in the kitchen.
Being football players, Joe and T. J. and Downes got
stag-line invitations to debutante balls; they would feed up
and then leave.

Joe operated alone. Tom Bilodeau had met him for
the first time on the ski train to the Dartmouth Winter
Carnival; everyone else had dates, but Joe's plan—more
or less successfully carried out—was to descend on the
carnival like a wolf on the fold, steal some Dartmouth
man's date, and save wear on his pocketbook: "Let some
other guy pay her way."

He loved to ski and would try anything. Bilodeau recalls
"skiing with him over and over, straight down a hill, neither
of us being able to ski worth a damn." He liked action. He
swam for Winthrop, played intramural squash, basketball,
golf, and sailed. Despite his activity, he was defeated for
marshal of the Student Council in 1937, but competition
was tough that year; Arthur Schlesinger, Jr. was running
for Odist and Richard Tregaskis for Poet. Joe was determined to graduate *cum laude* himself—he was disappointed in Tom Bilodeau for not bothering to do a thesis,
which would have assured him an honors degree—but he
never allowed studies to interfere with his enjoyment of
Harvard. When life grew dull, there was always the prospect of a good brawl on the ancestral sod of Boston; he
and a few fellow athletes could guarantee themselves
exercise on paydays by wearing coats and ties to an East
Boston saloon on a Saturday night and waiting for the
first snide crack from a drunken steelworker. None of his
varsity friends were ever sober enough at the outset to
recall specific battles today, but it is not hard to visualize
Joe, relatively sober and clearheaded, hardened by ranch-
work, football, squash, and tennis, pitching into a fracas
for the sheer joy of battle and cleaning out a waterfront
bar.

When not stirring up a brannigan, he was on the side of
law and order. Joe Timilty, his father's friend until for
some reason he fell from favor, was for ten years Boston
police commissioner and, despite the difference in their

ages, one of Joe Junior's closest cronies. They went to the races together at Suffolk and Rockingham and to the dog races at Revere; Joe would get so excited at a photo finish he would jump up on his seat to shout in a winner. He liked to drive after dark with Timilty in the police commissioner's car watching Boston's Finest perform in the nightclubs and bars of Stewart Street and South Boston.

Joe had a good left, apparently no fear at all, and occasionally the standards of the Round Table. Driving alone one night from Boston to Cambridge, he heard a woman screaming near Harvard Square. He found a man beating her in a parked car. Ignoring Harvard's one outside rule for undergraduates, "Keep your name out of the papers," Joe moved in. The police sirened up and Joe, to his surprise, was clapped into the cooler along with his opponent. He spent the night in jail and might have had to appear in court had not a Sergeant McLaughlin and Police Chief Timothy H. Leahy arrived with a proper Irish appreciation for the sanctity of women and perhaps the name of Kennedy. Joe slammed into his room at Winthrop in the morning. He was unshaven, hungry, and "mad as hell," according to Downes. Joe's chivalry never cooled, though, and in Downes' view he remained "the kind of a guy who, instead of ignoring some thing like that, would try to help a gal out." Later, when Joe dived into the Charles River after a drowning man—or said he had—he became known to those who cared to bait him as "the Lifesaver."

Harvard had never asked much discipline of its students. Harvard "riots" in the thirties were spring perennials greatly inflated by the press and the City Fathers, who greedily eyed the university's tax-exempt status. The "Yard cops" of the university were hired more as guides to drunken students and buffers against the Cambridge Police Department than as brakes on undergraduate enthusiasm. The tutorial system, in which Joe met alone or in a small group with his tutor Earl Stillson, did not strictly require his attendance at lectures; he could cut as many classes as he wished. The only house rules at Winthrop or any other residence club were those that prohibited him from keeping "dogs or women" in his rooms.

Today Joe would be a collegiate swinger; in the mid-thirties he was simply an active, handsome young student playing the field to keep himself free. His relations with the other sex required finesse and, Bilodeau recalls, considerable last-minute shuffling of the unhappy victims. He had vast energy and great impatience; it took a nimble girl to follow his train of thought, and he was intolerant of cloudy thinking. Mrs. George Pinto, "Dee-Dee" to the men of Winthrop, was in charge of the dining room. Joe assigned her an extracurricular social task: to approve of clothes, flowers, and even sometimes the girl he would date. When she didn't approve, Joe would question her relentlessly: "Why? What's wrong, Dee-Dee?"

"She's not your type. She doesn't speak your language, Joe. She's much too young."

"Well, Dee-Dee, if she's big enough, she's old enough."

He preferred to take a girl to a movie rather than a formal ball; he favored a stripper over a dull co-ed. In an era when a poll of his classmates showed that three out of four dated eastern college girls, Joe liked showgirls and those who worked. His looks and charm gave him a choice of high-Irish heiresses, debs, and Radcliffe girls, but he went with those who were on their own and likely to stay safely so: in the chaotic war years to come, they would be divorcees and often estranged wives. He found traditional New York society boring, but the café society of Brenda Duff Frazier, El Morocco, and the Stork Club was another matter. Here beauty and wit were better qualifications than family or wealth; as big, elegant Lucius Beebe proposed, "It is the only society of the day that amounts to a hill of *haricots verts.*"

As a girl collector in the flashbulb set, Joe had certain advantages over the average Harvard undergraduate. His father's empire was subterranean but available for part-time aid in youthful conquests. AM TAKING THE ONE O'CLOCK TRAIN, he wired one weekend from Cambridge to Paul Murphy at his father's Rockefeller Plaza office. WILL YOU PLEASE GET TWO TICKETS FOR TONIGHT BOY MEETS GIRL THEN WILL YOU PLEASE CALL UP MISS HELEN BUCK AT THE BARBIZON HOTEL AND ASK HER IF SHE HAS SEEN IT IF SHE HAS GET TWO OTHER TICKETS . . . JOE.

The prodigal son was heading home for a New York weekend, and you could hear the deserted Irish colleens sighing from Back Bay to the Charles.

5

Joe was intensely interested in people and sometimes his probing annoyed them. He speculated often with his own roommates on Jack's frivolity, wondering when he would mature. Congressman Torbert MacDonald, who roomed with Jack, recalls that "Joe had a sort of protective attitude toward Jack; he thought he was too small, for example, to play football, and he'd tell him, 'you shouldn't do it.' And they would have arguments like all brothers but in my judgment they got along very well. Joe was not overbearing, but he was a great needler too. You could never tell when he was saying something—he'd say it with a smile—you could never tell whether he meant it sarcastic, or if he was just saying the words. Joe was a very bright and nice guy, too."

Joe had, of course, real grounds for worrying about Jack's football, and the proof was the back injury that almost killed him when Jack ignored his advice. Where no real risk was involved, Joe's requirements could be tough. He determined simplistically that Teddy, baby of the family, must not be overly protected. At Palm Beach when Teddy was two, Joe announced that he was going to teach him to swim. He tied a rope around his tubby belly and tossed him in; Teddy showed no fear, having already learned to thrash from one to another of a circle of brothers, sisters, and parents off Hyannis. He remembers today his grown brother Joe daring him into higher and higher dives from Eden Roc on the Riviera until their father stepped in to put a stop to it.

LeMoyne Billings, who knew Joe at Choate and went often to the Cape with Jack, recalls acting as ballast in Joe's sloop on a seven-hour beat across the Sound to Nantucket Island: "It was a heck of a long trip—twenty-five miles—and a cold one. This was my first experience, very wet, I was just completely soaked the whole way, and Joe took a very great deal of pleasure in having Jack and me up on that windward rail. Joe enjoyed it."

Eunice, who crewed for Joe in races, remembers that "he was very good, but he had quite a strong temper and would be cross as a billy goat and would blame somebody else when he didn't win." He liked to tease his sisters, whom he saw seldom except on vacation. "He took us all to the parties over at the Wianno Club," says Eunice. "He was a terrific dancer. Great gusto! Great excitement! He had a terrific sense of humor. A real extrovert. If you got stuck with somebody else, he'd leave you there for a while just to sort of tease you and then he'd rescue you a little later." He teased Jean, sometimes to the point of tears, for putting on weight, but she was his godchild and he made that a special bond between them. He called her "Jeanah Darlin'" and took the sting from his quips with special little presents. He would write his sisters a postcard, en masse and in toto: "Girls: Never say I didn't write you. Joe."

He had, Billings remembers, "a terrific sense of humor." One year Joe's sailing mentor Eric, the Kennedy boat keeper, having towed the family fleet behind the *Davilis* to the week-long Edgartown regatta, became famously drunk and, though notorious with women himself, more virtuous with every glass. Joe, Jack, and Billings were using the cruiser as a base of operations and Eric took particular exception to their decadent collegiate habit of stealing every girl in sight. Finally he handed down an edict that boys and girls who boarded the boat together left together. Joe waited until his sermons were loud enough to disturb boatyard owner Chet Crosby, who was moored astern, and then Joe called the local constabulary; Eric spent the rest of the regatta in jail.

Jack Kennedy regarded his brother as having a keen wit and thought that he saw the humorous side of people and situations quicker than anyone he had ever known. But Jack spotted another side too: "a slight detachment from things around him—a wall of reserve which few people ever succeeded in penetrating. I suppose I knew Joe as well as anyone and yet I sometimes wonder if I ever really knew him. He was very human and most certainly had his faults: a hot temper, intolerance for the slower pace of lesser men, and a way of looking—with a somewhat sardonic half smile—which could cut and prod more sharply than words. But these defects—if defects they were—were becoming smoothed with the passage of time."

Joe Senior, happy to have the boys together at Harvard, has written of their personalities in college. "Joe used to talk about being President someday and a lot of smart people thought he would make it. He was altogether different from Jack, more dynamic, more sociable and easygoing." Jack failed to survive even the primaries for president of the freshman class; Joe, who had urbanely M.C.'d his own freshman smoker and snagged Rudy Vallee for it too, was elected junior year to the Student Council and senior year as chairman of his Class Day Committee.

After several seasons as a chorus girl in Pi Eta theatricals, Joe rebelled when he was given a role as a hula dancer. He soon discovered that his father's appointment as ambassador to the Court of St. James's had complicated even such a simple act of mutiny. Papers carried the news that the son of the new ambassador was quitting the troupe and Joe quickly denied it: he would perform, but as a Marine—to impersonate a grass-skirted Hawaiian would "take too much time from my studies. I am getting pretty tired of all this publicity, but I'm going to be in the show."

Jack, as a sophomore, joined his brother's house. He and Joe ate dinner together daily, exchanging family news. To the outside world the two presented a united front: when Joe Senior visited Winthrop to give a talk, both boys characteristically arrived late, but then moved without embarrassment to the speaker's table, embraced their father, and kissed him. And when, to the delight of the British press, the elder Kennedy in his first round of golf as ambassador sank a hole-in-one at Stoke Poges Course west of London, they sent him a joint cable: DUBIOUS ABOUT THE HOLE IN ONE. The childhood rivalry seemed dead: the chocolate pie stolen from Joe's plate a memory.

Joe had been trying for years to move close, like his father, to the world of show business. Before a Harvard dance one week he talked loosely around Winthrop of escorting Katharine Hepburn, currently appearing on stage at the Colonial Theater. There was a problem: she did not know him from Adam. When all of his bridges were well burned, he went to see Commissioner Timilty. "I *got* to take her, I told the boys!"

Timilty was aghast. "Joe *I* don't know her!" He looked at his stricken face and said: "I'll see what I can do." He went to the theater manager, Al Shayne, who was equally dubious, but finally told the commissioner to come in that night and talk with her. Timilty went to her dressing room. Miss Hepburn, whose mother had just driven up from Connecticut, thought it over and said, "I'll accept on one condition."

"What's that, Miss Hepburn?"

"You take Mother."

The four went together; Joe's face was saved for another day. Jack observed the triumph, cogitated, and invited to Harvard the beautiful young singer Gertrude Niesen, starting her film career in *Top of the Town* with George Murphy. Joe, his primacy at stake, moved in. "Get lost, Baby Brother," he said, grinning. "I'll take over." Jack flushed angrily. The rivalry was still alive. Gertrude found herself with two escorts rather than one. "I was very young," she says, "and it was very exciting, very flattering, very wonderful. Joe was a *terribly* good-looking guy. He was much better-looking than Jack at that particular time. If I'd been a little older and really understood what was going on—"

It may have seemed a game to her: to Joe and Jack it was perhaps more. In their earlier adolescence, Jack's oblique charm had been as effective with girls as Joe's flash of physique; now it seemed to desert him. Joe and Tom Bilodeau, passing through New York by special football train after a Princeton game, jumped ship against Harlow's orders. Cruising Manhattan nightclubs, they glimpsed Jack with a beautiful girl at the Stork Club ringside. Joe placed a call from a pay booth, Jack was paged, and while he jiggled with the hook, his silver-tongued brother pirated his date and the two football players took her home. "She lived somewhere on Fifth Avenue," Tom recalls, adding a little wistfully that "Joe took her up." Arriving later at the Kennedy Bronxville mansion, they found 150 pounds of raging Irishman stationed like Horatio at the top of the stairs, stripped to his drawers for action. Jack ordered Bilodeau from the house, obscuring the fight, if there was one, from history, but win, lose, or draw, Joe had got back his chocolate pie.

6

Collegiate football in America is supposed to have begun at Princeton in 1820 with "ballown," but that was simply a kicking game like soccer, and the true ancestor of American football was Harvard's "Boston Game." It was a lethal descendant of English Rugby born on the playing fields along the Charles. No other college in the United States but Harvard would play it for thirty years, but

Harvard continued with grand indifference, apparently preferring intramural mayhem to admitting to Princeton, Yale, Columbia, or Rutgers that she had chosen the wrong rules. When finally, to test her mettle and prevent athletic inbreeding, she was forced to invite McGill down from Montreal to a bastardized version of her game, her stubbornness paid off; she beat McGill and the melee looked interesting enough to attract Yale. The Sons of Eli accepted Harvard's suicidal impulse to run the ball and to tackle and played her next year, beating her four goals to none. In the sixty-odd years between Harvard's first Yale game and Joe Kennedy's last, she had not got much better. Only twice since World War I had she been named among the leading teams of the nation and in the Rose Bowl's thirty-five-year history it had invited the mother of American football to Pasadena just once. She had not won a Yale game since Joe had entered. In this, his senior year, though Harvard had—for Harvard—an exceptional team, Yale was undefeated and favored ten to eight.

Today the typical nonplaying Harvard undergraduate can take school spirit or leave it. Really militant ardor left the rooting section somewhere between blue-suede shoes and Vietnam. "Harvard Indifference" was of course there even in Joe's time, but then it was only skin-deep, born of the statistically supported truth that to save face most Harvard athletic contests were best approached with a careless smile, a pocket flask, and a Radcliffe date. But on the last blustery week of November in 1937, Joe Kennedy and those who ate at the long training table in the Varsity Club knew something that their fellow students did not: Coach Dick Harlow had prepared two surprises for Yale.

The great Yale back Clint Frank, Harlow knew, was going into the game with both legs heavily strapped; Harlow assumed that his reactions on defense would be slowed and so he designed a play for Frank Foley, a good Harvard running back, to take advantage of the star's bad luck. It was a simple in-and-out fake, but Harlow characteristically christened it the "Foley Special" to give it class; Harvard had been practicing it secretly for weeks. There was another trick in the bag, too, and Yale might be dumped on its Bulldog rump.

There is a legend among those close to the Kennedy family that Joe Junior played first string, or very close to it, during his Harvard career. It is simply not so; he made the forty-man squad each year, traveled with the team and suited up for games. End coach Wes Sessler

thought him steady, competent, and rugged. But always
between Joe and success had loomed his silent contempt
for Harlow, his refusal to hide it, and his frequent injuries.
Despite his calisthenics on the Hyannis lawn, his sweaty
months in Arizona, his intramural regime of swimming,
squash, and basketball, there were still four ends ahead of
him at the end of his senior year. At the beginning of his
last season the *Harvard Guardian* had predicted that the
keenest competition of all would take place at the ends,
listing the four to watch: Daughters, Downing, Green,
and Jameson. A substitute end behind Joe, Gibby Winter,
had got into the Army game and played beautifully, po-
tentially dropping Joe another step in the pecking order.

In his years of varsity football Joe had shivered on
benches from West Point on the Hudson to Dartmouth in
the mountains of New Hampshire. He had endured a torn
knee, a broken arm, and a concussion. The only reward he
or any senior substitute hoped for now on the eve of his
last game was a chance to earn his crimson "H." He was
not particularly worried, nor were the other senior nonlet-
termen on the squad. It was unthinkable that a coach at
Harvard, where after all, tradition was supposed to count
more than winning, would deny a last-year man the last
few seconds of play before the Yale game gun that would
bring him his letter.

But if Joe was confident, his father was not. He arrived
in Cambridge flashing the smile, but he had no confidence
in the theory that Coach Harlow was morally bound to
play Joe. His financial and political life was built on
carefully nurtured pessimism: in the stock market he had
been described as a "whole den of bears." He was worried
that Spanish communists would defeat Franco and
Chinese communists outmaneuver Chiang Kai-shek; that
England would go to war to stop Hitler, turn socialist in
the process, and drag the United States in after her. Now,
visiting his old room at Hollis House, surrounded by
classmates, swept into the hysteria of pregame rallies and
cocktail parties, dropping in on the Varsity Club (sporting
the letter to which he was entitled because he had himself,
by whatever means, got into that last play of the Yale
baseball game twenty-five years before), he began to
worry about Joe: his son's whole happiness seemed to be
held in the palm of Harlow's pudgy hand, and he did not
trust the coach to treat it generously.

Harlow that Friday sat in the outer athletic office with
Al McCoy, his backfield coach and confidant, going over a

list of seniors who should in fairness be played sometime in tomorrow's game. The phone rang on the desk in his private office and he left to answer it; when he came back his face was as red as the lobsters he loved. "Somebody called me," he exploded, "told me his name, and said he was close to Kennedy's father. He wanted to know if Joe was going to get his letter tomorrow because he wanted to tell the father. Well, nobody's going to high-pressure me!" McCoy calmed him and they went back to the list.

That night Harlow, protecting his high blood pressure, holed up in a Boston hotel suite to get a night's sleep, shielded from alumni and press by his assistants. After he turned in, the telephone rang and an assistant coach took the call in the suite's living room. The caller claimed to be Joe's father. The coach, to guard Joe from further reaction as much as his boss from apoplexy, refused to wake Harlow and the caller, after trying to charm him into some assurance that Joe would see action tomorrow, hung up.

Outside Soldiers' Field by noon the next day hawkers bundled against wind off the Charles asked fifty dollars a pair for tickets. Inside, fifty-seven thousand jammed the stands. Graham McNamee warmed up his voice on a pie-plate mike in the press box. Joe Kennedy, Sr., in the section reserved for the Class of '12, sat next to an old and humorous classmate, Tommy Campbell. On the bench, which actually was an extension of the stands above, sat Gentleman Dick, an impassive, immutable lump in a heavy overcoat. Harlow had no more decisions to make until half time. Coaching from the sidelines, if detected, was a fifteen-yard penalty, and if he pulled one of his starters, under the substitution rules, he could not return him until the second half. Barring injury or outrageous incompetence, he would probably not send in a substitute until after the mid-game break. Down the bench from Harlow crouched Joe Junior, tense and taut. As the teams lined up under fat-bellied snow clouds, the great Harvard band boomed gloriously behind him and the rooting section as always lost its detachment and promised to "fight for the name of Harvard till the last white line is passed." Across the field the blue Eli banners fluttered gustily; it was a miserable day, perfect for Ivy League football.

On the second play Harvard sprung the other of Har- before. Just as Yale had settled down to Harvard's six-man defensive line, it found itself faced with seven; before low's surprises: defensive signals. No one had used them it solved that one, the Harvard captain barked a number and the next time the tackles were wider and Yale's blocking assignments were chaos. Yale began against all logic to kick on first down every time it got the ball: Joe's teammate Daughters snagged a pass in the second period and scored. Harvard failed its point after touchdown and the contest turned so dull that a Dalmatian puppy loose on the field became, until his capture, the star of the game. On the bench substitute seniors began to shift impatiently. If Harlow was going to let anyone in, the seconds before the half-time gun, with a six-point lead, were as safe as those at the end of the game, but the coach made not a move.

At the break it began to snow. In the locker room nerves were strung wire-taut, but Harlow was complacent. He never gave pep talks, except when the press was around; he had picked the best men he had, and the rest was up to them. There had been a few substitutions for injuries or to illicitly run in plays, but he had not bothered to send in graduating seniors; that apparently would come later. Joe and the other last-game men trotted back to the bench in falling snow: the same team which had started the game started the second half.

At the beginning of the third period Yale scored, Harvard blocked the conversion, and all through the third the score remained tied as the Crimson washed against the sky-blue jerseys. The Blue broke through in the fourth period. It looked as if she were going to score, but Harvard held and Yale missed a field-goal attempt. Then the Crimson, sparked by the Yale failure, pulled the cork with the "Foley Special" and slammed eighty yards. Foley suddenly scored standing up and the stadium became bedlam. With six minutes to go, the Harvard bench writhed in anticipation: Harlow, in the lead, would surely start to substitute now. It was humanly impossible for the seniors to keep their seats. The coach sat impassively as the minutes flew. Some seniors stayed tight-faced; some, like Joe, fought tears; some could bear it no longer and begged O'Dell or Palm or McCoy to get them in. No player broke so miserably as to ask Harlow directly; his assistants sympathetic but powerless, remained silent.

Harlow called for an end and Joe leaped to his feet; Harlow pointed at Jameson and Joe sagged back to his seat. The clock jerked ahead, minute by minute, and then second by second, and somewhere in the last moments Joe, white with anger, had to face the fact that his fondest dream was dead. The gun went off with a sharp crack and so, high in the stands, did Father Kennedy. He turned helplessly to his old classmate Campbell, then fought his way blindly through hysterical fans to the field to comfort his son. He could not find Joe, but he cut off Harlow in the melee and what he said, even if known, would be unprintable.

The Harvard locker room was strangely quiet after the game. Reporters ascribed it to shock—a stunned reaction to a hope come true. It was not that at all: the nineteen men who had played were almost as bitter at Harlow for not playing their graduating teammates as the seniors were themselves: the next issue of the *Crimson* was critical even in its exuberance. In the entire game only eight substitutions had been made—only one end—and the paper did its best to heal the seniors' wounds by listing the most obvious candidates for letters who had remained benched. There were seven but still no solace for Joe, whose name was not even there. "After the game," reported the *Crimson*, "Dick Harlow said he would like to have given more letters, but added that 'the first debt is to Harvard football. We needed our strongest defensive combination up to the closing whistle.'"

It would have been an acceptable answer at Notre Dame, Army, or Southern Cal—you suspect that young Joe himself, after the initial disappointment, would have approved the sentiment—but it never placated the rest of the Kennedy clan. Next year Jack, writing to his father of one of his roommates, Ben Smith, reported gleefully that "Our good friend Dick Harlow only put him in against Dartmouth for five minutes and he scored a touchdown, which pleased us all, as it made Gentleman Dick look a little sick."

Harlow years later lost his job in a player mutiny. He retired from football but saw no reason to resign from the university, since he was theoretically a faculty member. Joe Kennedy, Sr., in 1936, running tenth in a dozen candidates, had failed to be elected to Harvard's Board of Overseers, or it would be hard not to suspect him of choosing Harlow's new honorific: Joe Junior himself could not have picked his old coach a better job. Harlow was given the title "Curator of Oology," a branch of ornithology, and ended his Harvard career in charge of the university's collection of eggs.

7

Ambassador Kennedy, disappointed at Harvard's failure to
award Joe his letter, learned now that he himself had been
blackballed again, turned down for an honorary degree by
the university, which had decided an ambassadorship, even
to the Court of St. James's, was of insufficient merit to
meet Harvard standards. The ambassador, to Roosevelt's
amusement, had hardly time to turn down the nonexistent
offer in the press to save face before the word was out. He
decided later that he had never liked Harvard anyway—
"I guess I have the old Boston prejudice against it"—but
Joe Junior was still giving it his all. He played Rugby all
spring, ending his season just before graduation when the
Cambridge University team sailed from England and defeated Harvard 50-0, almost braining Joe in the process
and effectively revenging those of their countrymen whom
Joe and Whitelaw had so roughly handled five years before on the playing fields of London.

Joe had a last chance to redeem his athletic honor at
Harvard in June: the McMillan Cup sailing races were
held in a three-day regatta that year at his own Wianno
Yacht Club. He was known as a natural helmsman: he
seemed to have a sixth sense for wind on sail and water
against rudder. An older friend, John Daly—"Black Jack"
to Joe—trailing in a race from New London to Marble-
head, had once given him the helm of his big sloop and
watched incredulously as Joe, puffing a black cigar, sailed
through the whole fleet and handed him back the wheel.
"Well, Black Jack, if you need any more help, just let me
know." Everyone had blamed it on a shift of wind, yachtsmen bleeding easily, but the gusts seemed always to start
when Joe took the helm and quit when he went below.
Perhaps the McMillan Cup competition, in which such
national stars as Bob Bavier of Williams would be sailing,
might heal his tattered pride.

The regatta began on a Wednesday. Ten colleges com-
peted. The first day neither Joe nor Jack scored, and by
evening Williams had outpointed the fleet, although Harvard's Loren Green won a first in the first division. As the
ambassador, back from England for Joe's graduation,
watched from the committee boat on the second day, Joe

and Jack grabbed their tillers and sailed out to do battle for the Crimson. A fine southwest breeze off the Sound ruffled the waters Joe had dominated since childhood. Family tradition and previous Kennedy literature has Joe, captaining the Harvard fleet, sailing to victory with Jack against the Williams College boat. It did not really happen that way. The captain of the Harvard team was James A. Rousmaniere. The regatta's fourth, fifth, and sixth races were scheduled that afternoon; Loren Green of Harvard won again, but Jack Kennedy was next to last in the fourth, neither he nor Joe placed in the fifth, and in the sixth Jack came in second and Joe fourth.

It is not difficult to understand the distorted legend. The *New York Times* somehow headlined: POINTS PROVIDED BY KENNEDY BROTHERS IN SIXTH RACE DISPLACE WILLIAMS, neglecting to point out that Merrick of Penn in one division and Madden of Trinity in the other had actually won it. Whoever was stringing for the *Times* at Hyannis wrote that "Joseph P. Kennedy Junior and John Kennedy sons of the Ambassador to the Court of St. James, gave Harvard the lead in the inter-collegiate sailing championship series for the McMillan Cup today. . . . The second and fourth by the Kennedys gave Harvard a total of 79½ points to 78½ for Williams." There is no mention of Harvard's Captain Rousmaniere, and very little of Loren Green, who was the only man to win first-place points for Harvard in the whole regatta.

It was hardly an individual triumph for Joe except in the *Times,* but the Harvard team held its lead the third day—with no points from Joe or Jack—and he won his "H" in sailing; not exactly a football letter, but better than none at all.

Leaving college, he was impatient to begin his political career. "From his father," Jack Kennedy would someday write, "Joe inherited a tremendous drive and a capacity for work and a flowing and infectious vitality. . . . I do not think I can ever remember seeing him sit back and relax."

But he was only twenty-two, three years too young for Congress and thirteen years too young to be the first Catholic President. Three months before graduation the Anschluss had shaken Europe; three weeks ago the Czechs, alerted to Hitler's plans, had partially mobilized and the Continent had thought itself teetering on the brink of war. Joe was unmarried and in peak health; there would never

be a better time to study international politics, working
with his father at the Court of St. James's.

He had become fascinated with the world political
scene. In the back of his mind was a trip to war-torn
Spain. To graduate with honors from Harvard had required an under-graduate thesis: Joe's paper was entitled
"Intervention in Spain," and dealt with the history of the
Hands Off Spain Committee, an isolationist group in which
he was interested. Laski's liberal teachings had been lately
diluted by Joe's much greater fear of U.S. involvement in
a European war, and Joe's later reports from the Spanish
front illuminate what must have been the theme of his
paper, since nothing happened in the meanwhile to change
his views. When he began his thesis, the sagging Spanish
Republican cause seemed suddenly to have come to life
with the last Loyalist drive to Teruel, but by the time he
finished writing it, Franco's troops, his Junker bombers,
his Krupp 88's, and his Italian allies had cut Spain in half.
Although it would be another year before Madrid fell
before Joe's eyes, to an objective Catholic college senior
the cause of Spain's Loyalist government must already
have seemed lost unless the democracies sent help. To risk
American neutrality in support of a dying government
riddled with Communists against Catholics trying to over-
throw it must have seemed to Joe the height of shortsight-
edness; one can assume that his thesis reflected the view—
almost treasonous on a liberal college campus—that Franco, if not the saviour of Spain, was at least no graver
threat than the Russian-supported government it already
had.

Whatever he wrote and however he wrote it, it earned
him his *cum laude*. Had it got him a *magna cum laude* it
would gather dust today in Harvard's Widener Library,
but it was simply graded and returned to its author and
apparently has sunk without a trace. His father read it and
was proud enough to mention it later to the British press;
his political-science professor, Arthur Holcombe, has no
particular recollection of it at all. The Kennedys save
everything, but Ted Kennedy quite honestly cannot find it
in the family records; perhaps it was lost with their thousands of feet of home movies in the flood which swept the
basement of the Hyannis home in the hurricane of 1944.

Whatever happened, there came a time when Joe must
have seen that if he returned from World War II, any
college thesis expressing even an objective view of Franco

would do him little good if it fell into adverse political hands.

Being a farsighted and intelligent young man, perhaps he lost it himself.

TWO

GOLDEN CRUCIBLE

1

JOE crossed the Atlantic with Jack and his father. He departed in a bowler with a black eye from a last-minute Rugby scrimmage. They embarked from Manhattan, and, except for Joe's eye, they were the image of three Harvard men bent on the Grand Tour. They sailed on the French Line's *Normandie* beeause the ambassador, who as chairman of the Maritime Commission had ordered striking American seamen put in irons and once purportedly swung on Harry Bridges in a hotel vestibule, had so little faith in the U.S. merchant marine that he would not trust his children's lives to an American ship. Their friend Arthur Krock happened to cross with them. He notes in his *Memoirs* that Joe soon found a beautiful actress aboard and that, despite Jack's marginal health, they lavished so much time on girls that the ambassador sentenced them to a midnight curfew. Krock, who liked young Joe and perhaps felt that in arranging his term at hard labor in Arizona he had done enough, never reported to their father that they were dressing and rejoining their dates in the ship's bar after he was safely asleep.

The ambassador had not got the degree from Harvard, but there was one waiting for him at the National University in Dublin. Joe disembarked with him and they visited Dunganstown in Wexford Field, from which young Joe's great-grandfather Patrick Kennedy had escaped to avoid the potato famine, and Clonakilty on the coast, from which his grandmother Mary Hickey's family had come.

At a state dinner in Dublin his father hesitated to begin a speech, he was so overcome with emotion at being on the Old Sod; he got it out, though, and was eloquent. Joe Junior arranged to return for some hunting in November; then they headed for the official residence in London.

2

The clean, buff townhouse on Princes Gate towers gracefully at the end of a row of its neighbors, staring out over Knightsbridge traffic toward Hyde Park and the bridle paths of Rotten Row. Today a plaque tells you that John F. Kennedy, thirty-fourth President of the United States, once lived here, but now the place, a gift to the United States from J. P. Morgan, houses a medical society. Inside, the great hardwood reception halls are empty; the French doors open on a bleak balcony overlooking deserted lawns. The red, white, and blue peonies which peeked patriotically from window boxes during Rose Kennedy's tenure as hostess are gone; so are the window boxes themselves, leaving the facade uniformly prim.

London in the summer of 1938 was an ostrich burying its head. A revolt of frightened anti-Nazi German generals was waving wildly for Chamberlain's attention, but he was not listening. Charles Lindbergh, touring Germany, gaped at the new, glider-trained Luftwaffe—how had they done it, under the Treaty of Versailles? He accepted an Iron Cross and flew to Paris to warn Ambassador Bullitt and to London to warn Ambassador Kennedy. Germany's air force, he told the ambassador, was the most powerful in the world; Luftwaffe bombers outnumbered the R.A.F.'s five to one and the U.S. Air Corps' eleven to one; if England and France fought for Czechoslovakia, Hitler would rule the skies from the first shot. Ambassador Kennedy added Lindbergh's evaluation to his own dismal estimates of British vulnerability and persuaded the Lone Eagle to tell Chamberlain too.

West Side London watched the newsreels (which Kennedy with his film contacts could sometimes influence in his friend Chamberlain's favor), heard the B.B.C., shuddered, and wormed deeper into the Long Weekend and the garden party. "You had the feeling," Jack Kennedy was to write of those days, "of an era ending, and everyone had a very good time at the end." London, for a while, embraced the Kennedys. The ambassador was "Jolly Joe" to the man on the street. The British press had secretly applauded when he refused to wear knee britches to present his credentials to the king. He was perfectly open with reporters, relying on their journalistic taste to censor his interviews and he could always furnish them a quote to encompass his family: "I would rather be the father of nine children with a hole-in-one than one child with a hole-in-nine," he had said after his first famous drive at Stoke Poges.

British affection enveloped Young Joe, who on his first night in town headed for the canopied gloom of the 400 Club, most exclusive of London's bottle clubs. He joined and had immediate access to what his friend Tex McCrary calls the "golden boys and girls." A British journalist found him that night at a table with an incognito Turkish pasha, Bergottis the Greek shipowner, Will Rogers' daughter, an Argentine polo player, the Dutch Baron von Haeften—inexplicably serving in the Scots Guards—and his beautiful blonde baroness. "A nice boy," the reporter wrote of Joe, "easily recognizable as the son of his father. I asked him whether Kennedy *père* had a chance of becoming President despite the fact that he is a Roman Catholic."

Joe was not about to pop any such trial balloon for his father, even in England. He pointed out that everyone had assumed Kennedy's Catholicism a bar to the ambassadorship, too, and yet here he was. His humor slipped out, too, unperceived by the journalist; ignoring such minor offices as secretary of state, speaker of the House, or Senate majority leader, Joe convinced the British newsman that a position as ambassador to the Court of St. James's was "considered the second most important post that an American can hold" and that "Mr. Kennedy's chances are pretty rosy even for the Presidency."

Rose, whom society columnists described quite accurately as looking as young as her daughters, had the residence on Princes Gate operating like a luxury hotel. She ruled a permanent staff of twenty-three house servants. The family had three chauffeurs and an additional reserve of twenty part-time employees for official functions. Even for the Kennedys, it was a little too grand. When the children traveled, they were made to go by bus to meet more people and retain the common touch. Joe Junior found his younger brothers and sisters tying up the private house-telephone from official calls by using it as an intercom to arrange which of the thirty-six rooms to gather in for backgammon and checkers. Nylons for the girls were arriving via diplomatic pouch. The terraced lawns outside were even better than the Bronxville grounds for touch football and Joe got a family league going. Bobby, a quiet, withdrawn aviation and camera enthusiast, was studying a book on how to fly and clicking candids from every nook. Teddy, six, had been inhibited at London's Sloane Street School for Boys by his father's warning that fighting would tarnish the American image and had suffered enough by his pacifism to arrange permission from Miss Cahill, his governess, to hit a classmate named Cecil in the nose. His room was a battlefield of soldiers carefully deployed against Bobby's troops. Both boys were forbidden, except on special occasions, to run the elevator, but Teddy was fascinated by it, and would leave it, door open, stranded and useless, as he made his escape on an upper floor if his father returned unannounced.

The younger children had been in London for six months when Joe arrived. Teddy had been to a costume party as a pilgrim and Jean as the Statue of Liberty; Robert had been introduced to Princess Elizabeth, his own age, at a garden affair and struggled with his eternal shyness until he hit on ski techniques and Saint-Moritz; after that "everything was all right."

For so brotherly a young man as Joe, Princes Gate was a delight. The family had not really been together except on vacations since he had left for Choate. Now everyone was a day student in a London school—Rosemary at Madame Montessori's, Eunice and Pat at Roehampton, Bobby with Teddy at Sloane Street—and everyone was home every night. Joe, though often sent on Embassy business for his father, saw them whenever he would return. He was still closest to Kathleen, but Jean was "my favorite godchild." He praised (to others) Eunice's wit and Pat's beauty; Rosemary he called to her face "the prettiest one of all." Bobby he tried to tease from shyness. But his favorite was "Teddy-Boy." Teddy's was the first room he would visit when he returned from a trip, and in the eyes of those who had traveled to London with the Kennedy household, Teddy began to take on his oldest brother's traits. Despite Joe's trimness and Teddy's childish chubbiness, they already looked alike. As Ted Kennedy grew older, the resemblance became startling: he is the model for the huge oil portrait of his brother in uniform in the Joseph P. Kennedy Memorial Foundation in Boston.

Louella Hennessy was a pretty young registered nurse, no older than Joe, whom Pat and Bobby had liked so much during a simultaneous hospitalization in Boston that the Kennedys took her to London as a governess for Rosemary and the younger children. Like Joe, she found Teddy her favorite. "Joe and Teddy both had dark-blue eyes and darker hair than the rest," she says. "They got along beautifully. Teddy idealized Joe. Joe was systemized and organized, like his father. The fairer ones—Jack, Eunice, and Bobby—went at things quickly. Teddy and Joe looked at all sides first. Joe was never late. He dressed right. He kept his hair combed. If we asked him to do something, it would be done in an hour."

The family became less insular. Anti-Catholic snubs in Boston and the famous blackball at the Cohasset Country Club had cooled its ambitions for high society at home; none of the Kennedy girls had ever "come out" as debs in New York; the ambassador had always claimed that no daughter of his ever "gave five cents for this society stuff." But here in London's real aristocracy they were accepted without question and they liked it. Kathleen and Eunice had a coming-out party at Princes Gate; to their awe, the Duke of Kent attended. Rosemary's welfare in a strange country had worried Joe Junior, but typically his parents had decided to let her be presented at Court with Rose and Kathleen. The whole family practiced at "curtsy parties" with the boys as extras, and when the great day came, Rosemary was a radiant success.

A Frenchman who met the Kennedy daughters in London said, "Eunice is the most intellectual and Pat's the prettiest, but Kathleen's the one you remember." Kick had beautiful blue eyes; she was quick-witted, bright, and energetic. While her mother convalesced in Europe from an operation, she acted as Embassy hostess. She was her father's favorite, the only one of his daughters who, like Joe, would stand up to him in an argument. She had a special quality of directness that no one who knew her has forgotten. She had studied art, was already a favorite of Princess Elizabeth, and was as athletic in her way as her eldest brother. Scarfed, derbied, and jodhpured, she cantered with Joe in early mornings down Rotten Row. She

baked cookies for the Great Ormand Street Hospital for
Sick Children and her picture was in the *London Times,* a
slender girl with her elder brother's flashing, slanted smile.
She had arrived in England allegedly in love with Peter
Grace, American heir to the shipping line. Interviewed at
debarkation, she and Rose had been noncommittal: the
two were just "good friends." She was linked in the
columns to Winthrop Rockefeller, too. Actually, she liked
Jack's roommate Torb MacDonald as much as anyone,
and her father, who liked Torb too, called the simpering
stories "rubbish"; anyway, she was only eighteen.

In later, grimmer years, photographed pedaling through
rubble in Red Cross uniform, Kathleen would become
London's "girl on a bicycle"; the city would grow to love
her and she would temper what Britishers came to consider her father's ingratitude. From the beginning she and
Joe liked England. Together they were invited to British
country houses for the weekends: Lady Astor's and the
Duke of Marlborough's and Sir James Calder's vast estate
at Lynford Hall. Kathleen made close English friends:
when Hugh Thomas, private secretary to the Prince of
Wales, was killed in a steeplechase accident, she invited his
daughter Cissie, who would later marry David Lord
Harlech, to live with her in the Embassy residence. David,
then an Oxford undergraduate, introduced Kathleen to the
Marquess of Hartington, informally Billy Hartington, at a
garden party for Princess Elizabeth. Billy was the firm,
strong-willed elder son of the Duke of Devonshire and
heir to the Cavendish fortune. The house was one of
the richest in land in Britain: 180,000 acres, Chatsworth
House, Hardwick Hall, Bolton Abbey, Compton Place,
Lismore Castle in Ireland, with stables and kennels as
good as any in the British Isles. Billy's home in London at
Carlton Gardens was as large as the ambassador's; Billy
himself was clear-eyed and good-looking, as handsome,
almost, as her brother Joe and even taller.

3

The present Duke of Devonshire, Billy's tall, friendly
younger brother, sips his whiskey in the sedate lounge of
Brown's Hotel on Albemarle Street. "My brother's romance with Kick," he says in his shy and halting manner,

"burgeoned fairly soon, so that we did see a lot of them." No one took the attachment seriously. Billy was considered a perfectly acceptable future suitor for the hand of Princess Elizabeth. The Cavendishes were among the leading Protestant families of England; most of their holdings, given Sir William Cavendish by Henry VIII, had been yanked from Catholic losers when the Church of England was established. Times have changed and the Duke can chuckle at it now, but Billy's father was head of the Freemasons and in 1938 it was still unthinkable that a wife of the young Marquess could be Catholic: she would traditionally become Keeper of the Robes. On the Kennedy side, the ambassador felt that he had endured enough Protestant rebuffs to last a lifetime: to Rose, an engagement was out of the question. Stubborn and headstrong as both Kick and Hartington were, they were too young and the odds too great. So they saw each other at garden parties and went to the cinema and the grand balls at Buckingham; with Joe and a horse-raising Irish friend Frank Moore O'Ferrall they went to the races at Ascot, and that was all. "Joe liked the racetrack very much," says the Duke, smiling. "And so did I. All of us were roughly the same age. Joe was more rugged than Jack. Joe very much *liked* being in England. He saw the point of this country, and one always likes to know that. Socially, and with the girls, he was a very great success."

He was a hit with the ordinary working girls as well as the titled. Terry McCulloch was a pretty Scotch lass who served as a receptionist in the vast Embassy building under the American eagle on Grosvenor Square. "Joe was an awful good-looking young fellow. He looked just like Teddy today. He and Jack used to kid me. We were about the same age. They called me 'Snow White' and they teased me and they'd pull my hair and chase me up and down the stairs. We had a lot of fun." Later when she helped Rose, Jack, and Bobby tape up the windows of a room next door in the establishment of Molyneaux, the dress designer, to be used as an air-raid shelter, she was amazed at their friendliness and informality: the ambassador directed the operation personally. "They were all very nice people, really great people."

The Duke of Devonshire remembers Joe and Jack competing for girls, and it must have been a relief to Joe when his younger brother left in the fall to begin his junior year at Harvard. It became Joe Kennedy Year in London, though there were holdouts untouched by his charm. One was a young peer who objected to Joe's Winthrop House technique of cutting in at dances; British gentlemen, Joe was informed, filled out dance cards long in advance.

No young aristocrat was going to change Joe Kennedy's techniques, but he had a lesson to learn about the unflappable British father. He dated tall, vivacious Virginia Gilliat, later to become Lady Sykes and mistress of Sledmere House. "I was very keen on him," she says. "He was one of my first beaux." One night after a date she invited him in for a nightcap in the drawing room. "The lights were dim, we were very young, there was a good deal of kissing going on, but nothing more than that. Well, my father walked in. Joe was absolutely covered all over his face with lipstick. Father put all the lights on. My father had the most beautiful manners, and he just made incredibly polite conversation with Joe and asked him how he liked being in England. . . . And there was Joe beaming, all over lipstick, and tears in my eyes, and my father not concerned, as if it were nothing, you know? Poor Joe!"

Poor Joe was having the time of his life. He dated the Argentine ambassador Carcano's daughters, Bebe and Chiquita, who was later to become Jacob Astor's wife. He met King George at a palace reception and "Wrong Way" Corrigan, en route back from Ireland and his navigational error. He did not neglect his political future: he would not be in England forever. He heard that Boston Councilman and political-writer Clem Norton, a "Last Hurrah" prototype, was in town, stringing for the hometown papers to pay for his travels. Two years later at the Democratic National Convention the two would be in a shouting argument in a Chicago hotel lobby, but now Joe phoned him at the Cumberland and asked him to lunch. Norton, a slightly built man, trotted innocently beside Joe along the Strand, noting with approval that the young millionaire paused graciously for some British girls who wanted to take his picture with a cheap camera, and that Joe's luncheon tastes were simple and American: steak and onion, medium; no wine; a glass of milk. Joe, buying a can of pipe tobacco on the way back, complained that it was "a shilling-six here and only cost thirteen cents in Boston." En route back—by bus—Joe gave him a sure-fire Boston quote from Honeyfitz: "You know, Grandpa—John F.— always tells us that we must never forget that years ago in Boston's North End, his family was poor." In the lobby of

Norton's hotel—"the best hotel buy for the money in Europe," Joe assured him—Joe left him primed to write the story of a humble young Boston millionaire abroad; it duly appeared in the Boston *Herald*.

Joe's popularity in London was gratifying, but he realized that his reflected glory would last only as long as the British did not catch sight of the ambassador's real isolationism. He liked England very much but agreed with his father that the ambassador's job was to protect the U.S. stake in peace, not that of an advocate for British-U.S. solidarity. There was still a lingering Irish distrust of the Englishman in the elder; while the two were in Ireland, Joe Senior had spoken bitterly and publicly of those English who had turned the Black-and-Tan loose on the I.R.A. Father and son often disagreed, but not on the best interest of the United States, which was to steer shy of the coming war: they were pro-British only until their granite isolationism was threatened.

Joe wrote bitterly to friends at home of unfavorable comments in the U.S. press when the ambassador spoke of getting along with the dictatorships, and his fears of U.S. involvement made him insensitive to the plight of the German Jews. He supported his father's "Kennedy Plan" (delegated to an Embassy aide) to get them out of the Reich, but he was annoyed that the cries of alarm from Jews everywhere seemed to threaten U.S. nonintervention. With uncharacteristic lack of objectivity he complained in a letter home that Jews everywhere were trying to mobilize opinion against the dictatorships, as if they were likely to do anything else.

But it was not so much Boston Irish anti-Semitism as noninterventionism that brought forth the outburst. Even his father's East Boston bias had been tempered by two generations in America; Baruch was his honored guest and mentor and Arthur Krock a trusted confidant. Next year in law school Joe would cultivate a crippled Jewish classmate, admiring his good voice and fine guitar, just as Jack Kennedy later was to seek out the friendship of Abe Ribicoff and Arthur Goldberg for their charm and intellect. And by the time Joe was in the Navy he seems to have shed most of his prejudice; in flight training and in combat two of his closest comrades were Jewish. An Irish Catholic squadron mate who knew him very well recalls with innocent sincerity that "He was just like me. He didn't like *kikes* but some of his best friends were Jews."

In the fall of 1938 Joe worked in Ambassador Bullitt's Paris office for two months, although he would never appear on its payroll. He went "on official business" under diplomatic passport to Prague and then Warsaw, where he met Jan Wszelaki, a Polish diplomat who became commercial attaché in London. Their meeting would later cause a diplomatic embarrassment, but Joe continued innocently to Leningrad, Helsingfors, Stockholm, Copenhagen, and Berlin. He decided that Russia was in deplorable condition, much worse than during his previous visit, but he found the Scandinavian countries "marvelous and I would love to go back there." To a former classmate he wrote: "Germany is still bustling. They are really a marvelous people and it is going to be an awful tough time to keep them from getting what they want."

His father had supported Chamberlain not because he had any faith in appeasement but because, in Boston terms, Chamberlain's seemed to be the only game in town. Perhaps the Prime Minister's policies could buy time for England to arm; if not, what else was there? The ambassador had never known of the plot of the frightened Wehrmacht generals to turn on Hitler if the British stiffened, a plan undercut by Chamberlain at Munich two months before, and now he promised Chamberlain that whatever course the Prime Minister took, the President would "go in with him." In September, at Nuremberg, Hitler shrieked for justice to Germans in Czechoslovakia, and it took Roosevelt's personal intervention to get Kennedy to strike a sentence from a speech he proposed to make in Scotland: "I can't for the life of me understand why anybody would want to go to war to save the Czechs."

When Joe returned to London from his travels in Eastern Europe the ambassador seemed suddenly to have more time to spend with his children. Perhaps it was because he trusted the Embassy staff; most of his own correspondence on the eve of World War II seems to deal with British film quotas on American films. Perhaps he felt he had done all he could; now, as his motto declared, "the hell with it." As lookout on the bow of the ship of state he had been yelling at the bridge, but by now he sensed that none of the State Department liberals handling the helm for Roosevelt cared to listen. He saw rocks ahead for America very clearly. "I have four sons," he had once said to an SEC colleague. "And I don't want them killed in a foreign war." Closer association with Secretary of State Cordell Hull had not eased his fears.

He began to ride horseback in the morning with Joe, and on Saturdays the two would walk with Teddy to the sailing pond in Hyde Park, and when Joe had set Teddy's model boat slicing across the water, they would sit watching the child skirt the shore to retrieve it. The ambassador had been hyperactive all his life. He was young and trim at fifty, but he seemed content these last peaceful English mornings simply to sit on a bench with his eldest son watching his youngest, as if they had not much time.

4

The ambassador, under attack as an appeaser in the U.S. press, accused by Roosevelt's advisers of White House ambitions and of intriguing against Roosevelt, returned to the United States to "do some thinking" and to calm the President. Young Joe, with Eddie Moore and his wife, herded the family to a Christmas at Saint-Moritz. He discovered on the Cresta Run a new sport exactly suited to his taste. He wrote Tom Schriber in New York: "They have a small sled steel-enforced weighing about ninety pounds. You go down on your stomach and reach a speed of about seventy-five miles an hour. It's a terrific thrill, going around the corners at that speed only a few inches above the ice." Bobsledding as a novice on the run, he came within seconds of the world's record.

There were other thrills, one of them Megan Taylor, eighteen-year-old figure-skating champion of the world. They were soon reported engaged, but Joe did not spend much time with her. He had learned nothing of skiing since schussing the slopes behind Cambridge with Bilodeau, and his daring ineptitude caught up with him alone in the Alps. In an epic spill he lacerated and broke his arm. Applying his scarf as a tourniquet, he skied back to Subretta House in Saint-Moritz, where the family was staying. He phoned Nurse Hennessy from the desk: "Louella, I need a Band-Aid." She came down, took one look, put on a pressure dressing, and called Eddie Moore. They started with Joe by sleigh for the nearest hospital, three hours away in Saint-Martin. She assisted the Bellevue-

trained German doctor in the operating room. "Joe—like
all of the Kennedys—had this high threshold of pain, and
he never complained," she remembers, "except afterwards,
he'd say 'Look at this! It sure looks awful, doesn't it?'"
He was soon back on the ice with Megan. There is a
picture of him skating doggedly with his arm in a sling as
the girl, off camera, presumably skated rings around him.
Then Megan, like most of the girls to whom he was
supposed to have been "engaged," drifted away into the
fogs of time. When the family got back to London his
father was still in America and Joe wrote Schriber: "I am
starting next week to work in some English banks to see
what makes the wheels turn, and then I am off to Spain.
From there I think Italy and Germany. Jack comes over
in February to begin his education."

His two-week crash course in international banking
over, he set out for Spain before the ambassador returned.
His father had been reluctant to let him go, since he
traveled on a diplomatic passport and it might not be
possible in Spain to maintain the strict impartiality demanded by the State Department. Taking him at his
word, Joe stopped off at the Paris Embassy and exchanged
his passport for that of an ordinary American citizen,
listing his occupation as "journalist." It was not as good
protection in case of trouble, but it had a certain trench-
coat flavor he liked.

5

When Joe Junior started for the Civil War, the anti-
Catholic Republic of Spain was on the ropes. Two years
before, at the very start, the International Brigade had
barely stopped Franco at the gates of Madrid; there he
squatted still, shelling the city daily. His Insurgent troops—
a quarter million Spanish professionals and 100,000
Moors, supported by 70,000 Italians and the Luftwaffe's
Condor Legion—had slugged amost insensible the half-
million-man Republican army of Loyalist Spain. A U.S.
embargo on selling arms to either side worked to the
benefit of Franco's Insurgents, who got theirs from Italy
and Germany anyway. The previous May Joe's father had
significantly contributed to Franco's victory by joining
other American Catholics in cabling a protest to Roosevelt

when Cordell Hull proposed to abandon the policy; Roosevelt followed his ambassador's advice, over-ruled his own State Department, and continued the embargo. The Republic's fate was sealed. Ernest Hemingway, missing the target, screamed in print that fascists in the State Department had done their "level, crooked, Roman, British-aping, disgusting efficient best" to defeat the Republic by "denying the Spanish government the right to buy arms to defend itself against the German and Italian aggression"; when it was too late, the President would express regret for not having supported the Republic; but in the meantime, Joe Kennedy, Sr., and the isolationists had won and leftists around Roosevelt were reduced helplessly to castigating his London Ambassador as pro-Franco.

Republican Madrid owed nothing to the Kennedys. Joe was heading into a city in which, if Communists or anarchists in the Republic won control before the final fall, American citizenship might mean little, and the Kennedy name might be a fast ticket to the local jail. There would be no help in sight, either; while most foreign diplomats had moved only as far as Valencia with the shaky Republican government, U.S. Ambassador Claude Bowers, leaving the Madrid Embassy to a Spanish caretaker, had fled all the way to the French Riviera. From there he shrugged off State Department efforts to prod him back at least as far as suburban Barcelona. In the final analysis he was right: Joe arrived in Barcelona the day it fell to Franco. He paused to survey the damage Italian planes had wrought, finding it "not staggering" in the city proper but in the port area "very great." He visited Nationalist Majorca, too, but he had really come to see Madrid, and he talked himself aboard a British destroyer bound for Valencia, last Republican port on the Spanish Mediterranean. There, as his newfound naval friends watched pensively from the deck, he clambered down to a motor launch, waved good-bye, and churned toward a battered dock.

6

Two decades had passed since World War I. Everyone had shuddered at the book *All Quiet on the Western Front* and gone to see the movie. At thirteen, Joe had seen *Wings* and reported it to his father as "a wonderful picture." Newsreels since 1931 had shown wide-eyed Chinese fleeing Japanese bombs; the classic shot of a baby crying in Shanghai rubble had been in *Life,* and afterward every photographer in China, Abyssinia, and Spain who could get his lens on a crying tyke had tried to duplicate it. Everyone had read Hemingway's articles in *Ken* and his North American Newspaper Alliance dispatches, and most Americans bled for the Republic, but vicariously. On U.S. campuses the Young Communist League passed the hat for the Loyalists and liberal professors cursed Franco; there were Harvard-purchased ambulances in Loyalist Spain. But few Americans under forty, unless they were starving in Franco's military prisons or had escaped the previous month with the remnants of the Washington-Lincoln Battalion, had ever heard shots fired in anger.

Joe Kennedy intended to hear them. He proposed to study this prelude to general war objectively. He had recognized fascism at eighteen, when he thumbed his nose at Mussolini's poster in Milan. Though he respected the German people's industry and apparently underestimated the Nazi threat to peace, he disliked Nazis now as much as he had in Munich with Whitelaw. But he hated Communists too and the reports of Nationalist and Republican savagery in Spain seemed to him to be at least equal: the Nationalists might have organized a mass execution at Badajoz, but the Communists in the Republican government had sacked convents and murdered bishops and burned the symbols of his Church.

When he landed in Valencia he certainly had no bias toward the Republic. He hoped not to be swayed by its propaganda, but he temporarily lost his objectivity when he saw the victims of the faceless German and Italian pilots. "Poor, helpless people," he wrote in a letter to the *Atlantic.* "I saw every few hundred yards home-made *refugios.* They're just rough tunnels with dugouts under the tumbled bricks and masonry, hardly more than uncertain protection from shrapnel. But people go right on living in them, without comfort and in perpetual danger. . . . Only a short distance from the port, just outside the immediate danger zone, everyone seemed undisturbed and happy enough. I saw children laughing and playing games. It made me sick. The sound of those little kids' voices . . ."

He walked endlessly through the city with the American vice consul, Woodruff Wallner, who pointed out that there was apparently no bread available that day since if there were, the people would be queued up for it. Joe grieved for the dogs, as he always would: "It's a mystery to me how the scrawny dogs, which prowl around the garbage cans in vast numbers, manage to exist."

They were caught in a fascist air raid and suddenly it was not a game, or a Hemingway dispatch, or *The March of Time*. "Wallner suddenly said, 'Here they come!' He was listening. I would never have noticed the sound against the noisy background of the city but Wallner's ears were sharpened by experience. Now I heard sirens going in various parts of the city to warn of the approach of enemy aircraft."

He saw his first white puffs of flak high against the blue sky, but none seemed very close to the little black specks of the aircraft, which kept coming on "as if they didn't give a damn." When nothing fell he noticed that people left their shelters, but they had left too early. "They began bombing the port. The noise was tremendous. It made our ears ache. The buildings vibrated like drums." Joe had lost sight of the planes in the sun and didn't catch sight of them again; he would have felt more comfortable knowing where they were.

"The thing that got me was the feeling of absolute helplessness. There is not much you can do about it after all." He noticed that a shoeshine man had kept right on buffing shoes while the rest of the people were huddled behind stone pillars or had dived into *refugios*. "I don't wonder that people develop a sense of fatalism after going through this day after day. I guess I'd acquire it myself in a little while."

He ached for the citizens but did not become an instant Loyalist. The stubborn government propaganda line offended his common sense. Now that the Republican cause was lost, he could not see how responsible men could lead their people further into misery. "The Valencia papers are just two-page affairs, but they're full of the stuff manufactured to appeal to men's finer sentiment—phrases like 'The fatherland is worth every sacrifice,' and 'the state needs the help of every man!' They carry only short bits of news from the outside world. Barcelona fell and they held the news back for several days, then released it with the phoney explanation that the High Command felt it best to retire a short way in order to consolidate their position. I wonder how many people swallowed that. Today's papers say that the Communist paper in

Madrid has been banned indefinitely—a hint for the pop-
ulace of a new attitude toward the Communists." He
didn't believe the Republicans could oust their Communists; the virus was too deep in the government's veins.
"How's anybody going to recognize truth when it's forever
wearing a mask of propaganda in print!"

Loyalist Valencia showed no sign of resentment toward
Joe for his father's views. Perhaps they were not known to
the officials there; maybe it was simply wise in view of the
coming defeat to treat any American well; perhaps it was
a favor to Vice Consul Wallner. If the crazy young American wanted to go to Madrid, from which everyone else
was trying to escape, O.K.: they placed a special bus at
his disposal and he jolted all day northwestward along the
road through the drab tan plain of Castile, bucking the
tide of Loyalist refugees.

In London, his father returned to Princes Gate and
found a cable: SORRY I MISSED YOU. ARRIVED SAFELY
VALENCIA. GOING TO MADRID TONIGHT. REGARDS. JOE.
"That," he muttered, "is the reception I get after being
away for two months. I wish he would stay out of the
firing. His mother will die when she hears he is in
Madrid." But he was secretly pleased and bragged to the
press of Joe's visit to Prague in the crisis six months
before, and of his prowling around Russia, too. Young Joe
became overnight the "Crisis Hunter" in the London papers and "Don José" in the New York *Herald Tribune*.

His first night in Madrid "Don José" Kennedy, leaving
his bag at the shelled and abandoned U.S. Embassy, settled down in the Calderón Theater for a variety show. The
city around him dangled precariously, connected to Valencia and the Mediterranean only by the Republican sash
across the belly of Spain along which he had come.
Madrid's defenders, down to lentils and dried fish for
food, without heat in the high arid cold, were dying by the
hundreds daily. It was all hopeless. Two years before, the
International Brigades, armed with Russian weapons—for
which Stalin had demanded half the gold reserve of the
Bank of Spain—had marched, singing, in from the east at
the last moment and barred the city to the Nationalist
troops. But the Brigades had been disbanded, the toasts of
Vivan los rusos, the camaraderie of German Communists
and French Socialists and Russian Bolsheviks and American volunteers in the Café Negresco and around the tables
in Puerta del Sol were dusty memories; there was little

bread left and very little wine; a smaller civil war was brewing in the city itself between Communists and Republican comrades-in-arms. Surrender would not be long, but the *madrileños* left in town were an unshakable breed and the show went on.

That first evening in the Calderón Theater Joe heard the guns and mortars of Franco's artillery limbering up in the Parque del Oeste, as they did every night; the shells hurtled in on downtown Madrid and the stagelights flickered. Some time before, Hemingway had observed in Madrid that "Shells are all much the same. If they don't hit you there's no story and if they do, you don't have to write it." The day before in Valencia, Joe Kennedy had noted that aerial bombing breeds fatalism: there is simply nowhere to hide. But to be the target, or even near the target, of artillery fire as he was in the theater is more personal and much more interesting. At first you are intrigued with the liquid, warbling sound of an approaching shell. It is the noise that you would expect if someone whirled a huge uncapped beer bottle at you: a fluid arpeggio which drops a whole octave as it passes overhead and ends in a chest-squeezing blast. You play with the thought that if the next one fails to pass overhead you will never hear the final chord.

So at first you are interested and then you become, in the presence of others, very aware of your own bravery, especially if they are nervous or try to leave. Hemingway, who thought passing shells sounded more like ripping silk, defined courage under fire as the ability to suspend one's imagination, but Hemingway had left Madrid for Key West three months before, and he had left something out of the definition anyway: the time factor. It is easy to suspend your expectations for two incoming rounds, or three; even five minutes is not unbearable, but soon your imagination begins to play with the law of averages and you know that if you sit there forever sooner or later you may well lie there forever.

The stage show in the Calderón was doubtlessly lively, but the imaginations of some soldiers and civilians, burdened by two years of similar exercise, grew too heavy to suspend: they decided that the performance was not living up to advance notices and left, though there was no panic of course and most people stayed. Joe Kennedy stayed too, but when he left at the end he must have been a subtly different person. He would at least never again be a young man who *thought* that under fire he might control his fears; he was a somewhat older man who knew he already had.

He had seen the Nationalists proudly take Barcelona, and tonight the Loyalists clinging with equal pride to their ancient city. Loyalist courage was evident, and he was fascinated, but meanwhile he knew that there were other wars beneath the city's surface, and other troops.

He began to grope for contact with Franco's Fifth Column.

2

IT was not easy for an American to make contact with the Franco underground, especially when he was billeted in the old U.S. Embassy building. It was deserted, but it occupied a whole block on Calle de Eduardo Dato, and it was too conspicuous a spot for a non-Spanish-speaking observer, even one whose motivation was simply curiosity, to commence clandestine operations. It was probably watched. Leased from the Duke of Montellano, it had been his townhouse: it was yellow, ornate, three stories high. Fine sloping lawns had once sprawled inside the garden walls toward Paseo de la Castellana and there was a stable and even a coach house, converted to a garage. When Joe Junior moved in, seven shells had already struck the grounds. Only one had hit the residence, passing through the absent ambassador's office and sparing six of the Duke's Goyas and a Boldini canvas. The lawns were tan now, for water in the semibesieged city was scarce. There were no cars in the garage or servants in the quarters, only one, Francisco Ugarte, a caretaker until the bad times were finally over and Ambassador Bowers found it safe to return and pick up the pieces.

Meanwhile, Joe had no one in whom to confide his desire to meet the Fifth Column. U.S. citizens had been ordered out of Madrid long ago; the Washington-Lincoln Battalion had suffered seventy-five-percent casualties along the Ebro and any fighting Americans not already in Franco's prison camps had been evacuated while Joe had been

119

skiing at Saint-Moritz. If there were any stray Americans manning the bleak trenches on the campus of the University of Madrid, no one now remembers it, and such would be obviously poor sources for information on Franco sympathizers, anyway. No American or British newspapermen remained in their favorite bar, Chicote's on the Gran Vía; when you ask correspondents who covered the Madrid front whether they were there when Joe Junior arrived, the answer is no, they'd escaped.

While Joe waited for a break, he studied the city. Food was desperately short, the daily ration miniscule. "250 grams," Joe reported later to his old *Choate News*, "of which 150 grams were bread ... about four American slices." The remaining ration of lentils and salt codfish was hardly enough to sustain life. Fuel he found nonexistent in the freezing city, with half the trees which had survived the shelling burned already. Women would walk for hours into the country to bring back a few twigs; when trees were cut down for official use, he saw guards posted against citizens "to prevent their great rush to tear off a branch." In the svelte department stores near Puerta del Sol there was nothing to buy, but some stayed open with one counter on the ground floor "selling old merchandise which really had no value."

Republican President Juan Negrín had waved good-bye at the French border to a succession of provincial Loyalist leaders—Azanya, de Aguirre, Louis Companys—and winged back to Madrid, Don Quixote in a DC-3, to lead the last defense and to ask Franco for terms. Franco was intractable—there would be no amnesty; Negrín decided that the Republic might as well fight on. That month as Joe Kennedy drifted past the Cibeles fountain, its shell-pocked lions sand-bagged too late, or poked around the Gravina barricades, non-Communist Republican Army officers, concluding that Franco's harsh refusal was directed at the Communists rather than at them, ousted Negrín in favor of General Miaja, who formed a new Council for Defense, expelling Reds. The Communists, along with other Negrín supporters, revolted immediately. Heavy street fighting broke out. The city crawled with bands of militiamen hunting down Reds, and Reds hunting militiamen, and everyone hunting the Fifth Column. The wide avenues and the narrow alleys between the barred windows of the old city became dangerous enough even for fast-talking *madrileños,* and Joe's Spanish was primitive. Armed bands roamed the rear of the battle lines, settling accounts.

Joe could stand hunger and shortages, but Madrid's fratricidal civil-war-within-a-civil-war gagged him. "The Communists ... with tanks, artillery, and hand grenades ... took over two strategic positions in the city.... Outside of the house in which I was staying we saw some ten men shot down, one-half of them soldiers and the remainder civilians. . . . It was touch-and-go whether they would take over the city and, if they had, the bloodshed would have been beyond description."

Franco simply waited in the suburbs, but his Fifth Column, Joe found out, was slipping desperately through the streets, trying to save imprisoned noblemen, Falangists, priests, before someone—Republican militia, SIM Police, Anarcho-Syndicalists, or Communist guerrillas—took long enough off from sniping at each other to get their prisoners before a last-minute firing squad.

At this point Joe learned that a lovely American woman was an operator with one of Franco's cells. She was the wife of a devoutly Catholic underground leader; now she is dead and he is the Spanish ambassador to the Vatican; in 1939 he was simply a young lawyer who had worked for the American Embassy before it ran for cover in France. His name is Antonio Garrigues y Díaz Canabate. His wife, Helen Anne, was the daughter of a U.S. general, and she was possibly the only American in Madrid. Joe set out to find her.

2

The Piazza di Spagna in Rome is very dark at 9 P.M., and the ancient Spanish Embassy is the darkest building fronting it. After checking in with an elderly guard, you climb a sweeping, red-carpeted stairway to meet a liveried butler with kind Spanish eyes, who leads you along a hardwood reception hall to a warm paneled study which, as a setting, would have pleased El Greco. Ambassador Garrigues is a gentle, graceful man, who used to escort Jackie Kennedy in Rome. He seems lonely in the vast Embassy now that his wife is gone and his children grown. He is attentive and a little wary, as becomes a diplomat. But as he talks of days when colors, seen for what might have been the last time, were perhaps brighter and men seemed braver and everything seemed bigger than life, he loses his reserve.

"My wife and I were active in the underground, living like characters in a book, no? And we were taking control of many things, moving all the time. That kind of activity is very interesting because it is very risky." The smiling butler passes caviar on toast, serves us drinks, and pads out. "Joe used to come very often to the house in those days and he found there some American ambiance. The Americans and most people were rallying to the Republican side, and here we are ... an American and her husband who are taking the part on the Nationalist side! And we explained to him the reason: we considered the Spanish Republic since the beginning of the war a kind of Communist government, no? And then he was very interested in knowing all the history of the war and the origin and the reasons."

Joe began to travel with them on their operations. To move through the chaos, Garrigues and his comrades carried several sets of false papers for police, militia, or Army units that might stop them. With a raging civil-war-within-a-civil-war and everyone in the same rag-tag uniforms or none at all, they depended on a sixth sense to guess which set to produce. Someone had lent them a little American car, an unusual item in Madrid for civilians, but necessary in their frantic haste. "At that time to move in Madrid was very bad. The streets would change often from one party to the other. Then you never knew with whom you were speaking—Communists or Republicans— and you very easily could make a wrong move and you have all kinds of false documentation."

Joe joined Garrigues and his group one day on a mission. "All of us very active in the underground, and then Joe. We went to visit the prisons and talk to the people who might release the prisoners, because it was near the end of the war and Franco was winning." They accomplished their task, or at least were not themselves clapped into jail, and were returning in the little car "along a street with the shape of an S—it is called Calle del Esse." Suddenly they found themselves in a roadblock of armed militiamen. They squealed to a stop, trying in vain to decide from their captors' conversation whether they were dealing with Communist irregulars, government troops, or anarchists. "They point their guns at us and they ask us for our documentation." Something in the tone of the leader spelled Communist to Garrigues. He had Red Cross documentation, and he tried it. It was no good. Joe and the Spaniards were ordered out of the car and lined up against the wall.

"In civil war the worth of human life is very, very little," murmurs the ambassador. "At that moment the worth of life was absolutely none. We thought that perhaps our last moment had arrived." He tinkles the ice in his glass and his voice drops lower, so that you have to lean forward to hear. "Joe Kennedy . . . I have to say that he was very timely. And very tranquil. Because at that moment he turned and presented his American passport. And then he showed his visa, which made these very, very low people—Spanish but low people—confused. American car and an American passport? They were surprised. They had a conference and they decided to proceed with discretion and to leave us alone and not get into foreign complications. They say all right to continue."

Shortly afterward Garrigues was picked up again, this time by the Communist-dominated SIM secret police, who interrogated and then released him. He never dared return to his home, knowing that he was being tailed. Thus he did not see Joe Kennedy again, and wonders if he left Madrid before its final fall. You know that he did not, and tell him so.

Back in Madrid, speeding from the airport through miles of Guardia Civil in their shiny lacquered hats lining the highway to greet a member of the royal family, you enter the city and find Calle del Esse. It is indeed serpentine, indeed isolated, a paved channel curving between a brick wall on one side and a gray stone barrier on the other; no windows front on it and its curves hide it from its intersections with the traveled street behind. You think of the first of the Kennedy brothers to face violent death against the wall in this lonely place, and you spot on the stone face of it an angry red scrawl: "Youth Now!" A student revolt at the University of Madrid has closed the campus, which the Republicans had clung to so tightly thirty-two years before. Your airport taxi driver asks that you not use his name if you write of the visit, and murmurs, in his soft Andalusian accent: "There is no freedom in Spain."

3

Joe stayed in Madrid to the end, sending reports to his father. They do not survive, but the ambassador read a portion of one aloud at a small dinner with Prime Minister Chamberlain, whose health he had just described in a cable to Hull: "He has failed more in the past week than he has the last year. He walks like an old man and yesterday he talked like one. He is a shade more hopeful of peace." At the dinner, *London Times* editor Geoffrey Dawson overheard Kennedy reading Joe's letter and praised its journalistic quality; the Prime Minister urged the ambassador to quote more, and Joe Senior ended by reading a whole batch. Chamberlain, who quite innocently at Munich had doomed the Spanish Republic by delaying the inevitable general European war until Franco had won his own, seemed interested.

Republican Madrid hung on finally beating down the Communist revolt after 3500 fatalities. Joe roamed the Salamanca Quarter, taking cover when he heard incoming mail from Franco's artillery across the dusty plain on Garabita Hill. He wandered through the Duke of Santa Elena's Palace, ruined by shells and bombs. On an evening of unusual violence, he turned up as scheduled at a Spanish professor's house for bridge: the professor, who "had never dreamed he would brave the bullet-ridden streets," never forgot it. The city had not been bombed from the air since the Condor Legion had helped Franco to his short-lived occupation of University City in 1936, but there were two thousand shells per hour landing downtown and always, if one got close enough, one heard the crack of rifles in the no-man's-land around the Clinical Hospital and the worker's district across the Manzanares.

The lines, which had not varied one hundred yards in position in two years, did not bend even at the end. Across the space between them, Franco's regulars and the Republican militia exchanged obscenities, jokes, and sometimes their own overly ambitious dead and wounded, but little moved aboveground except aid and burial parties. Franco's loud-speakers blared the serial numbers of banknotes that the Generalissimo would accept when he entered the city; storekeepers heard and would accept no others.

"Anyone who had anything valuable," Joe reported, "refused to sell it, for he had no use for the fast-depreciating currency." Loyalist loud-speakers bellowed their brave exhortations, and still no one moved above trench or barricade. The propaganda Joe had scorned in Valencia seemed to have taken root: the Republicans were apparently ready to die where they stood for their fatherland: the half-starved militia awaited Franco's final assault.

It never came. The Republic had simply been waiting for the miracle of general European war to save it; when Hitler moved against the Czechs unopposed, Loyalist Spain was through. The surrender started on March 29, two weeks after German troops entered Prague. It was clear then that nothing would bring the democratic world to its side against the fascist powers, and the Republic could wait no longer. The Loyalist capitulation was born somewhere in the trenches of the Arusuelas Quarter. Touched by some final weariness the Republican soldiers simply tore up bandages, sheets, clothing, whatever was white, mounted the firesteps of their trenches, and began to wave them. They were greeted with shouts of joy from Franco's soldiers. Both sides scrambled over their sandbags and the two lines raced together. In many cases they embraced. Mariano Aribas, a Loyalist propagandist with a high voice, already a faceless celebrity in Nationalist trenches from his taunting broadcasts over the loudspeakers, found himself slapped on the back, greeted as "the little Red with the girl's voice."

Finally the Fifth Column surfaced, as Franco had promised. "The entrance of the Nationalist troops into Madrid was not a glorious one, accomplished with a fanfare of trumpets," wrote Joe. "The city was taken prematurely by Franco sympathizers within the city. Some daring ones raced through the streets with the Nationalist flag in their cars." Ten men in a truck sped down the Gran Vía yelling "Franco is coming." Incredulous women stared from the barred windows, and when next they appeared, they were laughing and weeping and hanging out the scarlet and yellow Monarchist flags they had hidden throughout the siege. Anything with Nationalist colors was draped over the twisting alleys of the ancient quarter: tablecloths, curtains, kerchiefs. Joe reported that "soon the old city, sick to death of war, had Nationalist flags in nearly every building." Above the Republican barracks dripped white sheets of surrender. The

Fifth Column waited for the Fourth outside the city:
Nationalist uniforms, which would have cost their owners
their lives the day before, were suddenly all over the
place, jammed in the crowd at Puerta del Sol, impatient
for Franco, "the man on the white horse." Joe reported
that there were no Nationalist troops within the city until
nearly five hours after it was taken over. "It was done
most efficiently; the loss of life was practically nil."

Drifting in gray trousers and a sweater through the
elated, apprehensive crowd on this day of victory for some
and defeat for others, Joe turned down an offer—by Vice
Consul Wallner from Valencia—of sanctuary aboard a
U.S. warship. "I can take care of myself." He watched the
Loyalists, fearful of reprisal, streaming eastward on the
Valencia road toward exile in France; he studied Franco's
ordered phalanxes tramping finally in from the west.

The nobility began to trickle back. Joe's absentee landlord, the Duke of Montellano, visited the lightly damaged
townhouse he had leased to the United States. When he
saw his Goyas unharmed, he sobbed with gratitude: he
was probably the only grandee in Madrid whose house
had not been molested by Reds. Since Ambassador Bowers had never shown up, Joe, as the only even faintly
accredited American diplomat in town, had managed to
meet the moderate-socialist Julian Besteiro and Colonel
Casado, who had taken over from Negrín and ultimately
surrendered the city. To the newsmen flocking now to
interview him Joe confessed that he had been favorably
impressed by both; he was also keenly interested in the
report that the United States would finally establish diplomatic relations with the Franco government.

The Pope cabled congratulations to Franco. Palm Sunday would come two days after the fall of Madrid, so Joe
delayed his departure. The Church considered its Madrid
parishes to have been profaned during the war: among
other desecrations, Reds had dressed an image of a Christ
Child in militia uniform with a toy pistol in its hand. Only
twenty-two of three hundred churches in Madrid could be
reconsecrated in time, so forty thousand madrileños celebrated Holy Mass in the streets, using olive sprigs for
palms. Mantillas appeared on women for the first time in
almost three years, and there were prayer books and
rosaries; the tricornered patent-leather hats of the Guardia
Civil were everywhere, and priests in ankle-length cassocks.
Joe Kennedy went to Mass and afterward watched a

Falangist parade augmented slowly by bystanders shouting *"Viva Franco"* and *"Arriba España"* until at noon there were 100,000 marchers led by a band playing the national anthem. "Did you ever see anything like it?" he asked a newly arrived reporter. The weather had been miserably cold for weeks; now it warmed and there was a hint of spring in the thin dry air.

He left for London via Burgos and Hendaye on the French border. He had seen no Nationalist reprisals and hoped that there would be none. In a few weeks he would motor back through Spain en route to the Kennedy villa near Cannes with Kathleen and Hugh Frazer, a British friend who is today a Conservative member of Parliament. On the subject of Spain, Frazer found him "objective, certainly to the left of *my* point of view." Kathleen wrote with some sisterly prejudice of that tour together through Madrid: "I remember thinking then of how brave Joe was when different Spaniards told me of how he, the only American, used to walk about the streets during the bloody horrible days of the siege.... He understood and had pals on both sides and was the only person in Madrid who had them and lived."

Swimming off the beach at San Sebastián they laughed over their first hint of the spirit of Franco Spain, a sign on the sand which read: "Spanish women! You have just passed through the perils of a bloody Civil War. Beware now of the dangers of peace. In particular beware of the cocktail and the one-piece bathing suit." In a few moments Joe was tapped on the shoulder by a Guardia Civil, who read him a copy of Spain's new beach laws and ordered him to find a top for his trunks.

Joe withheld judgment. "These are the formative months," he wrote, "and it will not be until Franco has worked out his program more thoroughly that one will be able to judge the government of New Spain."

At the rented villa near Cannes the family swam from a chartered yacht and played golf. Joe Junior's Riviera vacation was the end of his European fun. Before the ambassador had left London he had talked to Chamberlain, who already felt that Hitler had decided to "take England on." The Prime Minister thought that the attack would come "probably just in time to spoil our vacations—in August." By July 19, Foreign Minister Halifax in London was asking Kennedy how long it would take him to pack his bags and return: Kennedy estimated five hours.

But he took his cue from the Prime Minister, who left on vacation August 5 "for a reasonable time," and the Kennedys did not actually break camp until August 25, when the ambassador returned to London and sent Joe and Jack to Berlin to assess the situation with U.S. Chargé d'Affaires Alex Kirk. Kirk estimated that war would break out in a week. Jack left for London with the message; Joe stayed on. Their father relayed a secret request from Chamberlain to Roosevelt that the United States put pressure on the Poles not to fight. Roosevelt refused and the ambassador fell into gloomy lethargy.

In Berlin the weather turned hot and sultry. Joe noticed Berliners in the railroad stations starting for the weekend cool of the country; the last frantic English and French citizens were heading for home. A Nazi rally at Tannenberg at which Hitler was to have spoken was called off; so was the "Party Rally of Peace" at Nuremberg. That Sunday night the radio blared news that rationing of food, soap, shoes, textiles, and coal would begin the next day, and Monday Kirk told Joe that there was grumbling in the streets. German troops began to rumble through the city heading east. On Friday, September 1, they crossed the Polish frontier: the Poles fought back. Joe Kennedy, Jr., left for London.

By nightfall he was at Princes Gate. On Sunday Chamberlain summoned his father and read him the speech that he would deliver at 11 A.M. that day: "Everything that I have worked for, everything that I have believed in during my public life has crashed in ruins," he said. By noon England would be at war again.

Kennedy wept. He phoned Roosevelt, told him, and made arrangements for the family. A year before, during the Czech crisis, he had moved the younger children for a while to the south of Ireland in fear of a surprise German air raid; now he moved them to a country house in Windsor Great Park outside London. London blacked out: Joe found the city suddenly "dark as a deep forest." He discovered that carrying a newspaper at night helped to prevent sidewalk collisions and that nightlife behind the darkened nightclub windows endured, but not for him: ten hours after England declared war, German U-boat commander Lemp, mistaking the British liner *Athenia* for an armed merchant cruiser, torpedoed her two hundred miles west of the Hebrides.

She was jammed with 1,400 passengers. Three hundred

of them were Americans. Twenty-eight Americans died but the rest were brought to Scotland, where they demanded a U.S. convoy for their next attempt. The ambassador sent Jack to Glasgow with Eddie Moore to calm them: Joe got steamer space for the survivors, but that was just the beginning. It turned out that there were 9,000 Americans stranded in Britain. The family gave up its own reservations in favor of fellow citizens. The Kennedys intended to return in relays of no more than three—like the Krupps, the U.S. President and Vice President, and the King and Queen of England, they never flew in the same airplane and now, with U-boats infesting the shipping lanes, they would split up for the voyage home. Joe found freighters for those Americans unable to afford a ticket on a passenger liner and formed a financial committee to loan passage money to those who could not afford even that. He arranged sailings for thousands, and finally he arranged his own.

He still liked England, his prayers were with her, his temptation was to drop law-school plans and to stay in London with his father. But to fight the ambassador's lonely battle against intervention at home while his father, gagged by diplomacy, fretted here, seemed more important to him than anything he could do in England. Even as a law student his voice might be heard in America: it was certain to be lost in London. Waiting for his sailing orders behind those he had helped, he celebrated his father's birthday. Then, on two hours' notice, he was called to Southampton and reported to the British Cunarder *Mauritania*. Armed with a six-inch gun and painted battleship gray, she crept quietly from her dock. Escorted by an R.A.F. bomber all the way to the Isle of Wight, she zigzagged west.

There were no submarine scares en route except when the gun crew blasted unexpectedly and unsuccessfully at a wooden, red-flagged target. Joe landed in Manhattan to find himself regarded as a world traveler and two-week expert on the war. Walter Winchell commented favorably on his *Atlantic* article on Spain and *We the People* had him on the air. To reporters he made certain that he mentioned the family's work with American refugees and the *Athenia* survivors; on questions regarding American neutrality he warned that "the British hope we'll go in; they'd like us to help them." He admitted that England, whatever her false hopes for U.S. aid, was beginning her fight seriously, without flag-waving, and seemed to have "a grim determination to do the job." Then he headed north to Cambridge to begin his own.

3

JOE had been gone from Harvard only a year. As an undergraduate he had been just another good-natured athlete wandering about the Yard with his green bag full of books, but something in England, France, Spain, or Hyde Park, where he had reported on his travels to the President, seemed to have sparked him into leadership. Now, at law school, he had the assurance of one who had talked with British royalty, carried diplomatic messages, and heard shellfire in Madrid. When some of his experiences in the Spanish Civil War began to lose their glitter, his Irish imagination took over. He liked to test the credulity of his listeners. Joe always claimed that he knew where a fortune in jewels, entrusted to him by a Spanish grandee, lay in a castle moat, he having tossed them there when pursued by angry Reds. And a story of being thrown into a Spanish jail, stripped and searched, has actually filtered into some of the Kennedy literature.

He rented a fifty-dollar-a-month flat in the Bay State Apartments at 1572 "Mass," fronting the wide avenue leading to Harvard Yard. He got it cheap because the owner, Mrs. Alice Harrington—"Alice in the Palace" to Joe—was a friend of the family. He staffed it with George Taylor, a tubby, tan, and dignified Negro whom he called "his gentleman's gentleman," and another Negro, part-time, named Holmes—"Justice" to Joe. Joe was too Irish not to laugh at his own extravagances. In an age of quiet, unchallenged Northern prejudice, if Joe dined out with friends, Taylor often had a seat at the table too. "He befriended everyone with whom he came in contact," Taylor writes, "Jew, Negro, and Chinaman, irrespective of race, color, or creed."

Joe's first roommates in the Bay State were his friends from undergraduate days: Tom Bilodeau, two years ahead of him in law school and struggling through under financial pressure, and Bob Downes. They used Bilodeau's furniture, which remained when Bilodeau graduated from law school. He suspects that Joe sold it when he joined the Navy. "We ran on a strictly cash basis," he says. "If you borrowed a pipeful of tobacco, you paid it back. If you were in real trouble, Joe wanted to *give* you money, not lend it to you, but he was very tightfisted for normal expenses."

Although in Joe's two years in law school he had always at least three law students sharing the apartment's expenses with him, it was always Joe Kennedy's apartment, Joe Kennedy's cook, Joe Kennedy's houseman. Landlady Harrington remembers that the local tailor's delivery boy, if she reprimanded him for breaking some rule of the house "in a most superior way would declare that he was Mr. Kennedy's valet." Joe Kennedy had a cretinous Florida alligator named Snooky, who lived in the bathtub. The first operation in taking a bath was to remove it. "Chubby-Bubby" Downes, having done so, was happily splashing around one afternoon while Joe was hosting a mixed group at a cocktail party in the living room. Joe, noticing that Snooky was out of his intellectual depth anyway and perhaps to test Downes' Spartan nature, opened the bathroom door and flicked Snooky back into the tub. Downes, who still believes the beast to have been the least intelligent living thing he ever knew, flung it back into the living room and took off after Joe. Snooky somehow disappeared in the excitement. Joe searched for weeks before he found him behind a couch, apparently frozen to death under an open window in the fierce Massachusetts winter. Experimentally, he put him back in the tub and ran warm water over him. Sure enough he arose from the dead and lasted until Bilodeau, trusted as guardian one vacation, managed to lose him for good.

Three law students in one flat strained the resources and the patience of the Bay State Apartments. Joe tried, when he planned a party, to stifle criticism in advance. He invited the families living above, below, and alongside, sending invitations through the mail and even having flowers delivered. For formal occasions he drafted janitorial personnel as doormen, waiters, and maids. He was always on the verge of making the apartment over. "Everything was wrong," Mrs. Harrington has written, "the shower, everything, and he turned the roof into a sun deck."

Joe gave songfests in his apartment, and another law student in the same building, Walter Klockau, had a guitar and accompanied Joe in the songs of the day: "Deep in the Heart of Texas," "A Tisket a Tasket," and the Harvard football marches.

"Joe always had to be directing traffic," says Bilodeau. "If he wanted to go someplace for a hot dog and you wanted to go along, O.K. Otherwise, he'd just go himself. He would just brusquely leave a conversation where he felt his train of thought wasn't being followed." He had developed an irritating habit of skimming the financial page or the sports or a lawbook while carrying on a conversation. "He had a photographic memory," says Bilodeau, "and he'd never miss a word."

Howard Clarke, who moved into the flat later and is now president of American Express, found Joe at the time: "Goodlooking, articulate, attractive, energetic. A very tough guy. Just a little bit unfeeling; he wouldn't have been elected the most popular man in the class." Tom Bilodeau, whose affection for Joe was so deep that he has to force himself to be objective, admits: "His whole style was: 'I'm going to do this and you can follow along if you want.' Like the rest of the Kennedys he never felt he owed anybody anything."

Tom was engaged and his fiancée, later his wife, tried to interest Joe in some of her friends, but they were "nice Irish girls who wanted to get married, and they scared him off." Debutantes still bored him. He entered into competition with Tom Watson, Jr., for Olive Cawley, a beautiful Powers model who first dated Jack at Choate, then Joe, and later married Watson. "Joe was a lovely person, and great fun to go out with." There were singers from Coconut Grove. "We had a terrible time trying to keep his girls apart," remembers Bilodeau.

Tex McCrary characterized Joe's later reputation in the European theater as that of "the greatest swordsman in the E.T.O."; some of Joe's correspondence with Jack seems to hint that the brothers were engaged in a neck-and-neck international race for female conquests, but down deep Joe was emotional, vital, and honest with women, losing his arrogance when he truly cared. Some vestigial trace of the old Irish tradition that a man should not marry until he is old enough to own a plot of ground seems to have inhibited close entanglements: Eleanor excepted, he had no childhood sweetheart. Pending financial or political success of his own, he would stay clear of engagements. Later, in the riot of war, he fell comfortably into the traditional naval officers' view of stray Navy wives as legitimate prey: they were, if you cared to risk the unexpected return of the husband, perfectly safe. Lorelle Hearst, ex-showgirl, ex-publisher's wife, and ex-war correspondent, a little older than Joe but a charming and beautiful woman who was to become one of his closest friends, recalls that with girls he was "terribly sweet and immediately made you feel very close to him and that you'd known him forever. He had a tremendous physical atraction and also there was a tough side to him. I don't know what would bring it out in him, but sometimes he could be cruel. He preferred girls a little older than himself because they had a little more sense. He never would have married anyone who wasn't socially prominent, mostly virginal, and Catholic, I think."

The Bay State apartment was a fine Cambridge base of operations. T. J. Reardon, anxious to make good in a new job that Joe had helped him to get in a Boston advertising agency, slept in the living room one Sunday night after a raucous Homecoming weekend and a football game. He awakened to find Joe shaking him angrily: "I recommended you! You want to get fired down there? Look at the time!" Reardon gaped at the clock. It was almost noon. He glanced at his watch, threw on his clothes, and sped to his new office. He rushed around apologizing to bosses and secretaries, drawing speculative frowns. Finally he caught a glimpse of the office clock: just after nine. Joe had set every timepiece in the apartment, including T. J.'s wristwatch, ahead three hours.

Joe himself still groped for his father's financial touch. Tom Killefer, a handsome Stanford Phi-Bete at Harvard Law, who moved into Joe's flat the second year and became one of his best friends, was driving with Joe down icy roads to Bronxville one weekend when they were stopped at the end of a long line of cars behind a truck which had skidded into a ditch. Joe spotted a nearby highway café and invested all their cash in scores of sandwiches. He was approaching his first stalled customer, all charm and ham-on-rye, when the truck was freed and the line started up. That weekend they ate sandwiches for breakfast, lunch, and dinner.

Joe played the stock market without marked success. He still went to the races with Police Commissioner Timilty and kept his own horse, Kentucky Charles, at Smith's Stable by Jamaica Pond. He rode in the early morning and often invited Reardon, Bilodeau, and Downes; Reardon and Bilodeau were leary, but one day Downes went along. Joe picked him a horse. On a wide bridle path he started a race and Downes' mount bolted. He hauled on his reins without effect until the horse slipped on an iron drain and fell on him; from that day on Joe cantered along the wooded roads around the pond alone.

Law school was informal. On football weekends Joe would bring his date to his Saturday lecture, as tradition allowed; he joined the Easterner's Lincoln Inn Law Club and lunched there almost daily, arguing politics with fellow students and professors. But the easygoing atmosphere was deceptive; he discovered that he had to work harder than ever he had before. The thirties were the golden age of Harvard Law. Graduates were set for life, but the competition was relentless. At the indoctrination lecture at the beginning of each year, freshmen were told, "Gentlemen, look at the man on your right and the man on your left. By next year one of you will not be here." They say that everywhere: at Harvard they meant it.

Harvard Law used the method Professor Langdell had invented in 1870; few good U.S. law schools today, save U.S.C., use any other. Its object is to make the student think like a lawyer. Casebooks, compendiums of significant arguments and court decisions, such as *Property* by Langdell, *Equity* by Chaffey, *Contracts* by Williston, were the basic texts and in huge lectures in Langdell and Austin Halls the questions were Socratic, minute, and blarney-proof. "Mr. Kennedy, state the rule of law in *Palsgraf* vs. *Long Island Rail Road.*"

There is a story that Joe, stumbling through a question in Barton Leach's course on property, finished by claiming lamely: "You know, I *can* say that—" at which point "Black Bart," as Joe called him, was supposed to have growled: "You can *say* it, Mr. Kennedy, but only because you have the protection of the First Amendment." Leach labels the story "part of Harvard mythology," and "about a hundred years old," but the picture itself is true: the Harvard Law philosophy was: "Humiliate the student, it's good for his mind."

There were certain scholastic advantages to living with Joe Kennedy, if you survived his female fallout, his bridle paths, and his barbershop quartets. Tom Bilodeau remembers his two law-school years before he shared digs with Joe, as academically "a horrible time." Then he moved to the Bay State. Dean Landis and Judge Burns and professors Joe's father had known began to drop into the apartment for bridge. Tom lost his anonymity and his marks began to improve. As the bridge games progressed, Joe would load their teachers' drinks with whiskey from his father's Somerset Importers: "We got our Scotch pretty inexpensively," remembers Killefer. "*We'd* stay sober—we had to. Joe would bid pretty high, but we'd come out all right."

"Work goes on as always," Joe wrote his father in London, "with the boys really starting to put on the pressure for there are only two more months to go. We have started to review and I am counting on Judge Burns to give me a few pearls of wisdom." But Joe wanted no nepotism from those he disliked, and when an instructor who had served his father as an SEC counsel began patronizingly to drop the Kennedy name day after day in class, Joe finally rose to his feet. "I don't want any favors," he said harshly, "and if you continue this I want to change my class."

Neither Joe's mother nor his brother Jack thought that things came easily for Joe, and according to Tom Killefer he seemed to "work like a slave"; but Jack had the best IQ in the family, Tom was a brilliant student, and their opinions reflect the ease with which they themselves learned. Most of Joe's law-school classmates and professors had a different slant. "Joe could cut every class," marvels Bilodeau, "buy notes on Harvard Square, and memorize entire courses. He didn't work any harder than he had to." But he loved to read and he utilized every moment, even studying on winter weekend trips with tall, aristocratic "Big Dick" Flood, to the Cape to check on the house and boats. Joe's handwriting was notoriously poor, so he taught himself to hunt-and-peck and got permission to type his exam in criminal law so that his mark would not suffer.

Perhaps because as a millionaire he had a special interest in the subject, he did best in property under Leach, but all of his marks were good. Two hundred of his class of five hundred failed the first year, but Joe was in the upper ten percent of his freshman law class and ranked 69 out of 371 at the end of his second year. Charles Garabedian, now a Boston attorney, lived in a Bay State flat and studied with Joe and Bilodeau in "Kennedy Corner," a battered nook in Austin Hall Library where they could put their feet on the table and smoke. "Joe was a born lawyer," he says. In the moot-court Ames Competitions he was sharp and aggressive. "He could cut you apart; the best natural speaker of any of the Kennedys."

His style was not entirely natural. He crossed the Charles River to Staley's School of the Spoken Word, where Michael Curley, learning public speaking, had hauled himself up from street urchin to mayor and eventually into a prison cell at Danbury. Joe's ambition ranged beyond moot courts or even real ones. He had no judge or jury but an electorate in mind.

2

The war in Europe was phony, London seemed safe enough, and Joe, Jack, and Kathleen were still sensitive to British criticism they felt they had incurred for leaving England. Kathleen, tired of giving teas at Armandos for British War Relief or perhaps longing to see Billy Hartington, wanted to return; her brothers agreed and Jack wrote their father that he didn't think the anti-American feeling in England would hurt her "due to her being a girl." The ambassador had no intention of letting her come and so she stayed in New York, but she visited Boston often and Joe would pry his law-school friends away from their books to date her.

He still ate Sunday dinner after Mass with his grandparents in the Bellevue Hotel near the State House. One weekend a few months after his return from England he had an idea. With Roosevelt stalling on the third-term issue, anything might happen at the Democratic National Convention this summer—there had even been a short-term "Kennedy for President" boomlet in Massachusetts until the ambassador buried it with moist bathos, as usual mentioning his family as the reason: "I know I'll die young," he said tragically. "Therefore, after this job, I want to quit public life. I want to establish my older sons firmly enough so they can look after the younger children."

Even though his father would be no candidate, Joe wanted to go to Chicago to see the show. Why not go as a delegate? He was only twenty-four, but he had the carefully nurtured Massachusetts address and the Fitzgerald blood. Honeyfitz exploded into action. William Burke, chairman of the Massachusetts Democratic Committee, lived in the hotel too: they breakfasted together daily. Burke knew Joe already and liked him: "He was a very brilliant young man with a great political future. One of the finest young men I ever met in my life! His grandfather came to me and I was more than glad to put him on the slate."

There was a problem. Ordinarily Democratic party endorsement would be tantamount to automatic seating, but this year a group of young state legislators and politicians wanted to run too. Joe and John P. Brennan of Cambridge went on the slate as the endorsed candidates, good for one-half vote each and pledged by the committee to James Farley; three other candidates run as unpledged.

There was an immediate protest from one John L. MacDonald of Cambridge that Joe was not a registered voter in Brookline, from whence he had filed. Joe consulted Superior Judge John J. Burns, his father's friend. "Some so-and-so," Joe wrote the ambassador, "has protested me as not being a registered voter and the papers have carried a story about it. Burns says that it is OK . . . I am a registered voter of Cambridge. I don't know how long you have to be one which might be the only catch."

Joe appeared that day before the State Ballot Law Commission and won his first and only case. Now he was on the ballot, but two weeks later he got a strange and unexpected knife-in-the-back from Adolf Hitler. When the Nazis took Warsaw, they claimed to have captured unburned Polish diplomatic correspondence, some of it consisting of reports forwarded to hard-drinking, flamboyant Polish Foreign Minister Beck from Jan Wszelaki, Polish commercial attaché in London. From these reports the German Foreign Office published a White Book purporting to show that Ambassadors Bullitt and Kennedy had promised to whip up American enthusiasm for the Polish cause before the invasion, pledging U.S. cash and support and thereby inciting the Poles to their useless fight. The White Book was a national bombshell, headlined in the *New York Times*. It quoted Wszelaki, whom Joe had met in Warsaw and again with his father in London, as saying that Ambassador Kennedy told him that "his two sons, who recently had traveled all over Europe, had an opportunity to see and learn a great deal," and that they intended to make a series of lectures after their return to Harvard. Ignoring the fact that such lectures would have been, had they occurred, *non*interventionist, the White Book quoted Wszelaki as writing that: "The ambassador placed great importance on these lectures in forming American opinion."

"You have no idea," Kennedy had allegedly bragged to Wszelaki, "to what extent my oldest boy, who was in Poland a short time ago, has the President's ear. I might say that the President believes him more than me. Perhaps that is because Joe presents a case with such conviction and enthusiasm."

With considerable conviction and enthusiasm and a great smile for *Time,* Joe labeled the story "a lot of bunk," following the lead of his President, who suggested that it be taken with not one or two but three grains of salt. Of his undelivered series of lectures Joe said: "This is pretty touchy stuff and I don't wish to comment on it," leaving the door open for the project in case he decided to undertake it. "My studies at the Harvard Law School take up pretty much all my time."

Jack had escaped on "Easter Vacation" from the reporters. From the Harvard Spee Club, he wrote his father that "the White Book revelations fizzled ... the Bullitts receiving what criticism there was ... the remark about Joe and the President's ear seemed too ridiculous for anyone to put much credence in."

Joe Junior seems not to have been so sure. His father's remark about their relative influence with Roosevelt had a certain dry and bitter ring: the ambassador had in truth lost the President's ear somewhere between Spain and the outbreak of war and knew it. Furthermore, his father was not denying it in London. While the whole thing was vaguely flattering to Joe, the image of a twenty-four-year-old Harvard Irishman influencing U.S. public opinion and advising the President might not sit well with the iconoclasts in the Irish wards. Ignoring the almost certain assurance of victory as an endorsed Democratic candidate, he decided to stump for the delegate seat.

The district was a conglomerate, ranging from the upper-middle-class wards of Brookline, Newton, Waltham, and Wellesley to the apartment-house districts of Brighton and down to the poorer "Brick Bottom" wards of Cambridge. He moved through barbershops and cocktail lounges, beauty parlors and saloons: "I'm Joe Kennedy Junior. I'm pledged to Postmaster General Farley. I'd like to represent you at the National Convention."

It is a good thing that he did. Two seats were up and five candidates ran. 22,188 ballots were cast. Brennan, his official running mate, won easily. When the count was over Joe Kennedy, Jr., had barely squeezed out Edward Mullonney, the next contender, by 129 votes. The first of the Kennedy brothers, running endorsed by his party's State Committee for the privilege of paying his own way to Chicago to cast a minuscule one-half vote for a candidate in whose choice he had had no voice, would have lost had he not got out to campaign.

That spring he read Jack's undergraduate thesis. Conceived first as "England's Foreign Policy Since 1731," it had finally become "Appeasement at Munich," an explanation of Chamberlain's conciliation. Joe wrote their father that "Jack rushed madly around the last week with his thesis and finally with the aid of five stenographers the last day got it under the wire. He seemed to have some good ideas so it ought to be very good." Then the onetime editor of Choate's yearbook passed literary judgment: "It seemed to represent a lot of work but did not prove anything."

Jack's thesis won him a *magna cum laude*, bettering the *cum laude* that Joe had won with his own paper on Spanish intervention. Arthur Krock suggested that Jack publish it, and even supplied a title: *Why England Slept.* The ambassador, author of *I'm for Roosevelt*, concurred: "You would be surprised how a book that really makes the grade with high-class people stands you in good stead for years to come." Jack asked Krock to write the foreword; the ambassador decided that Henry Luce should do it instead. The book, hurriedly printed by Wilfred Funk, got Jack's own grinning picture into *Time*, which found the volume: "startlingly timely, strenuously objective ... a terrifying record of wishful thinking about peace when peace was impossible." It sold eighty thousand copies and earned Jack $40,000 in royalties before he was twenty-four. En route to Chicago, his older brother, who had yet to earn his first dollar at anything more intellectual than the fourth at Narragansett or the rear end of an Arizona shovel, read *Time*, blinked, and presumably retired as a reviewer.

3

The city was hot, gusty, and heavy with the smell of stockyards as the special train rolled in. Everyone had known that a Chicago convention in July would be miserable, but Roosevelt, undeclared and evasive, had made certain that it would be held here, where Mayor Kelly, panicked into supporting him by Republican strength behind Willkie, could pull the strings. Joe moved into a room at the lakefront Stevens, where the Massachusetts delegation stayed. He called Bob Downes in Oshkosh and their classmate Charles Garabedian, who was visiting a Chicago eye surgeon. He promised them passes if they would come to the convention. They arrived and the three law students began to drift through the hotels, curious to see how Presidents were nominated.

All the main headquarters and most of the front men were at the Stevens; no one there had the courage to mention any name but Roosevelt's above a whisper. Across the street in a suite at the Blackstone, Harry Hopkins sat locked in a toilet to keep himself isolated. Into the bathroom ran a private line to the White House. A few floors up James Farley, Roosevelt's only serious opposition, Democratic Conservative and National Committee Chairman, was beginning to realize that, despite the encouragement of well-wishers, it was the old old story: the chairman might think that he ran the party, but the political machine that ran Chicago could swing the nomination on its home grounds. The machine was Kelly-Nash and Mayor Kelly had the strength. Farley had no more real chance of the Democratic nomination, if Roosevelt agreed to run, than Republican Willkie, whose Willkie Democratic Headquarters were seven blocks away at the Palmer House.

Heavy, suave Postmaster General Farley, loved throughout the party, did not intend to wreck the organization, but he would not budge either. Roosevelt, who had once said, "I have never heard Jim Farley make a constructive suggestion or even criticism regarding anything of importance to the country as a whole," had just expressed favor for Cordell Hull over Farley as a candidate and the postmaster general was just bitter enough to risk the President's wrath, lead an anti-third-term movement, and wait. Someone asked him if he thought there would be a move to make the nomination unanimous for Roosevelt before the balloting began, and Farley suggested that even if he as national chairman made a decision it would have no effect. "But let's go through the regular roll call and put all the names to the vote," he pleaded. "That's the proper procedure, isn't it?"

Newsmen asked if he actually thought, once Roosevelt's name arose, that any of his Massachusetts delegates would stay with him. "I think those delegates who were elected are pledged to me," he said. "If they think differently, that is up to them. I am not forcing anyone to vote for me—I don't want anyone else to force them."

Someone else was trying to force them already. Edward H. Flynn, scared like most party bosses that anyone but Roosevelt would lose to Willkie, was twisting political arms; John McCormack of the Massachusetts Delegation had reserved the right to vote for Roosevelt if his name was placed in nomination; Delegation Chairman William Burke, who had put Joe on the ballot, was a Roosevelt appointee to collector of Boston customs and ready to bolt Farley. He wanted to cast the Massachusetts vote for Roosevelt, and he wanted it unanimous. None of them saw any difficulty; no one dreamed that the delegation's youngest member would stand in its way. His father, after all, had said as early as last December in support of Roosevelt that the problems were becoming so great that "they should be handled by a man who won't take two years to educate."

The convention opened at night. The grimy old Chicago Stadium was ringed with policemen: Mayor Kelly was taking no chances on any spontaneous demonstrations but his own. It was so hard to get in that the spectator seats were only half-filled. A hundred people crashed, including One-Eyed Connelly, but Mayor Frank Hague of Jersey City forgot his ticket and couldn't get in until someone identified him. Texas and Minnesota delegates arrived battered after a fight in the Hotel Sherman. Elliott Roosevelt, a Lone Star delegate, passed out sandwiches. Radio crews in a cool, air-conditioned booth above the speakers' platform were comfortable but everyone else sweltered.

James A. Farley loomed on the platform in a white double-breasted suit, his bald head glistening. Joe Kennedy, Jr., sat sweating behind the Massachusetts banner. He listened to a soloist sing "God Bless America" and to Mayor Kelly eulogize Chicago as a city of "stand-uppers from start to finish," a sanctuary where the delegates could "ward off any telegraphic bombardments from Wall Street," and where no Morgan shadows—"those who would corner the market even on humanity"—would walk at their heels. Kelly mentioned Roosevelt at the end, touching off the first premature, one-man demonstration by a Tammany delegate who paraded the New York banner halfway around the hall before he noticed that he was alone. There were only a few dispirited cheers. But when the session broke up, the delegates had consumed fifteen barrels of beer and 163 quarts of whiskey.

Joe Kennedy was revolted at the spectacle of Harry Hopkins dictating a national convention from the Blackstone bathroom. Joe was not the only one; a reporter noted that "delegates resented being used as scenery like Hawaiian leis and brass bands." Roosevelt's third-term forces, surprised at the first night's apathy and outright delegate anger, begged the President himself to come; he refused and offered Eleanor. "She has a fine way with her." When she would not come without an invitation from the chairman, Farley gallantly tendered it but she did not arrive until after the nomination.

Joe Junior and Bob Downes went to Van Schuller's bar and restaurant, a famous magicians' hangout, and watched Blackstone cut a girl in half; the next day they were back for Mayor Kelly's second performance in the stadium. Hopkins had decided that anti-third-term feeling was rising and that there was no time to lose. He picked Kentucky's Senator Alben Barkley to read a message from the President giving permission for his name to be placed on the ballot, and Barkley would save that magic name for the last sentence; this would touch off a giant demonstration which would stampede the convention. Mayor Kelly took no chances. He hired a marching band to augment his sitting band and brought a bevy of costumed "Rainbow Girls." Straw hats, noisemakers, tin horns, and placards were distributed to hired demonstrators, ward heelers, and

to fifty precinct police captains in mufti who were filtered
into the galleries. Thomas Garry, Commissioner of Sewers,
remembered that the old public-address system had been
left intact when a new one was installed for the convention. He locked himself in the electrician's office and
awaited the cue.

Barkley began his speech hesitantly and got worse.
Fourteen minutes into it, long before he meant to, he
mistakenly popped the name of Roosevelt. The delegates
on the floor reacted spontaneously. For twenty-five minutes they howled and milled, while the galleries, instructed
earlier to wait, held firm. State standards pitched and
bobbed in the tides; six stood immovable, including, for a
while, the Massachusetts banner. Finally a free-for-all
erupted around it. Joe sat still. "They went wild," remembers Downes. "Jumping over chairs, trying to get at the
damn banner. One delegate named Wheeler told Joe he
had more guts than anybody and turned in his credentials
and left." The banner finally was swept into the mass of
demonstrators, followed by Chairman Burke and half the
delegates. Joe, aghast that grown men could be so "ani-
mal-like" sank deeper into his seat in disgust.

From the platform Farley watched the riot, chewing
gum impassively. Senator Barkley pounded the gavel for
fifteen minutes. A fight over the Texas banner brought
down a squad of policemen, and Barkley began to plead
with the delegates to take their seats. A knot of men in
front of the speaker, chanting "We Want Roosevelt,"
drowned him out, and it was not until he called for a
doctor and announced that "a lady has been seriously
injured" that he was allowed to finish his speech.

The demonstration seemed to have stiffened the Ken-
tuckian's weak delivery. Now he began to pound the
rostrum, shake his head for emphasis, and shout. He even
attempted humor: a henchman handed him a twist of
tobacco from his native state and he waved it before the
crowd, offering it to Willkie "to stop him from chewing
the rag." He castigated Willkie for an eternity and finally
read his long-awaited message from the President: "The
President never had and has not today any desire or purpose to continue in the Office of President, to be a
candidate for that office, or to be nominated by the
convention for that office." Below, shock and consterna-
tion. He continued to read: "All of the delegates to this
convention are free to vote for any candidate."

This oblique and almost incomprehensible phrase presumably included freedom to vote for Roosevelt, and was to have set off the staged demonstration. It was too subtle. The delegates sat stunned in silence, trying to decide what it all meant. The Kelly-packed galleries sat too, just as puzzled. Suddenly Sewer Commissioner Garry, deep in the bowels of the stadium, figured it out and began to bellow: "We want Roosevelt . . . We want Roosevelt . . ." The stadium exploded. For forty-five minutes this time, the banners paraded, led by the New York delegation. Barkley beamed and leaned over to hug Kentucky's standard as it swept by. The brass band in the Illinois section blared, the marching band marched, the Rainbow Girls glowed, the police captains bayed, the noisemakers rattled, and the tin horns tooted. Little Claude Pepper of Florida captured a microphone on the platform and announced that Florida wanted Roosevelt: Senator Josh Lee yanked it from him and bellowed that the world wanted Roosevelt, and Alben Barkley announced unnecessarily, "That's all right by me!" Someone handed him a giant, framed portrait of the President, and he waved it aloft, starting the demonstration afresh. A New York delegate screamed, "Tammany wants Roosevelt!" New Jersey boss Hague and Chicago boss Kelly jumped to chairs to lead the cheering on the floor. Above it all the dismal voice of the sewer commissioner reverberated: "Louisiana wants Roosevelt . . . Kentucky wants Roosevelt . . . Massachusetts wants Roosevelt . . ."

Big Jim Farley, his jaws moving rhythmically on his gum, looked down on his party. There were tears in his eyes. Joe and Bob Downes left.

4

The next day was just as sultry and miserable, and nerves were fraying. The demonstration, labeled in the morning press as rigged, did nothing to ease Hopkins' fear that unless the President was nominated by acclamation or at least unanimously on the first ballot, the inviolate third-term prohibition would defeat him at the polls in November. All day the squeeze on Farley increased, but he would not move out of the way. His name would go into nomination, and no one could stop it.

The pressure shifted to delegates, primarily Massachusetts delegates at the Stevens. Chairman Burke paid off Roosevelt for the Boston customs collector job: in caucus in the ballroom he formally switched from Farley, explaining to the delegates that he had always reserved the right to do so if Roosevelt became available. John McCormack, who had actually reserved this right and remained unpledged from the beginning, backed him. Clem Norton, the politician, writer, and world traveler with whom Joe had lunched in London and who had described the thrifty young millionaire so fondly in the Boston *Herald*, went to work on the subject of his sketch. He found quickly, in the lobby of the Stevens, that he had got it wrong: Joe was more than a simple, respectful All-American boy; he was a stubborn, red-faced Irishman. With all of his considerable eloquence Norton tried to convince him that not to switch to Roosevelt was to wreck his own political career and to bring the wrath of Roosevelt onto his father's head. He was a voluble, loud little man but Joe's voice was just as raucous, and the argument attracted a crowd of reporters. Finally Joe stalked off. He never wavered, but he wanted advice. He found Arthur Krock in his *New York Times* suite at the Stevens, window open to the breeze off the lake. They moved to the bedroom for privacy, and Krock suggested that if Joe really wanted to change his vote he ask Farley to release him, and that Farley would agree.

Joe refused. He had pledged himself in the saloons and flats of brick-bottom Cambridge; voters who had given him their ballot had trusted him to vote for Farley, and he would not ask a way out.

Krock beamed. "What do you think your father would want you to do? Keep your word or not? Keep your commitment, which is not only a legal but a moral commitment? I'll tell you what he would want you to do, I'm quite sure: that's stick to your moral and legal commitment."

Thus fortified, Joe returned to the ballroom below to find that the Roosevelt men had actually phoned his father in London begging him to straighten out his son. The ambassador answered: "No, I wouldn't think of telling him what to do." To ensure that he was not misunderstood, he sent a cable to Joe: DO WHAT YOU THINK BEST. Joe talked to his father by phone, too, as Commissioner Timilty, who had gone west to the convention, listened: then

Joe cast his vote for Farley in the hotel ballroom and went to the stadium.

Hopkins had picked balding Senator Lester Hill of Alabama to nominate the President. Hill in his hour of glory so flexed his oratorial muscles and whinnied a speech so similar in delivery to the fabled "Mr. Speaker" address that even his hometown papers laughed at it. It was enough to set off another demonstration, though, and it looked as if no one would capture the microphone long enough to name anyone else. But before the tumult died, tiny Carter Glass of Virginia, eighty-two, tottered to the microphone to nominate Farley. Kelly's henchmen in the galleries began to boo. The little old gentleman, his head hardly high enough to reach the mike, enraged at two anonymous anti-Catholic telegrams he had just received, stood stiffly in the swelling dissent. When Farley could stand the spectacle no longer, he moved from his seat to the floor; Barkley, to his credit, went with him. "Those two guys came down there hotter than hell," Bob Downes remembers, "big strapping guys, and collared Kelly and Nash and told them to call their goon squads off and let the old man talk and let him talk *now*, and Kelly and Nash did."

Perhaps to protect those Massachusetts delegates who had climbed with him onto the bandwagon for the Boss, Chairman Burke stood and announced a mathematically impossible Massachusetts vote: 21⅓ for Roosevelt and 11⅔ for Farley, enabling Delegate John Coan of Swampscott to demand a public poll of the delegation. A groan went up from the soggy, impatient galleries, but Barkley granted the request. This time the vote was accurate. Twenty-three delegates cast their 11½ votes along with Joe. Farley forever after remembered Joe's "resolute young voice" over the tumult: "James A. Farley."

Now that the Democratic convention had indeed been democratic, now that those pledged to him had had a chance, if they dared, to voice the will of their districts, James Farley stood and moved that Roosevelt be nominated "by acclamation." The stadium trembled with the roar, the bands struck up "When Irish Eyes Are Smiling," and the convention adjourned.

Joe Kennedy headed west to California for fresh air.

5

Joe had been invited to California by William Randolph Hearst, Jr., and his wife, Lorelle, to visit "Wyntoo," the great Hearst ranch on the McCloud River in the shadow of Shasta. Joe brought Tom Killefer too and they spent weeks riding through the stately redwoods, fishing, and hunting. They met Princess Pignatelli and her daughter and Joe developed what Hearst describes as a "schoolboy crush" on Lorelle, an ex-Follies girl. For her benefit he insisted on swimming the swift and frigid McCloud, which had its origin in the ice-cave country of the Shasta National Forest, and which Hearst had been trained to regard since childhood as almost certain death.

He survived and headed south to Tom's home in Hermosa Beach. They spent the summer swimming, body surfing, and capturing girls. Tom's mother thought Joe a charming house-guest, if not the neatest. "Every letter he got from his mother she'd say 'Now remember, Joe, do pick up your room!' and he actually made a few half-hearted attempts. But he'd take everything out of his pockets at night and in the morning I'd go in there and there would be clothes all over, and bills—you'd never see anything less than twenties—behind the door, under the desk, behind the furniture."

He was greatly loved. He would entertain Tom's father, a former big-league ballplayer who managed the Hollywood Stars, with imitations of FDR. Tom had a summer job in a local law office and needed his battered Ford to get there, so Joe would hitchhike when he wanted to go someplace. "He just loved to go to church," Mrs. Killefer says. "He'd come back just beaming. He'd say, 'It just makes me feel so good.' I had a hard time remembering to serve him fish on Friday and sometimes he'd forget and eat a hamburger on the beach, but no matter how late he was out on Saturday night, he was right up and going to church."

While he was there the phony war in Europe caught fire. Congress passed the first peacetime conscription bill. Lieutenant Colonel Lewis B. Hershey was named its coordinator. Joe and Tom hoped to finish law school before they were drafted, but if their numbers came up, they decided to try for naval aviation. Tom envisioned a fighter, where he would not have the responsibility of a crew; Joe wanted a big patrol plane, where he would. Joe made a quick trip to see Mexico City. Then he returned to Harvard Law to do all he could for Roosevelt, nonintervention, and his own education before Hershey caught up with him.

4

THREE weeks into his second year of law school, Joe registered for the draft along with seventeen million other American men between eighteen and thirty-five. In June, Churchill had pulled the British Army from Dunkirk with thirty thousand casualties, leaving most of its equipment. France had fallen. Now as the Germans massed to invade England, the Luftwaffe slugged London for twenty-three nights straight; in the last two months they had hit 1,400 factories in the metropolitan area alone. Coventry was wrecked: John Kennedy donated his British royalties on *Why England Slept* to the city and neither he nor Joe wrote any more to their father of Kick going back to London to improve the family image: instead she got a job on the Washington *Times Herald,* owned by the ambassador's friend Colonel McCormick, writing the column *Did You Happen To See.* The ambassador, fearful that his death by bombing would bring the United States closer to intervention, slept nights in Great Windsor Park. The estate was bombed. He found a piece of incendiary with, by coincidence, the initials J.P.K. on it, but he wrote Rose that he was not going to be killed by a bomb. A shot-up Messerschmitt crashed with its pilot so close to him that "I could see the fuzz on his face and almost count his buttons."

He told British newsmen that "bombing, as far as it interrupts the night's rest, is nothing new to married men who, like myself, have many children," but suddenly it was harder to get smiles for quotable quotes. He had been through 245 raids and blown off the street and onto the sidewalk in a car, but London chatter had him sleeping for protection in a bathroom in the Dorchester or spending his days as well as his nights in the country. He had strongly endorsed the sale to Britain of ammunition, machine guns, and field artillery to replace that abandoned at Dunkirk; he had publicly praised British courage under fire: "I did not know London could take it. I did not think any city could take it. I am bowed in reverence." But no one was listening: his pessimism already showed and, after all, he had sent his family home. Londoners traded bitter rumors in the underground shelters that the Kennedys lacked courage. The ambassador had lost his popularity and he wanted out. He was lonely. He was an isolationist and he wanted his views known in America. He wanted them known before the election while he had leverage, not afterward, and he suspected quite accurately that Roosevelt was keeping him in exile to shut him up.

In Cambridge, Joe prayed for his father's safety and began to make his own voice heard. A week after he registered for the draft, Secretary of War Stimson had blindfoldedly picked a number from a jar. Joe would be subject to an early call; there were no deferments for students, and he had not much time. He began to talk anywhere, everywhere, on any subject to any group. He was so good a speaker that invitations flowed in. He refused to tailor his views to his audience: invited to speak to a club of Townsend Plan oldsters at the Brookline Town Hall, he accepted and then blasted Francis Townsend, explaining first that his position was his own and not his father's: "I have not the money at my disposal to discuss the pros and cons of the Townsend Plan over the transatlantic telephone, and I do not dare reverse the charges." That got a chuckle, but nothing else did. The Townsend Plan, he said, was the most dangerous of all pension schemes put forth. "I do not blame any of you for favoring it," he admitted, "for it is much the vogue today to get as much as possible from the government," but he labeled the plan unworkable, economically disastrous, and impossible to administer.

In October his father pried himself loose from London by threatening the State Department to release his views on intervention anyway, through Eddie Moore in New

York. He arrived in the States carrying an air-raid siren for Hyannis to call the children in from swimming. He visited the White House, where Roosevelt, by again taking his side against his own State Department, recharmed him. Within two days the ambassador was on the radio, nationally, at his own expense: "England's valiant fight is giving us time to prepare. . . ." He denied a secret commitment by Roosevelt to Great Britain to lead the United States into war, and finished as always: "My wife and I have given nine hostages to Fortune. . . . I believe that Franklin D. Roosevelt should be reelected President of the United States."

Joe Junior heard the speech and pitched ardently into the campaign for Roosevelt. He distributed FDR badges on the steps of the State House during the National Roosevelt Youth Day Program. Two days after his father's speech, when Roosevelt visited Boston on the eve of the election, Joe dragged his Republican sidekicks Bob Downes and Tom Killefer to the station to meet him. The three rode with Grandpa Honeyfitz and the President to the Boston Garden, where Joe Junior spoke for him before the jammed galleries and Roosevelt returned the compliment, glowing over his father: "that Boston boy, beloved by all of Boston and a lot of other places, my ambassador to the Court of St. James, Joe Kennedy." They heard Roosevelt make the famous statement that would haunt him forever after: 'And while I am talking to you mothers and fathers, I give you one more assurance. . . . Your boys are not going to be sent into any foreign wars."

Five days later Roosevelt squeaked into office, defeating Willkie with the smallest plurality since Wilson had campaigned on roughly the same issue—"he kept us out of war"—in 1916. That Saturday Ambassador Kennedy gave his ill-conceived interview at the Ritz-Carlton to Louis Lyons of the Boston *Globe:* "Democracy is dead in England. . . . It may be here. It isn't that she's fighting for democracy. She's fighting for self-preservation, just as we will if it comes to us. I say we aren't going in. Only over my dead body."

It was enough to finish him with England, and with Roosevelt. He didn't care about the first: he had already submitted his resignation. Loss of favor with the President was another matter. His plan, after Christmas in Palm Beach, was to "devote my efforts to what seems to me to

Left: Joseph P. Kennedy, Sr., star pitcher for the Boston Latin School, 1907.

(Wide World)

The right end of the Harvard freshman team, 1934—Joseph Kennedy, Jr.

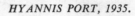

HYANNIS PORT, 1935.

Left: (l. to r.) Eunice, Bob, Joe Junior, Jack (holding Jean), Rosemary, and Pat, seated.

Below, right: Bob on young Joe's shoulders.

Below, left: Joe Junior supporting Eunice and Bob.

Left: Mrs. Kennedy and her eldest son, Joe Junior, Palm Beach, 1935.

Below: A wonderful summer—all together.

(Photograph by Bradford Bachrach)

Above: Two Palm Beach pals: Teddy and his older brother Joe.

Below: The Kennedy men captured London: John, the ambassador, and young Joe at Waterloo Station.

(Pictorial Parade)

Joe Junior found Rugby exhilarating.

CHRISTMAS AT SAINT-MORITZ, 1939

Right: Joseph Kennedy, Jr., at play.

Above: Young Joe with skating champion Megan Taylor.

(Wide World)

Right: Having broken his arm skiing, Joe was still skating.

(Wide World)

Above: Having toured the Spanish combat zone, Joe Junior sat in the U.S. Embassy gardens in Madrid. On his left, Francisco Ugarte —the caretaker and sole resident of the Embassy—and, on his right, Arturo Cardona, journalist.

(Wide World)

Below: Back in London, Joe Junior took Kathleen and John to the special sitting of the House of Commons, September 1, 1939, as war threatened.

(Wide World)

Left: At the Democratic Convention, young Joe stuck to his commitments and voted for Jim Farley despite pressure to switch to FDR.

Right: Joe Junior reported to the Squantum Naval Air Base to begin his training in July, 1941.

(Wide World)

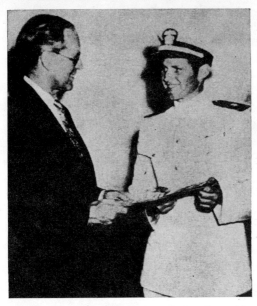

Above: He received his commission from his father, May, 1942.

Left: On leave in Palm Beach, with Countess Ravenska and Tom Killifer.

Above: Young Joe flew his submarine patrols, and his final mission, in a PB4Y-1.

Below: F. Jones (l.) and Mark Soden (r.) stand in hut at Dunkeswell Air Base. The hut immediately behind is where Joe Junior lived.

Above: The Marquis of Hartington and Kathleen on their wedding day. Joe Junior is standing behind Kathleen.

(Wide World)

THE TARGET: a V-1 site.

Below, left: Jim Simpson, the next-to-last man to see Joe Junior alive.

Below, right: Wilford (Bud) Willy, who was killed with Joe Junior.

The Lost Prince.

(Wide World)

Lieutenant j.g. John F. Kennedy and Ensign Joseph P. Kennedy, Jr.
(Pictorial Parade)

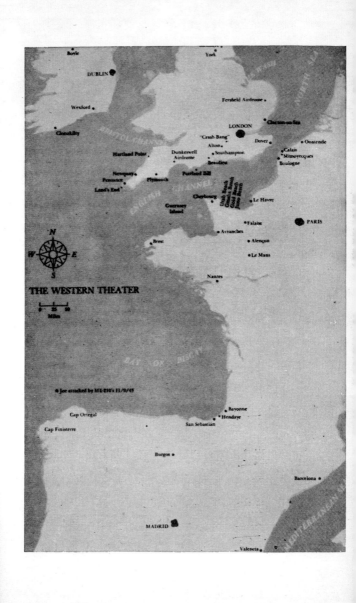

THE WESTERN THEATER

TARGET AREA

Cap Blanc Nez

BEACH

C 122°

Wissant
(900 pop.)

Cap Gris-Nez

BEACH

N

W E

S

0   0.5   1
Miles

Marquise
(880 pop.)

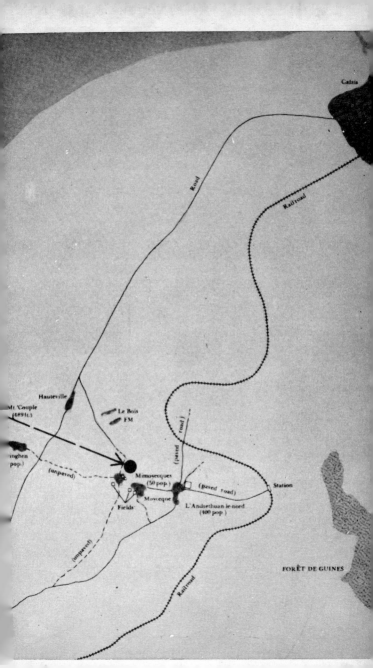

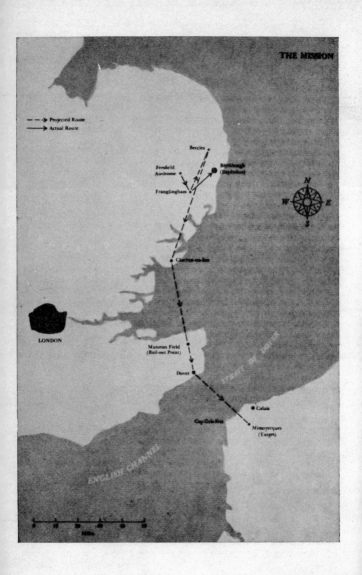

THE MISSION

- - - → Projected Route
———→ Actual Route

Beccles

Fersfield Airdrome

Blythburgh (Explosion)

Franglingham

N
W   E
S

Clacton-on-Sea

LONDON

Manston Field (Bail-out Point)

Dover

STRAIT OF DOVER

Calais

Cap-Gris-Nez

Mimoyecques (Target)

ENGLISH CHANNEL

Miles

be the greatest cause in the world today . . . to help the President keep the United States out of war."

It was a cause, he would find, that meant much less to Roosevelt than to Kennedy himself, or to Kennedy's oldest son.

2

Kennedy Christmases were always spent in Florida, and they were frantic. This year there was even a moratorium on sisterly squabbles. The family itself had no time to decorate the tree; everyone had been too long away from each other, and had too much to say; the tree was dressed and lighted by the help, eventually, and simply appeared on Christmas morning in the great tiled living room. There was always a last-minute rush for presents, and no one was really certain when it was all over who had given what to whom.

Tom Killefer had gone to Palm Beach with Joe. They swam and played golf—Joe losing to Jack—and watched unhappy Barbara Hutton on the course, and sometimes played with her handsome fiancé, golfer Bob Sweeny. Killefer was impressed at the crowded breakfast table with Rose Kennedy's ability as a dispatcher of transportation: one car went here and dropped Kathleen, picking up Bobby and dropping him somewhere else, and was back in time to take the ambassador to the Golf Club, while a second car was similarly engaged and a third was on an errand to Miami. He and Joe liked to talk to the ambassador while he lay on a table in the solarium by the pool, under the hands of his masseur. He would pick up a poolside phone and call anyone, Killefer recalls: "Winston Churchill . . . Chiang Kai-shek . . . and actually speak to them . . . get right through. . . ." Tom and Joe watched in fascination. "He would talk about the war, the way things were going, anything."

It was a good Christmas, but perhaps a sad and frightening one too. The ambassador with his long line of communications was obviously informed and increasingly distrustful of the President's Boston promise to the parents of America. Roosevelt's signed and smiling portrait dropped suddenly to a minor level below the family pictures on the wall of the den. Joe's brothers began to drift

back to prep school and his sisters to their Catholic
academies in Philadelphia and New York; Rosemary, who
had become increasingly irritable and unmanageable, went
back to her special school. Jack left for the Stanford
School of Business Administration and Kathleen for her
desk on the Washington paper. Flying back to Cambridge,
Joe must have wondered if next Christmas they would all
be together again.

3

The America First Committee, dedicated to keeping the
United States out of the European war, had grown to
sixty thousand members with eleven locals and was gaining hundreds of students daily on campuses across the
country by the time Joe returned to Cambridge. It was the
creation of a Yale law student named Robert Douglas
Stuart and perhaps that is the reason Joe Kennedy
did not actually join it. But with his classmate Robert
Taft, Jr., Quentin Roosevelt, grandson of TR, and other
anti-interventionists, he helped form two ad hoc committees dedicated to the same ends. Joe's opinions, publicly
stated over the next few months, had been held before
America First existed and derived from his own observa-
tion, salted with his father's sentiments. They are nevertheless almost precisely parallel to the three cornerstones
of America First philosophy: that Germany could not
invade America even if Britain failed, that the United
States could and would if necessary do business with Nazi
Germany, and that if the United States convoyed British
shipping, the act was sure to put America into the conflict.

Joe had always been outspoken in class and now he
began to debate faculty interventionists who were members of the Committee for Militant Aid to Britain. He
argued the issues at lunch in Lincoln's Inn, over the bridge
table in Taft's home—Taft was married—and sometimes
more formally on the speaker's stand. Joe and his isolationists, reluctant to tie themselves to the parent America
First movement, called themselves the Harvard Committee
Against Military Intervention in Europe. Forming it, Joe
said bitterly, "Since contrary to the assertions of the
Committee for Militant Aid to Britain there is every
reason to believe that America is not now at war, it is

incumbent upon us to consider the possibilty of remaining at peace." His law professor Barton Leach was a leader in the interventionist group. "Joe was all fired up by this America First business," he recalls. "He was head of the Harvard part of it and got very emotional about it. And he was very active in it and spent time on it that he ought to have been spending on his studies."

Joe seldom needed to call for help in a debate, but when he did he knew where to look. He gave a cocktail party at the Bay State apartment for the lion-maned Norman Thomas and turned him loose on Leach. "He took me like Grant took Richmond," admits Leach. "I had never been up against a thoroughly competent debater before. He was wrong as hell, but this was his meat, and he just toyed with me."

Mostly Joe spoke for himself. He believed that the United States would be better off under a barter system with a Nazi-conquered Europe than engaging in total war on the side of Great Britain, a war "which the American economy cannot stand. All our trade," he protested to a Ford Hall Folks Meeting in January, "would *not* be cut off if Britain lost." To guard transatlantic shipments to Britain, he warned, would inevitably demand that "we send an air force to Britain and battleships to convoy supplies, and we shall be in the war, a total war which may last six or seven years." He was no apostle of disarmament; he would have nothing to do with the pacifists of the World Peace Group; on the contrary, he wanted to strengthen the Army and Navy against the Nazi menace while there was yet time. But now the U.S. Army, he asserted, could not stand a total war.

His view of American potential was overly pessimistic, like his father's: his view of her present strength was very clear. The first batch of U.S. draftees were training with broomsticks: in the *Harvard Lampoon* a cartoon showed troops with a fireman's net under a falling bomb while their commander explained to a bystander: "It's the only bomb we got." There were campus peace strikes everywhere and in the Army an OHIO movement—"Over the Hill in October"—began to grow.

Joe was on the losing side and undoubtedly knew it, but he continued to tangle with anyone, anywhere. At a Foreign Policy Association luncheon in Boston's Copley Plaza, sitting at the speakers' table with his former political-science professor Arthur Holcombe and Harvey Bundy, he took the stand to sharply question President James Baxter of Williams, asking what effect on American morale would be if U.S. soldiers or sailors were "drowned like rats" in convoys headed for Europe. Although he urged all possible aid to Britain short of war and disagreed with Lindbergh's recent statement that destruction of the British fleet would *not* be a serious blow to America, Joe said nevertheless that if America convoyed shipments at all it must be prepared to go the whole way, send men overseas, and undertake a five- or ten-year war. He was very effective. Holcombe, who shared his views, remembers that "he had a great natural aptitude and made a fine and effective appearance on the platform."

It was a lonely fight and growing lonelier. The Lend-Lease Bill was passed in March. In Madison Square Garden Wendell Willkie brought a crowd of twenty-three thousand to its feet as he ended a speech in favor of convoys, spacing his words ponderously: "We . . . want . . . those . . . convoys . . . protected!" Lindbergh, rapidly becoming an ex-hero, protested: "Britain is obviously losing the war, and the U.S. will only be beaten if it tries to intervene." Eighty-three percent of the United States was still against the war in a Gallup poll of April 7, but if the *only* way to beat Germany and Italy was for the United States to go, sixty-eight percent would have gone then. The Atlantic Patrol was extended, and Winston Churchill thanked Roosevelt, quoting Clough's line: "But westward look, the land is bright." Navy Secretary Knox announced that the Navy was "readier than ever to assure delivery of supplies to Britain." Magazine ads began to show uniformed men and Navy nurses; *Life* ran a section on military dress so that Americans could tell a marine from a soldier and a private from a colonel.

Joe Kennedy signed up for the Naval Aviation Cadet Program in May and passed his preliminary physical and psychological tests. Like most students, he was granted a delay in reporting until his semester was over.

On June 24 he stood by the dingy steps of the recruiting station at 150 Conway Street in Boston in suit, and tie, and suede shoes, and was sworn in as a seaman second class, U.S. Naval Reserve. It was an elite group of Ivy Leaguers: the President's son John was there, to become a supply officer. John Thomas, with whom Joe would fly in England, was there too, just out of Amherst. Reporters and photographers milled about: the richness of the catch was still, in pre-Pearl Harbor days, good copy.

They took Joe's picture. He looks uncomfortable, a little shy, and very thoughtful, and for once the smile is missing.

THREE

THE MISSION

1

JOE TIMILTY wanted to drive his young friend to his first duty station, so Joe Junior put aside certain reservations he must have felt and arrived at Squantum Naval Air Facility as a seaman second, in an official car driven by the Boston police commissioner. The station lay on a little peninsula which divides the waters of Boston Harbor from Quincy Bay to the south. It was a tiny base and dedicated, like scores of other "elimination bases" that hot and frantic summer, to quickly purging from the strong red blood of naval aviation those corpuscles judged too weak to survive later.

Joe thanked Timilty, watched him drive off, and found himself in a strange and rankless status. Because a successful candidate would eventually become a naval-aviation cadet, he was issued a cadet's khaki shirt and pants; because he was technically a twenty-one-dollar-a-month seaman second he was still denied the tiny gold collar anchors of cadet rank. On the streets of Boston he would have felt like a Boy Scout or a service-station attendant, but his reception in Boston was academic, anyway, for he was not going to see it for a month, and everyone on the base knew what he and his fellows were, insignia or not. What they were was nothing.

The preflight cadet was subhuman, less than a boot-camp trainee. Further, he was a potential victim of a cruel philosophy. Naval pilot training held coldly to the

premise that it was better to remove the accident-prone
early, before too much time and money had been wasted
on him. The Navy would have preferred to eliminate him
with a pencil during his aptitude test, or a spinning chair
during his physical, or with a "down" from a hard-nosed
instructor during his first dual flight. But if the fledgling,
suicidally negotiating all of these barriers, insisted on re-
moving himself terminally in flight, the establishment preferred losing an untrained seaman or cadet soloing a
$2,000 biplane to sacrificing later a highly trained ensign
with a dozen crew members in a $250,000 patrol bomber.
Attrition through medical washout, academic deficiency, or
the unpredictable tendency of certain students to leave too
little air under the aircraft was traditionally fifty percent:
the odds only slightly better than Harvard Law.

Ambassador Kennedy, had he been aware of the Navy's
desire to bury its mistakes early, would probably have
been even more uncomfortable at his son's choice of
services than he already was: to all who would listen, he
was already complaining in a mixture of pride and genu-
ine anguish: "Wouldn't you know? *Naval aviation*, the
most dangerous thing there is!" But knowledge of military
aviation's cold-bloodedness was not general among parents: even the potential victims themselves welcomed the
early solo as a sort of airborne puberty rite, perhaps not
realizing themselves that, like the deliberately built-in
ground loop in primary trainers, it was designed to uncover
the aerial spastic—not later but immediately.

What was hard for Joe and most of his classmates to
take was the new extension of the eliminate-them-early
philosophy to the fields of physical endurance, courage,
and aggressiveness. The ground portion of the V-5 Pre-
Flight Program had lately been turned over to the "jock-
strap commandos," professional and college athletes and
coaches swept into the Navy by patriotism, promise of
rank, or fear of the draft. The potential U.S. naval cadet
had always been screened for intellect more carefully than
the Army Air Corps candidate—ground school was more
arduous, Navy pilots were trained as navigators, too, and
flight training itself was longer: the Navy required a
college degree long after the Army dropped its standards.
But now the Navy was apparently demanding that its
candidates be supermen as well. The naval *E* base on the
brink of World War II was earning a reputation as a cross
between Andersonville and Dante's Inferno.

Joe Kennedy and his fellow martyrs, who assumed correctly that their future duties would require nothing more strenuous of them than the ability to push forward a throttle or climb onto a barstool, found themselves thrown into a ring with fellow wretches and enjoined by potbellied ex-athletes to "fight until one of you goes down"; they scrambled around commando courses like demented marines, knowing that the last one to finish would do it again; they did push-ups and climbed ropes and marched interminably on the asphalt parade ground—the "grinder"—in the sultry Boston sun. When they went to class, they double-timed. Joe Kennedy, who had always kept himself in shape, suffered not nearly so much as some of his classmates. He welcomed the contact sports and endured the commando courses. Harvard had been poor practice for military discipline, and he had never joined the R.O.T.C., preferring to keep himself free to choose his own service if war came, but in childhood he had learned to treat rank if not too overbearing with outward respect and at Choate he had survived considerable hazing, so he learned to say "sir" and survived. The flying he loved: he sat happily on a chute in the rear seat of open-cockpit Stearman "Yellow Peril" biplanes, peering past his instructor's shoulder as they jounced and bumped through the thermals over Boston. He began to get the feel of the plane through the stick—it was not unlike a sailboat's tiller in his hand—and to sense the pulse of the rudder through the pedals under his soles. Some of his instructor's aerobatics made him squeamish, but he kept down his lunch and tried to follow his teacher's movements through the dual controls. The reward finally came one afternoon: the instructor landed on a grass field down the Cape, climbed to the wing, looked him in the eye, and said, "Once around the field."

He was all at once airborne, by himself, free and alone. He must have wanted to fly forever, but he did what he had been told and circled and landed; when he reported to Jacksonville for primary training, his logbook read ten hours dual and five minutes solo.

That night in Boston, finished with Squantum and *E* base, he met Ted Reardon, who was going into the Army as a second lieutenant. They celebrated Joe's solo, and then he went to the Cape. He had five days to get to Jacksonville, where, if he survived, he would really learn to fly.

2

The naval air station at Jacksonville was a great sprawling base with green lawns and alabaster buildings. It had never been intended for primary flight training, but the glut of would-be aviators had engorged Pensacola and then Corpus Christi and even here, Joe found, he would have to wait two months as a seaman before he was sworn as a cadet and saw the inside of another Stearman cockpit.

There was little to do, fortunately, for the Jacksonville Naval Air Station in August was an inferno. For a while after "elimination base" it felt good to play golf and swim and visit the city with Tom Killefer, who had joined up in Long Beach and survived an *E* base in California. They had liberty until 11 P.M. every second night. They met the local belles before wartime swamped the area with servicemen, while the welcome mats in the great mansions along the St. Johns River were still out. They went to the beach and Joe wrote his sister Jean, twelve, that it was not half as nice as their own beaches, "the sand so hard that you can drive along it in a car."

Bored, he began to golf with the chaplain, Father Maurice Sheehy, who was also public-relations officer and edited the station paper. The father put him to work as a reporter and found that he had a natural newsman who went after one story so hard that he antagonized a navy captain. Joe fit in well with his shipmates, mostly graduates of the Ivy League. His classmates grew used to his kneeling to pray in the barracks and reminded him if he forgot. He became president of the Holy Name Society, entitling him to wake up the Catholics in the barracks for early Mass. He had always liked to wake up people and often he used heroic measures, with great gusto, on the wrong people. When the Jews in the barracks complained, Father Sheehy called him in.

"Don't they have souls?" Joe asked. "Aren't you interested in saving them?"

"Try to use persuasion," suggested Sheehy. "I don't think you're making friends for the Church by dousing them with water at five in the morning."

"The trouble with you, Father," said Joe, "is you're anti-Semitic."

After eight weeks of loafing, Joe was discharged as a seaman and sworn as aviation cadet, U.S. Naval Reserve. His salary was more than tripled: now he got seventy-five dollars per month. Finally he could wear the tiny gold anchors, but that week Jack wrecked his accomplishment. His younger brother, after having been turned down by the Army, had built up his back through exercise and had finally passed a Navy physical and put on the golden bars of an ensign. As an elder brother, Joe was proud of him; as previously undefeated contender for family honors, he was shattered. Lorelle Hearst found him worried about his brother's bad back and bitter at their father for not doing something to keep Jack out of uniform. He was annoyed, too, at having been so quickly and easily outranked. He was still a cadet and now his brother was an officer. Joe already knew that naval precedence, unlike the Army's, was assigned for life, depended on date of commissioning, and marched ponderously on, blind to merit, forever. For the first time Jack had passed him, and no matter how Joe strained, he could never catch up. He had a grim suspicion that if their paths ever crossed in uniform, his younger brother would never let him forget his seniority. The only note of cheer was that Jack was safe from glory at a Pentagon desk, preparing a daily news digest for the brass.

Joe had plenty of problems besides that of being outranked by his younger brother. Primary flight training here at Jacksonville was no easier than *E* base had been at Squantum. Reveille was at 5 A.M. It was still dark when Joe would stagger forth in tennis shoes and khaki shorts for calisthenics on the concrete outside the sprawling barracks. Breakfast was from steam tables in the mess hall and then there were eight hours of ground school classes and three hours of drilling on the macadam. There were Friday field days with swab and bucket in the barracks and locker inspection Saturday morning, and "full-dress" reviews in the blazing forenoon. He had so little time of his own that when Grandfather Fitzgerald came to visit, Joe had to get an officer friend, Ensign Chuck Warren, to meet him at the gate.

In the cadet regiment there was cadet rank and even a certain Annapolis-like arrogance that inevitably came with it; Joe had a low threshold of tolerance for minor Hitlers but put up with them for the sake of his goal. When a cadet officer forgot to sign him out for early Mass and the regimental office assigned him extra duty for missing morning formation, Father Sheehy offered to square the report away. Joe refused, apparently not wishing to appear to trade on their friendship, and marched the extra duty, wearing a navy web belt and learning something about the unnatural gain in weight of a Springfield '06 lugged hour after hour in Florida sun.

Cadets berthed two to a room. Joe lived with Bill Ash, a cadet officer, and learned to make a Navy bunk and to stow a Navy locker, but he somehow accumulated thirty demerits. He was unimpressed by this sword of Damocles and continued a floating illegal blackjack game with Phil Kind, a wealthy Jewish classmate from Philadelphia, behind the hangars. Phil found him the best blackjack player he had ever met, and on the long "cattle-car" bus rides to outlying fields, Joe cleaned up at bridge.

He was a natural leader with sea-lawyer tendencies. When a telephone operator off the base claimed that an anonymous cadet in his barracks had used abusive language on the phone, the duty officer ordered everyone out of the barracks and announced that until the culprit confessed the cadets would stand outside in ranks, all night if necessary. Mass punishment and an attempt to force a confession seemed to Joe such a cruel and unusual punishment that he urged the criminal to stand mute and promised that no one would turn him in. At 1 A.M., as the cadets shivered and coughed in ranks, each apparently on the verge of pneumonia, the officer threw in the towel. Having saved the U.S. Constitution, Joe marched off to bed with the rest.

He was elected immediately as his class representative to the board of governors of the Cadet Club, a lively institution which served beer and liquor and was the hub of social life. To be a governor was gratifying, but real power and prestige lay in the board's presidency: the president of the Cadet Club got invited everywhere. Election was by majority vote of the board of governors. Joe started late: Cadet Edwin M. Wilson, a Floridian who thought he had learned politics in student-body elections at Duke and as president of a Willkie College Club, had by scurrying frantically through the fast-moving currents of cadet life already managed to find enough governors to sew up a majority. The attendance at the meeting on election night seemed sparse: Wilson discovered that none of his own delegates were there. Joe generously agreed to a

delay while Wilson searched. Wilson sped furiously around
the base but could find no governor who was not night
flying, on watch in the barracks, or serving as messenger
in the regimental office. Joe won by a landslide, and it was
not until the next day that he told Wilson the awful truth:
out-numbered, he had sought out not governors but the
yeomen, cadet officers, and the friendly instructors who
had made up the previous night's duty rosters.

There was not much time for politics, or social life
either. Ground school was tough. Later he would claim
that he had wanted to fly fighters, but from the first his
papers show that he had wanted command, not of a
single-seater Wildcat or even a three-man torpedo plane,
but a real crew and a multiengine aircraft. In the fall of
1941 that meant flying boats. Navigation would be important to him as a patrol-plane commander over the long
ocean reaches; it was the terror of most cadets but Joe
wanted to know it better than his potential navigators and
earned a starring grade, 3.45. He wanted to understand
his engines as well as his mechanics would; in Aircraft-
Engines and Aircraft-Structures classes, competing with
some classmates who held engineering degrees, he stood
very near the top of his class. Sweating under his earphones
in the cubicles of the code room, he learned the fifteen
words per minute that would enable him to back up his
future radiomen. Patrol planes, he knew, interrogated
shipping at sea, and his grades in international signal flags,
semaphore, and blinker were almost perfect.

The flying was another matter. Six weeks after Joe was
sworn as a cadet he walked, seat chute flopping astern, to
a "Yellow Peril" like the one he had soloed so briefly at
Squantum. His instructor was an ensign named, appropri-
ately, Hardie. Suddenly Joe found himself launched on a
rough, nerve-straining, and frustrating sea of instructions,
counter-instructions, exhortations, and pleas. In the air,
academics didn't count. Mental habits of law school,
where he had been taught to question every ruling, were
detrimental. Flying is more closely allied to blowing a
tuba than to building a case in court. Lieutenant Commander Lester McDonald, Medical Corps, the flight surgeon at Jacksonville, had concluded from a study of training records that "musicians make the best pilots, which is
why all aircraft carriers have good bands. Lawyers make
the worst." A certain relaxed ability to do two things at the
same time, such as turning sheet music without breaking

rhythm or rubbing your belly and forehead in different directions, makes the good flier. A mind conditioned to practicing the last move while accepting complex instruction on the next one is a great aid in getting through flight-training.

It was apparent that this lamblike acceptance of orders from the man in the front cockpit would in Joe's case have to be learned. It is simply the ability to take his word against all instinct that when your engine fails on takeoff and a cement factory looms ahead, it is better to drop your nose and try to land in the cement factory than to turn and try to get back to the field. You do not interrogate him—which is why primary students flew at the receiving end of a gosport tube, with no way to talk back to their instructors over the howl of the slipstream. You do not weigh the odds or try to figure out for yourself why the cement factory is a better landing field; you simply dump the nose and hope it was the man up front rather than the Man Upstairs who cut the engine and that he will remember to add throttle in time.

Joe's previous training was obviously not directed toward such good-natured trust of authority, but he was about to get an assist in earning his wings from Admiral Nagumo at Pearl Harbor. As news of the naval disaster swept the base on December 7, the cadet regiment was assembled by Lieutenant Commander Roger W. Cutler, USNR, a wiry Bostonian with a crisp and salty tongue. He was officer-in-charge of the regiment, and now he ushered in the new age. Cadets would sleep that night outside the barracks to avoid being trapped like rats in an imminent German dirigible attack; civilian clothes were *verboten* henceforth on liberties; if any dog-face Army troops insulted the U.S. fleet in town, cadets were to swing and ask questions afterward; he would back them all the way.

Two days after Pearl Harbor Mr. Hardie certified Joe as safe for primary solo, but he qualified the honor after later hops: "This student does not absorb instruction readily. . . . He cannot remember things from one day to the next . . . student does not look where he is going. . . ." He echoed the age-old cry of the instructor wearied by a student who is trying so hard to maintain the proper altitude, compass heading, and air speed that he cannot relax and fly: "Student flies with head in cockpit too much." He added on subsequent hops that Joe's judgment was poor and that he could only do one thing at a time, and finally wrote and underscored in Joe's record like a judgment from on high: *"Student is afraid of inverted spins; consequently recovery is uncertain."*

It was the first and only time that anyone had ever questioned Joe Kennedy's courage, and it all sounds worse than it was. The marks assigned the flights after the stinging remarks were at least average; Joe had accumulated no "downs" so far. *Everyone* was afraid of inverted spins, except perhaps Mr. Hardie; they are ordinary spins except that, instead of being pressed snugly into your seat you hang by your creaking safety belt, eyeballs popping, until the plane resumes normal flight. Only the animallike will of the old Stearman to survive made inverted spins possible even then: they are almost unknown to the new breed of pilot, having disappeared from any civilized syllabus.

There was airborne trauma, but there were good days, too. Hardie himself finally admitted that Joe had a feel for stunt flying, and with no trouble the student was certified by another instructor as having an aptitude for flying at night. He graduated to his first real airplane, the SNJ low-wing metal monoplane, and showed "average ability in adapting himself to a strange plane." He liked to fly solo, where he made the decisions, and hated dual, where the instructor did. He still charmed almost everyone, naturally and instinctively, but charm was of minimal value: flying was life-and-death and no one could forget it. Marine Lieutenant James Otis, who traded a student with another instructor to get Joe because they were both New Englanders and his father knew Joe Senior, remembers him as "one of the nicest gentlemen I have met," but found his airwork only average. R. G. O'Connor, another instrument instructor, found him faulty in orienting himself over the radio ranges at Daytona Beach, but passed him when he discovered that Joe had learned to recognize the "cone of silence" over a station by a change of signal; he had no natural ear for the beat of a radio beam, but his quick intelligence made up for it.

The instructors' comments were confidential. Joe never saw them. On the face of his record he might have convinced himself that he was doing fairly well but now he was getting occasional "downs," and in his own eyes that meant he was failing. He became tense and preoccupied on the ground; worse, he was still trying too hard in the air. Chaplain Sheehy noted his nervousness and took him to a dance in Jacksonville. Joe glanced at the bovine, starry-eyed belles, gestured generously to the padre that they were all his, and disappeared. Sheehy asked Joe to see Flight Surgeon McDonald, and when Joe had squeaked through his present stage of training, he presented himself to McDonald's board of fellow flight surgeons, which diagnosed "accumulated stresses," found him temporarily incapacitated for flying, and recommended seven days' leave of absence.

He headed for Palm Beach and spent a week with his parents. When he returned to Jacksonville he was awarded "extra time" to get back into the swing, and then he was ready for the old PBY Catalina twin-engine patrol planes flying off the St. Johns River. He still had problems and his instructor wrote: "Student is tense in cockpit. Did not perform cockpit check when I asked him. . . . Does not know course rules. . . ." Orville Dean, a P-boat instructor who would later be executive officer of Joc's squadron in England, thought that at Jacksonville his "appearance left something to be desired." He discovered while checking Joe and another student out that Joe, instead of squatting in the traditional third-man-seat between instructor and student lapping up spilled knowledge, was asleep in a bunk in the rear; Dean never quite forgave him. When Joe's turn came to fly that day he was "completely lost as to the location of the plane," and made two downwind landings.

But the capacity for improvement which had served him at Choate worked again. "Student shows much improvement since my last flight with him. . . ." wrote an instructor. Flying boats are big and awkward and flown through brute strength, but it takes a certain delicacy of feel to skim one so gently onto the water that no one aft knows you have landed until the plane stops short, suddenly wallowing in the swells; Joe finally mastered it and his record reads: "Normal landings okay." Flying boats are treacherous. To land in rough water takes a firm hand on the yoke to haul up the nose as you would rein in a runaway horse, until suddenly, a yard or so above the wave tops, the aircraft stalls beneath your seat and crashes in a sheet of spray, rivets popping and hull creaking, lurching in the troughs. It was hot and miserable baking behind the Plexiglas in the Florida sun, and when you are as tall as Joe, your head hits the top of the cockpit as the plane stalls and drops. Instructors grow easily irritated as the sweat flows faster, but finally Joe mastered this phase too:

"Full-stall landings okay. . . . Safe for solo." He graduated from flight training with 192 hours. His inability to take instruction in the air had pulled him down to a rank of seventy-seven out of a class of eighty-eight, but he was considered good officer material. His fitness reports had been above average: "A likable personality and a splendid character. . . . Very cooperative and industrious. . . ." The final report of his last instructor read: "Cadet Kennedy has a cheerful, co-operative disposition and a strong, forceful character. His handling of his regular and additional duties has been satisfactory, but he is expected to improve considerably in this respect as he gains experience in the naval service. He is average instructor material."

A story of his winning so-called "Cutler Wings" as an outstanding cadet is perhaps apocryphal. Commander Cutler was a generous man with a wealthy wife—he once spent six hundred dollars out of his own funds to provide footbaths for cadets during a fungus epidemic in the barracks—and so he might well have informally presented a pair of $2.50 wings as a prize for military bearing or qualities of leadership or just for a likable disposition. There is no official record of it, but Joe had at any rate survived an attrition rate through death, accident, and washout of almost fifty percent, and in the U.S. armed forces there was no more elite group than that which he was joining, and this was enough for now.

The family planned a cocktail party at Ponte Vedra Country Club. The ambassador came up from Palm Beach to address the graduates. During his talk he looked at his son and his eyes watered and soon his voice became shaky and all at once he broke down and could not go on. But it was he who pinned on Joe's wings of gold.

3

Today Banana River, Florida, where Joe went to "operational training," is part of the world's greatest launching pad, and is named for Joe's brother. There is plenty of action in the town of Cocoa, but in 1942 it was a filling station and a beer bar: Joe curled up every night with a book. But fishing was good, and he found himself a pretty fishing companion and sent her picture, with that of their catch, to the family, instructing them to send it to Jack. Joe was a hotshot naval aviator now, but he was still Big Brother, too, and he called Hyannis often. Once Jean was crowded off the phone, so he wrote her the next day, repeating the conversation, which centered around a sailing race. "Teddy made it quite clear that he was extremely disappointed in not having an answer to his letter, which arrived yesterday. Was quite surprised to learn that he came in third in the race, when his whole letter dealt with the subject." He sent her a pair of gold wings. "Tell your sisters if they get jealous that I shall send them something, but my godchild comes first." He told her that he liked the luxurious PBM Mariners he was being trained to fly, despite some odd characteristics which he was perhaps too inexperienced to note. "These planes are much better . . . a great deal more fun."

When he was through operational training, his normal course would have been to go to an antisubmarine squadron. But he wanted command of a plane once he got there, and he wanted it fast. He had less than three hundred hours in the air, and even in the pilot shortage of 1942 it was unusual for an ensign to be rated as patrol-plane commander, a designation just below God, with less than a thousand hours in flight. He suspected that before he was actually given his own aircraft and moved to the left-hand seat, he would face endless hours shooting stars, plotting fixes, carrying his "PPC's" briefcase, and stirring his coffee.

He studied the matter. There was a serious instructor shortage. No one except married men trying to stay in the States wanted to teach flying to newly commissioned ensigns like himself, but there would be no quicker way to build up time, to learn the aircraft, and to emerge an experienced leader ready for the left-hand seat. It looked like a long war, and if in six months he was still mired in Banana River he would somehow pressure his father into pulling the right strings to get him into action.

He requested instructor duty. Someone apparently forgot to read the unanimously dubious reports of his instructor potential, and he got it. He donned a Frank Buck helmet, drew more books on the PBM Mariner, took a few instructor-training hops, and became a sudden expert. "At present I am teaching other young ensigns how to fly these planes," he wrote Jean, "and my famous patience is sore-taxed. They pull some of the dumbest maneuvers possible, so as a result, you have to watch them every minute, which tires you a lot."

He instructed for six months, accumulating air time and the true understanding of an aircraft that comes only to instructors, who have to anticipate not only the questions of students, but also their mistakes. Harry Lawrence, one of his students, had himself been an instructor in PBY Catalinas but had never flown the PBM Mariner: "A peculiar airplane. It had a most flexible wing. The airplane really got about six knots additional speed by virtue of the fact that the gull wing actually flapped like a gull—about six feet up and down—at the wingtip. Joe was an excellent pilot, very calm, very smooth, and very confident. He knew his airplane—the mechanics of it, the fuel system, he could explain it very very well as he was teaching, and the appropriate emergency procedures. It took about six weeks for pilots who had learned other kinds of seaplanes to learn to fly that particular aircraft."

After six months as an instructor Joe was ordered to his first operational squadron, which was leaving for Puerto Rico. His plan had worked: he was a veteran now, with nearly a thousand hours. He would almost certainly pop directly into the left-hand seat. He had outthought the system, but he could hardly have anticipated what his drive for command would cost him.

4

As Joe left Banana River in January, 1943, oil from torpedoed tankers smeared the Florida beaches and bodies of merchant seamen washed ashore from Key West to Cape Hatteras. U.S. troops supporting Montgomery were meeting their first Germans on the sands of Africa. In the Pacific U.S. Marines were trying to dig the Japanese from out of Guadalcanal. Jack Kennedy, having made Lieutenant (junior grade) just in time to be photographed in blues with Joe while his older brother was still an ensign, had sprung himself finally from a series of desk jobs and diverted by last-minute efforts of his father's friends from the boredom and inactivity of a Panama Canal torpedo-boat squadron. Now he was heading for a more active one at Tulagi.

Joe had eight days' leave en route to his squadron: he

graced the nightclubs of New York in his new braid and uniform and delivered his friend Tom Schriber and his young wife, Betty, a live pig, boxed and wrapped, as a belated wedding present: the pig escaped and ran squealing all over their apartment. When Tom drove Joe to a country-club party, Joe discovered half way that he had left his officer's cap: he was out of uniform, he insisted, in danger of courtmartial or worse, and they had to drive back, gas rationing and all, to retrieve it. It was a good leave, and he barely made the last ferry flight of his new PBM squadron, VP-203, to Puerto Rico. They were en route to what they liked to describe as "the battle of the Atlantic." The squadron consisted of a dozen PBM Mariners. It arrived at San Juan in the midst of a gas shortage which forced it to detach a third of its strength to Guantanamo Bay.

They began to patrol the South Atlantic at speeds not much over that of the blimps operating out of Miami and Key West, and with hardly less luxury. There were bunks aboard, a head, a refrigerator, and a complete galley; the wings might flap and there was not much room for war-like accessories such as guns or depth charges, but they were flying hotels. To get into a real war zone might be futile and even risky: there was little chance of overtaking a U-boat at their speed and their best defense against fighter attack would have been to land and dive out of the plane. They were underpowered for the load they carried, and undergunned, but once off the water there was hardly a more comfortable plane short of the Pan-American Clippers, in which to fight a war. As Joe had anticipated, he knew more by now about this particular flying boat than anyone in the squadron, and had nearly as much time in it. The trouble was, nobody realized it except the skipper, the operations officer, a few logbook yeomen in the flight office, and the exec, a stubby, blue-eyed former Navy football star named "Sunshine" Jim Reedy. Joe had seen no need to brag about his considerable Mariner experience and did not realize when he was made a patrol-plane commander that to everyone else in the squadron, including the enlisted men, he seemed to be a millionaire ensign just out of Jacksonville pushed untrained into the left-hand seat simply because his father was an ex-ambassador to the Court of St. James's. When he did realize the problem he was too stubborn to make excuses.

"We knew he was wealthy," says William Sherrill, a

hulking mechanic who flew with him. "I thought he was a typical Harvard type, all stuck up. Everybody was down watching him when he checked out as PPC." Hard-nosed regular petty officers had never known so new an ensign to make patrol-plane commander. "He was pushed up to PPC in a few weeks ahead of many others who deserved it, in my opinion, ahead of him," complains Frank Haines, a retired chief mech. Hostility in Haines bred hostility in Joe. One sultry night as Haines signaled the waddling Mariners down a ramp into the water, Joe got impatient with the planes testing their engines ahead of him and told Haines to get them out of the way, he was ready to launch. Haines pointed out that he, Joe, would launch when he, Haines, told him to: Joe waited.

Even some of the officers in VP-203 thought they spotted arrogance in their new ensign. Norm Rudd, for whom Joe flew as copilot for a short time, believed he lacked the ability to mix with those who were not of his background. Eugene J. Martin, a tiny Indiana navigator who joined Joe's squadron later, says, "First, there was the Harvard accent ... to a midwesterner, this automatically attached a label. Secondly, I seemed to be invisible to Joe. Just a brief analysis," he admits, "should have resolved this puzzling phenomenon. Joe was at least six inches taller than I was and with his sights set so high it was probably physically impossible to see me when we passed. Later I was told that New Englanders are not bound by the rule that you at least nod the first time you meet someone each day, so belatedly I understood."

Even the men Joe was most interested in at first failed to reciprocate. Chief Jack Degman, an ordnanceman who was leading chief in the squadron, found him intensely concerned with the performance of each of his crewmen. "He stood for perfection in himself and expected the same from others. This at times led to a strained relation between him and his crew. At one time the relationship became so bad that it came to the attention of the squadron skipper."

The flying-boat pilot is more than an airman; he is half windjammer skipper too. He needs the help of his crew much more than the pilot of a landplane does. Seaplanes on the surface weathercock into the wind and no matter how delicately throttle and rudder are played, tend to work themselves into unmanageable positions. In any respectable breeze or current the pilot is a one-legged man trying to cross a sheet of ice in a wind with a pane of glass. For that reason, planes waiting on the water for the trunk-clad, tanned beach crews to trundle them into position to clamber up the ramp, moor to a buoy first. The pilot cannot see the buoy under his nose at the last minute; it is grabbed from the bow turret by a crewman. Bob Wurdack, a feisty little man from Kansas City who served in VP-203 as Joe's bow gunner, says, "The measure of your ability was not how well you could shoot the gun, it was whether you could hang on to the buoy. In Joe's case, since he taxied so fast, that was quite a trick." Wurdack, after having been chewed out by Joe on one hop for letting the buoy go, cured the whole situation by clinging to it so tightly next time that he was yanked from the bow-station and when next Joe saw him was in the water under the wing hugging the buoy and grinning up at him sardonically.

But Joe made friends in San Juan with those who were not fooled by the apparent favoritism he was shown. Mark Soden, a smooth-faced young ensign from Wisconsin, roomed with him: so did George Papas, a vivacious, chipper young man who liked the Navy and intended to stay in. They found disadvantages in rooming with a young millionaire who had always had servants: his housekeeping was still primitive and his idea of picking up was to throw dirty laundry into his closet until it was filled; then he would call for a steward's mate to bag it and send it out. George Charno, a wiry-haired Jewish law student from Missouri with lively, close-set eyes, would argue politics with him; Executive Officer Reedy would take him along on his liberties into the wilds of San Juan. It was a country-club life of swimming pools, white uniforms, and tennis: patrols were long and got longer when the planes were stripped of some of their hotel-type accommodations to provide room for extra gas, but the only action anyone engaged in was staged for a *March of Time* crew which arrived to shoot a film on antisubmarine warfare called *Clear the Way to Africa*. Joe, "Sunshine" Jim, and a stubby little pilot named "Sleepy" Wissman, who purportedly only woke up for landings, flew the cameramen slowly over U.S. submarines, wings flapping on the verge of stalling, for weeks, but no one ever found a U-boat.

Joe liked San Juan. "Jeanah Darlin," he wrote his godchild. "I am having a very pleasant time down here, though we are flying an awful lot. I have only been to town a couple of times. They have very fancy nightclubs with gambling in all of them." He was not allowed to say where he was, so he lobbed a hint past the censors. "The senoritas are quite good looking. If you want to take one out, you have to take their mother along, or about ten of their cousins, so it is quite an undertaking."

He gambled and sometimes his luck was incredible. At a roulette table in a local casino he found Sleepy Wissman down to one chip and ready to quit for the night. Imperiously Joe picked it up and plunked it on a number; the number came up at thirty-five to one, and Joe, poker-faced, simply cashed it in and led Wissman to the next stop. Joe's favorite hangout was the bar of Pedro Montáñez, ex-lightweight pugilist. Joe and George Charno were valued patrons for their gratuitous, law-student advice on the legal problems of Pedro's friends, which revolved around a minor domestic murder: his barber had just shot his wife and her lover.

On one of their visits to town, Joe met Paul Brabazon, an old Boston buddy from Holy Cross, with whom he had double-dated in Cambridge. Actor Pat O'Brien, another friend of the Kennedys, stumbled on the two in the street and all three celebrated at the Pan American Club; Brabazon, exec of the Navy refrigerator ship *Tarazan*, had them aboard for filets mignons and air-conditioning.

San Juan was choice duty, but the squadron was running the island out of gas. No one had yet spotted a German sub anyway, so the outfit was ordered back to Norfolk to continue its battle against the Axis with less strain on the local economy. Back in the States, Joe began to become restless; if he was going to see any subs in the Atlantic, it would apparently be off Newfoundland, where Ensign "Sighted-Sub-Sank-Same" Don Mason seemed actually to have finished one off.

Bobby, now a brooding, unsure seventeen-year-old, came to Norfolk to see him. Joe described him to Jean as "hard-up for conversation," but sneaked him quite illegally into his plane for a wartime patrol; he let him fly it from the copilot's seat. Twenty-five years later, Bob Kennedy described the flight to the author: nothing happened, but Joe had risked a reprimand or worse to take him on the hop and you felt that it mattered very much that he had, for Robert's sapphire eyes, remote and speculative at first meeting, softened with the memory. Afterward he joined the V-5 naval-aviation program. Though he later would leave it for Harvard and R.O.T.C., it was Naval R.O.T.C. he chose, and he stayed in it until Joe died and then enlisted to get into the war.

At Norfolk the endless, sterile patrols continued for Joe, but ashore the lonely Navy wives were everywhere and Joe and the other squadron bachelors tried to alleviate their boredom. Lorelle Hearst turned up with silver-blonde Lady Sylvia Ashley, another ex-showgirl; Joe introduced them to Mark Soden and they played bridge and swam at Virginia Beach. Soden bought a star boat and became a minor Bligh; Joe rented an apartment. Joe, Mark, and Jeff Marshall, a handsome, flamboyant pilot from Chicago whom Joe fondly christened "the naval aviator with the mind of a child," rented a Ford for a week at a time. Each Friday when the lease on the car expired, Joe would negotiate freshly on the same terms in a rising rental market, pleading the case of three underpaid naval aviators risking their lives for fat-cat civilians, leaning all the while against a crumpled fender to hide it from the owner.

Joe, who had just made lieutenant (junior grade), put his mind to work on the long patrols. He became fascinated with the elaborate radar in the Mariner and invented a radar-landing technique for the squadron which enabled it to return long after other planes were diverted by weather; the system was primitive, but no one had thought of it before, and it was in widespread use when he left.

Not until June, 1943, was the first of the squadron's submarine attacks made, by an ex-enlisted pilot named Kiefert. He sighted a periscope a hundred miles east of Norfolk and dropped four depth charges, but only one exploded and the sub escaped. After six months' work, this seemed slim pickings. Jack, in Rendova, was seeing action: he had been attacked by U.S. B-25's on patrol, had been bombed by the Japanese, had two of his crewmen wounded. Even their sister Kick had finally got to London, as a Red Cross girl. Joe wanted duty in the Pacific, Newfoundland, North Africa, anywhere. England, where he really would have liked to go, seemed, with antisubmarine warfare in the hands of the R.A.F. and the U.S. Army Air Corps, completely beyond reach. He did not know that salvation was in sight.

2

IN THE summer of 1943 German U-boats operating in the Atlantic were nearly all based in French ports below Brest on the Bay of Biscay. To get to their stalking grounds and to return, they had to negotiate the bay. It was here that the Royal Air Force Coastal Command, from bases in southern England, were trying to force them to "run the gauntlet" submerged. For a U-boat to have to dive for the long passage north was to decrease the endurance of her men and her batteries on the shipping lanes. The Coastal Command was operating without naval help. The Royal Navy had been pushed from the bay by long-range Luftwaffe fighters and bombers using, among other weapons, strange new glide bombs, apparently radio-controlled. R.A.F. Coastal Command patrols were so thin and infrequent that U-boats were scornfully fighting their way through on the surface to save their batteries. The U.S. Army Air Corps had come to help with B-24 Liberators, but Army pilots had little training in navigation, ship identification, or antisub work. Furthermore, though the Army B-24 Liberator was superior in all respects to the slow Navy seaplanes built for the task, the Army needed every B-24 it had in England to soften the continent for the invasion a little more than a year away.

Admiral Ernie King in Washington and Twelfth Fleet Commander "Betty" Stark in England, ex- Chief of Naval Operations dropped to a command of European forces after Pearl Harbor and still smarting, saw a chance to get the U.S. Army out of the antisubmarine business in the geographical area where the submarines actually lived. They began with a squadron of PBY Catalina seaplanes operating from Pembroke Dock in Wales. The PBY, which had endeared itself to generations of Navy pilots by its simplicity—it seemed to climb, cruise, and dive-bomb all at ninety knots—proved itself infamously unsuccessful in the Bay of Biscay, where people were playing for keeps. In Norfolk Joe Kennedy heard certain rumors in the BOQ. They were incredible, and for once they were true. For the European theater the Navy had procured Army B-24 Liberators. The B-24 was an aircraft, in the eyes of a Mariner pilot, so hot, fast, and dangerous that it had always seemed beyond reach. But the Navy was training its seaplane pilots to fly them and one of the first contingents to England would be drawn from VP-203.

On July 15 Sunshine Jim Reedy, who had been crying to Washington for Pacific carrier duty, passed the word to nine of his crews to meet in Hangar SP2 by the Norfolk seaplane ramps. He confirmed the rumors and said that he had been picked as commanding officer of the new squadron, "Patrol Squadron One Hundred Ten": VB-110. It was no fighter squadron but the next-best thing. He left in a rush to organize the delivery of planes, after turning over the details to his new exec, Lieutenant John Munson, a tall, gangly officer who looked like James Stewart. "No one is compelled to accept this assignment," said Munson. "Undoubtedly it will be a dangerous one. If there are any here who would prefer to remain with VP-203, let me know after the meeting. No questions will be asked. We'll be flying Liberators and we have just six weeks to check out in them before going overseas. The time is short and we need the cooperation of every single man. Good luck."

To an Army pilot doomed to daily action over the Ruhr or to a Navy carrier pilot tangling with Zeros, the word "dangerous" applied to antisubmarine patrol might have seemed faintly pretentious. But to the officers and men of VP-203, who had never expected to see a Messerschmitt closer than the ready-room projection screen, and to whom unflyable weather meant an afternoon thunder-shower off the Virginia coast, the prospect of meeting the Luftwaffe in winter flights off Europe must have seemed exciting and a little fearsome; nevertheless, no one wanted out. "The meeting," says Demetrios "Dee" Vilan, a

Greek-born artist, actor, and theater director who grew to be Joe's favorite radioman, "ended in cheers and applause. The most excited man in the room was Joe Kennedy. He was bursting with enthusiasm." Chief Jack Degman noticed it too: "I can recall quite well how enthused he was. . . . He was an eager beaver. He wanted to get with that war and get with it fast." The excitement was warranted, and so was Munson's warning. The group in the hangar and those who joined them later would win two Navy Crosses, four DFCs, twenty-seven Air Medals, and two Purple Hearts. They would lose two planes to enemy fighters and ten to weather and mechanical failure. Sixty-eight of them would die in action.

Joe elbowed himself into the initial group of pilots to be checked out, and took his first good look at his future plane. The B-24 Liberator, or Navy's new PB4Y-1, was strangely menacing: an underslung, split-tailed monster squatting on huge main tires and a nosewheel. Its four big engines were mounted so low on the wings that a tall man could peer into the nacelles by chinning himself. Loaded, it weighed over thirty tons. Its cockpit was one of the most complicated in aviation's history. Pilot and copilot sat a yard apart in low seats sunk below the long and bulbous nose; the cockpit always smelled faintly of gasoline from the fuel panel aft of it, of ozone from the radioman's station, and of sweat-soaked leather from the seats. In front of pilot and copilot were spread fifty dials and 150 switches. The plane taxied in a liquid, bobbing motion not unlike that of a seaplane on calm water, but when unburdened, it was so overpowered on takeoff that to Joe it must have seemed like a fighter. It was a stable plane in firm hands, but in uncertain ones it flew like a boxcar and landed like a weary truck. Joe, who had never flown anything bigger than a twin-engined seaplane, managed somehow on the blazing runways of Norfolk's East Field to check out in it in six days. Then he began to shuttle from the factory in San Diego back to the East Coast, bringing more for his mates.

While he was ferrying aircraft, his brother's PT-109 was chopped in two by a Japanese destroyer in Blackett Strait. For a week Jack Kennedy was missing, and Joe did not know it. The ex-ambassador did, though, for the last three days of the week, and suffered in Hyannis in silence; he had decided not to tell Rose, and could not have reached Joe had he tried. When Joe learned that his brother had been rescued, he must have thanked God, and Sunshine Reedy found him proud of his brother's courage and coolness in the water. But now Jack was not only a combat veteran but a full-fledged naval hero who had managed to save his crew. Chief Degman sensed a subtle change. "When news came about Brother John's PT-boat activities I think it inspired him to try harder. I don't think anyone was any more intent on seeking out the enemy and meeting him than Joe Kennedy." Navigator Gene Martin, still unimpressed with Joe, complains that "when I tried to make casual conversation I got the positive impression that I was talking about firecrackers to a man valiantly trying to perfect the atom bomb before an impossible deadline."

The deadline for Joe was the end of the war. It was a long way off, but there was no time to lose. For six weeks the new squadron practiced gunnery at Elizabeth City, North Carolina. Antisubmarine work required more sophisticated electronics than the Air Corps had bought so new radar was installed. Bow-gun turrets to strafe U-boats on the surface were added where Air Corps bombardiers had squatted. Flights began at dawn and ended at dusk. The pace became brutal and the new squadron had its first casualty: Lieutenant (j.g.) Jim Rowe tore off his elevators in an antisubmarine bombing run, but somehow crash-landed at the field. No one was injured until his navigator, Ensign M. E. Graff, leaped from the wing and broke his leg. Training in instruments was accelerated: English weather would not be like San Juan's or even Norfolk's. The crews spent their days on tactics, recognition, even small-arms practice to sharpen gunners' eyes for the Luftwaffe or to fight off capture by a U-boat if they ditched in the Bay of Biscay. Reedy, the ex-Academy athlete, even sandwiched in an athletic program. To condition crews to escape from southern France? Excitement rose. Joe flew to Quonset Point for a one-week course in antisubmarine work; there he met a Squadron Leader Macdonald of the R.A.F. Coastal Command and a U.S. Navy j.g. who had spent two years flying with it. Control procedures over Britain, the two warned, were so complicated and weather so treacherous that it would take a month after the squadron arrived to learn to fly the Bay of Biscay patrol.

There was time to go to Hyannis for his father's birthday party. Police Commissioner Timilty was down from Boston for the traditional Kennedy dinner; he would share Joe Junior's room. A prominent Massachusetts judge was there too. Joe must have felt like a slacker at the table, with even his sister Kathleen in London and Jack, though injured, still to his father's disgust making patrols in the South Pacific. While Joe, in uniform and ready to ship out to Europe, listened, the judge proposed a toast: "To Ambassador Joe Kennedy, father of our hero, our *own* hero, Lieutenant John F. Kennedy of the United States Navy."

Everyone waited, but that was all. The judge sat down. Joe Junior, face flaming and a sturdy grin plastered to his face, lifted his glass to his father and absent brother. But it was the final straw. That night as they turned in, he could hold in his frustration no longer and Timilty could hear him crying in the other bed.

The next day Joe returned to Norfolk to pick up his crew. Tom Killefer, flying a fighter from the *Bunker Hill* and bound for the Pacific, turned up and they had a farewell drink with Paul Brabazon, whose supply ship was in. Joe's spirits rose. He packed all of his considerable gear, bought a crate of good Virginia eggs for Kathleen, and took off for England. His first stop was New York, where he, Sunshine Reedy, and C. Horton Smith, the squadron administrative officer, spent a night at the Stork Club and a morning chatting informally with Lady Sylvia Ashley as she lay in bed in her Sherry-Netherlands boudoir. Suitably prepared for the dangers they would encounter in her homeland, they winged aloft from Floyd Bennett Field, bound for the war, with stops at Presque Isle, Goose Bay, and Bluie West One in Greenland. Joe flew in company with George Charno's plane and that of Norm Rudd, whose copilot was Joe's friend Jeff Marshall. Rudd and Marshall developed engine trouble somewhere off the ice cap.

"You better not ditch her, Jeff," warned Joe Kennedy, off his wing. "I can't stick around and circle, I've got a crate of eggs for my sister."

They limped into St. Eval in Cornwall and moved into a resort hotel near Newquay. They settled down to learn to operate the British way. Joe knew that it was essential to master British ground rules, but he was impatient. He wanted action and he wanted it fast.

2

The Cornish coast, pendant from the southern edge of England, was windy and wet but beautiful: fishing craft and private yachts danced at anchor behind the stone breakwater at Newquay; the coastal villages, with their homes climbing the cliffs behind snug harbors, had a Mediterranean look that reminded Joe of Cannes. This was the "English Riviera," country of Trelawney and the *Pirates of Penzance.* The officers were billeted at the gleaming white Trevelgue Guest House on the cliffs four miles from the airdrome at St. Eval and the men at the Bedruthian Steps two miles closer. The best place to eat was the great gingerbread Imperial Hotel; Joe found that he could always get a table by dropping a titled name from his London days. He found the food shortage bearable but the night life deplorable. The country was supposed to be a resort area, but it was an official evacuation area and stifled by aged Londoners escaping the bombing. On sunny days the gravelly beaches of the little coves would fill with striped beach chairs and graying evacuees; a few children would scull in rowboats, but no one ever swam. Bob Sweeny, the wealthy American amateur golfer and longtime London resident with whom Joe had played in Palm Beach, had years before become a British subject to compete in the Walker Cup. He was flying from Joe's field with the R.A.F. Coastal Command. He had already sunk his sub the month before and had read of Jack's exploits in *Time.* Joe felt more left out than ever. "He asked about you," Joe wrote Jack. "He is a hell of a nice guy." Jack had written that he was in good shape and finally on his way back from Vella Lavella and Joe added, irritated at the delay: "I understand that anyone who was sunk got thirty days' survivor leave. How about it? Pappy was rather indignant that they just didn't send you back right away."

But at least Jack was out of danger of further injury or heroism and safely on his way to New York. Joe was "delighted to find you in such good health and such obvious anticipation of the pleasures which await you in the Big City. I know that you will be disappointed to hear that before leaving I succeeded in dispersing my first team in such various points that it will be impossible to cover all the territory. If you give me a rough idea of your itinerary I will try to fit in a few enjoyable evenings for you en-route. If you ever get around Norfolk, you will get quite a welcome if you mention the magic name of Kennedy, so I advise you to go incognito."

He talks of a girl friend of Jack's he had met before he left, "just after your burst into the front pages. She doesn't think you will even speak to her now. She was looking extremely well, having taken off about 15 pounds. I was tempted to take her out myself but knowing how you feel about that sort of thing and knowing what a swell job you are doing in winning the war I decided to lay off."

He complained that the pubs ran out of beer at nine o'clock and that then the town folded up. The blackout was really black, and when the night fell their day was about over. "We are not allowed to say where we are, but it is raining here and muddier than the devil. The English are the same as ever. They have a lot of damn good ideas on aviation and I think in many respects they are far ahead of us. I much prefer working under them in the work which we are doing. My crew is cocky as hell and probably in for a hell of a surprise. The navigator on the other hand is terrible, and what a place for a terrible navigator. . . . But what the hell, we can always make a landfall at Brest. There are a million landing fields there. I will keep you posted on my doings. It doesn't look like I will get home for quite a while."

In a few months, on a horrible night over Beaulieu, Joe would become disenchanted with British "good ideas on aviation." Now he was learning that there were no radio ranges, since they would help Luftwaffe bombers: pilots instead called ground stations for "QDM" fixes or more precise "Darky" short-range instructions from the ground. A pilot could get a rough position and sometimes a heading home but never his altitude; it was apparent from the first that no matter what they faced over the Bay of Biscay, their worst enemies were hidden in the low gray clouds over England: sleet and ice and slamming turbulence, the cables of barrage balloons, radio static, and the threat of a hundred other planes. The R.A.F. Coastal Command, Bob Sweeny told Joe, had a higher casualty rate than the Bomber Command.

On October 20, 1943, "a black day for Admiral Doen-

itz," according to VB-110's squadron diary, Sunshine Jim
Reedy and Lieutenant John Munson flew the first two
patrols over the Bay of Biscay. The squadron had not yet
moved to its ultimate operating base at Dunkeswell in
Devon; it was just that Reedy and his flight officer could
not wait. Their crews were tense, confident that they
would be the first in the squadron to bag a sub. Dee Vilan
went as radioman in Munson's plane; when he returned,
Joe buttonholed him in the squadron office and learned
that Doenitz's black day had not yet quite dawned: "What
did you see out there?"

"Water," said Vilan. "A lot of water."

London and Kick were 250 miles away, beyond reach
until he could get leave, and her eggs were getting no
fresher. Joe got Reedy to send him to northern England
for some materiel. Then, by what he described to his
parents as "some very deft arranging," he managed to
land at a field near London. He would find the next day
that it was a fateful bit of artistry. He delivered Kick her
eggs at the Red Cross Club at Number One Hans Crescent
in Belgravia; the stately brick townhouse swarmed with
servicemen and Kathleen was their confidante and dream
girl; she was in fact, after a picture in the *London Daily
Mail* on a bicycle in uniform, the darling of wartime
London. After winning three pounds from her at gin
rummy, he extracted her from the festooned oaken halls
and blaring jukebox music and took her to the velvet
gloom of his old 400 Club off Leicester Square.

It was still the place to go. You signed a book to get in.
You had to be a member, and your bottle carried your
name. A huge plush canopy gathered at the top like a
medieval tent covered the main room; it was so dark
inside that the place needed no blackout curtains. "Too
dark," complained Joe to Sweeny, "to see anything, but too
light to do anything." Nevertheless, anything could happen
in its shrouded booths and frequently did. During the
Battle of Britain a party of Spitfire pilots from the Eleventh
Fighter Group moved in on a table and never left:
they would rush to their field at Tangmere when their
turn came, hurl their aircraft at the Jerry, and if they
survived, return to the same table. The party never stopped
until the last of them had fallen.

Except for the mob of American and British pilots, the
place had not changed since Joe left it four years ago. The
same crowd groped to the same tables: the "Dukie Wook-

ie" of Marlborough, as Joe and Kick called him; "Luscious Lucius" Ordway, a 9th Air Force intelligence officer; the Argentine ambassador's daughters Bebe and Chiquita Carcano. Joe danced with Bebe, who inquired "most ardently after Jack," despite her current affiliation with Bob Sweeny. It all looked promising to Joe, but Kick could not stay long. She had just had a weekend off to visit Lord and Lady Halifax in the country, and it was hard to get free time from the club. There was no way to get a cab after dark, so as Joe hovered invisibly in the background, she conned an Army MP lieutenant into a jeep ride back; when big brother materialized from the darkness and climbed into the rear the soldier boy was reduced to muttering something about the court-martial he was courting for taking her home when he was supposed to be inspecting guard stations.

The next day at the airport Joe learned that the Cornish coast was weathered in and that he was doomed to another day in London. He could find no room in any hotel. Finally he located William Randolph Hearst, Jr., in London as a war correspondent, and moved in with him. They had a drink with Tex McCrary, acting as an Air Corps public-relations officer, and went to the Savoy. There they dined with Virginia Gilliat, the girl whose father four years before had found Joe plastered with lipstick in his living room. She was Lady Sykes now, expecting her first baby, and she had a friend who dined with them too: a lovely witty Army wife with sky-blue eyes and a warm mischievous laugh. General Robert Laycock, head of the British commandos after Mountbatten, joined them reluctantly with his beautiful wife, Angie. For a while the atmosphere grew chill. Laycock was the ruggedest of combat men. He studied the millionaire American journalist Hearst and the wealthy and untried young naval aviator, wining and dining two English girls, with a certain cynicism. The British serviceman's complaint that Americans were "overpaid, oversexed, and over here" was as heartfelt at General Laycock's level as among the Tommies in Piccadilly Circus.

Joe, though he admired Laycock and envied his wartime experiences, could not have cared less. The girl with the sky-blue eyes, barely older than he, had once been a countess married to one of the wealthiest peers in England and was married now to an artillery officer in Libya; but it was wartime, and when Joe told her that the squadron was moving to Devon, she asked him to visit her and to meet her children and to bring some of his friends, and Joe looked into the sky-blue eyes and said that he would.

Ten days later the squadron finished its training and moved a hundred miles toward London to Dunkeswell Airdrome, not far from the coast. There were two other Navy squadrons there ahead of them: all would come under Captain Tom Hamilton, Fleet Air Wing Commander, who worked with the R.A.F. Coastal Command Group Headquarters in Plymouth. VB-110 relieved an Air Corps squadron which had been flying antisubmarine patrol; the Army outfit would henceforth face long flights through skies still swarming with hostile fighters over a continent bristling with flak, but they seemed very glad to leave.

3

DUNKESWELL Airdrome lies neglected now on a grassy
plateau in the Devonshire country of King Arthur: tradition holds that he is buried at Glastonbury, twenty-eight
miles away, but there is little of Camelot on the bleak flat
plains. Rain has just fallen and the gray concrete strip
glistens under scudding clouds. A sign warns you that the
place is still R.A.F. property and entry is prohibited; the
hired driver is nervous, but you tell him to ignore it and
he drives down the runway, cracked concrete tufted with
grass. Flanking the strip are huge black hangars, and the
Nissen huts which served as squadron offices stand like
giant sewer pipes half buried and neglected in the dirt. It
is very quiet. The place was used until recently as a launching site by an amateur glider club; now a quiet Englishman,
working out of an office trailer, pores over plans for a
factory which will build prefabricated Swiss chalets for
export, presumably to Switzerland.

Site One—"Mudville Heights"—where Joe and the officers and men of VB-110 lived, was dispersed far from
the strip as a protection from bombing. It lies along
a twisting dirt road, down a little valley and then up
again. The Nissen huts in which they lived are gone; so is
the mess hall and the officers' club. Robert O. J. Streuber,
a heavy-set, gout-tormented New York Central Railroad
magnate who once flew as a navigator in Joe's squadron,
looks at the cement foundations, shakes his head, and

though he had flown an ocean to come here, does not care to get out of the rented car. About the site he remembers very little, or perhaps too much. He is uncomfortable here—his gout or his recollections—so finally you leave.

When the sixty-four officers and 106 men of Joe's squadron landed here in October, 1943, it was at the end of the wettest fall that Devon had experienced in living memory. Joe Kennedy had thought Cornwall was mucky, but now he learned what mud was. The base seemed to float in a sea of it. It was impossible to walk: you lost your boots. "We hopped, skipped, and jumped," radioman Dee Vilan remembers, "like a troupe of Martha Graham dancers executing a fertility rite." Joe was assigned the extra job of squadron secretary, and the squadron diary, "secret" no more, is an extraordinarily nonnaval document bearing his stamp: "Roads were narrow and a constant sea of mud bathed all hands' pedal extremities, or was splashed on their nether regions by passing jeeps or trucks. During the winter months an intermittent drizzle, occasionally whipped into a solid wall of water by the capricious winds, made it almost impossible to stay dry. Inadequate heat—miniature coke stoves sparsely scattered around the base—made it almost impossible to get either dry or warm. Plumbing was nearly stone-age and even more widely dispersed than the living sites or aircraft. There was no toilet paper, although rolls of what seemed to be laminated wood were provided plainly stamped with 'Government Property.' Ablutions were located near the officers' mess which, unfortunately, was about a half mile, as the herd grazes, from Site One. No heat either for the body, the soul, or the water was available in this chamber. Food was quite good and plentiful and the quality improved as time passed. Conditions in general also improved, particularly after the arrival of a detachment of Seabees, whose task was to get the Dunkeswell Air Group out of the mud."

Dunkeswell, after the pukka-sahib life of San Juan and the parties in whites at the Norfolk O-Club, was miserable. There was one local pub—the white-plaster Royal Oak—down the road, if you could get there. Over the cigarette-scarred oaken tables, behind the battered benches lining the wall, hung signs, relics of Air Corps and British Army trade: "No singing allowed in this bar," "Owing to loss of cups, customers must bring own containers," "All breakages to be paid for." One "Gran"

Driver, a local mother to the squadron, had the welcome mat outside her cottage for tea and biscuits, but everything else was too far away in the mud and rain. Exeter, the nearest good-sized town, was almost an hour by jeep. The only nearby salvation was the bleak little officers' club in a Quonset at Mudville Heights, and Joe, who enjoyed alcohol so little that he traded his liquor ration for chocolate bars with Louis Papas, found little solace there.

His next trip to London seemed a distant dream. "If everything goes according to plan," he wrote his parents, "we are going to get one week off in every nine. I hope it works out but if it does, it will be the first thing that has worked since we have gotten over here. The more I see of the Army the better I think it is."

Joe shared a room in Mudville Heights with Mark Soden. The tubular Nissen huts were left whole as twelve-men barracks for enlisted men but partitioned into four rooms for officers, two pilots to a room. The tiny space smelled forever of pipe smoke, moldy fleece-lined flying boots, and soggy woolen socks. Each compartment had the tiny British stove. On the wall was a washbasin with a drain and plug but no drainpipe; a bucket under the basin served to catch dirty water. If the British "batman" assigned the room was not around—and he usually wasn't—when the bucket got full you dumped it yourself. This necessitated a trip through the mud, and there were trips enough to the distant latrine—"head" to the Navy, even ashore—without any extra ones. The trick when you drained the basin was to make sure that you didn't quite fill the bucket under it, so that your roommate would finally fill it and get stuck with the job. This, Joe found, developed a nice sense of the volume of liquids, useful in bartending.

"Joe was always spitting his toothpaste all over the basin," says Soden, "and never dumping out the water and we were so close together that we really got mad at each other and it got so I couldn't stand him and he couldn't stand me. Just about before Christmas I complained to him and told him that he ought to do his share even though he *was* Joe Kennedy or whoever he thought he was. Until that time it was really pretty tense but he had a bottle of whiskey and he offered me a drink and I took a drink and from then on we were fast friends again."

Commander Reedy, gung-ho and ambitious, began to lose drinking buddies at the crowded bar as his twinkling eyes grew hard with strain; still, he was no desk skipper and no one ever accused him of asking anything of his officers or men that he had not already done himself. Four days after the move to Dunkeswell, he was the first pilot to sight enemy aircraft. He spotted six JU-88's off the coast of France and lumbered into a cloud before they closed.

Patrols were ten to twelve hours long, cold and miserable. The PB4Y was an icebox aft; up forward the cockpit climate shifted from tropical to polar at the flick of a switch. Despite the fleece-lined flying boots and electrically heated leather suits that made Joe's crew look like a troupe of trained bears, no one was ever comfortable. Food in flight was sandwiches and coffee; there was no galley like the Mariner's, nor would there have been time to use it: everyone was too busy looking for fighters above while they pretended to look for subs below.

The year before, Marine Ace Pappy Boyington had described World War II flying as "hours and hours of dull monotony sprinkled with a few moments of stark horror." Joe Kennedy was an expert on monotony from San Juan and Norfolk, and was beginning to tell passing war correspondents—and Skipper Reedy—that he had wanted to be a fighter pilot. Now, the day after Reedy's brush, he was introduced to the stark-horror phase. On distant patrol with a crew of nine over the Bay of Biscay, Lieutenant W. E. Grumbles broke radio silence with a garbled message: "Oboe-Able, Oboe-Able . . . I am being attacked by enemy aircraft." It was intercepted by another PB4Y but never received by Group Headquarters in Plymouth or at Dunkeswell. An hour later he was somehow still in the air calling for help but no fighters ever found him and he never returned.

Everyone suddenly became aware that most of their patrols would be spent much closer to the hostile coast of France than to England. What had seemed an exciting business in the Norfolk hangar suddenly took on grimmer lines. A run on R.A.F. flight clothing developed: the Germans would obviously be unfamiliar with Navy enlisted men's dungarees or even the officers' naval aviation greens worn beneath flight clothing: a rumor started that if they were forced down in occupied Europe they might be shot as spies. A look at the intelligence maps in the briefing shack showed the coast of France from Brest to Bayonne, near the Spanish border, to be pocked with

enemy fighter bases. Luftwaffe airstrips on
Peninsula, which stuck like the barrel of a
the flight path from Dunkeswell to the sourc
on the Biscay coast, were lined with ME-100, -210, and
-410 fighters. Twin engine, long-range JU-88's flew from
Bayonne, which Joe had visited with Kick on the way to
Spain; now it was used as a finishing school for Luftwaffe
pilots. There was even a markedly unneutral German
radar at Cape Finisterre on the northwest tip of Spain to
pick up the PB4Y's as they approached the Iberian coast.

The enemy fighters operated in groups of six to twelve.
The PB4Y's, thrashing along at low level, flew singly, since
there were not enough planes to go in pairs. They were
unescorted because the Allied fighters were busy over the
Channel. R.A.F. briefing officers had claimed that the
Germans would not molest a patrol bomber unless they
outnumbered it six to one, but Bob Sweeny had told Joe
of being jumped by four Focke-Wulfs, which he evaded in
clouds to continue his patrol only to meet again on the
way home. R.A.F. Spitfires, Beaufighters, and Mosquitos
were supposed to be somewhere in reach, flying high cover
if the weather permitted, but if so they were usually
invisible and no one, after all, had come to help Grumbles.

The day after Grumbles was shot down, Joe took off on
a ten-hour patrol at dawn with his copilot Gil Rapp, later
shot down in the same area. Reedy had told him to
modify his patrol legs to stay within reach of clouds, and
if attacked to turn westward to the sea, drawing the
fighters farther from their bases. But for once there were
no clouds. As he closed the northwestern tip of Spain
toward "Junkers Junction" on his first leg at 1,500 feet
and 170 knots, his crew felt very lonely indeed. Joe, as
was his habit, had his head buried in the cockpit radarscope backing up his radarman. Fifty-five miles north of
Cape Ortegal, a hundred miles from the illegal radar at
Finisterre, he spotted a blip on the scope. It was off his
starboard beam at 7½ miles, between him and open ocean.
It showed no friendly IFF signal; it had to be hostile
anyway, for nothing friendly was within a hundred miles.
He alerted the crew, already at their guns.

There was still not a cloud in the sky and to turn
westward away from France as Reedy had suggested was
to head toward the German plane. The radar target began
to draw astern, cutting off his escape to the north, and a

w moments later was sighted by his port waist gunner off the quarter. The gunner identified it as a twin-engined, single-tailed fighter; it had closed to two miles. It drifted under their tail and they lost it for a while astern. Joe turned a little to port. Now he was in a box: on his left was the French coast with its fighter strips, Spain was dead ahead, retreat northward toward England was cut off. The German had disappeared from the scope momentarily; Joe continued on course and twelve minutes later the target reappeared on radar and began to weave from abeam to astern, keeping always between Joe and the open ocean. Another fighter arrived to join it; Joe's waist gunner finally identified them, from his vast experience with silhouette playing cards and pop-up slides, as ME-210's. Everyone agreed with studied calm that this was indeed so, and the two continued to herd Joe toward the coast. The first moved in to eight hundred yards, just out of range, while Joe pondered a dive to wave-top level to restrict the fighters to high-side runs when they made their attack. He decided to save that desperate measure for later and poured on more throttle, whipping the bomber up to a laboring 180 knots. The fighter abeam began to jink and feint at 290 miles per hour. At six hundred yards Joe said, "Commence firing," and the PB4Y shivered suddenly under the shock of his starboard guns, the cockpit filling with the smell of cordite. Joe peered past his copilot and saw the Messerschmitt pull ahead to a position six hundred yards on his starboard bow. Now the bow turret, manned by his stubby, red-faced plane captain, Ray Corcoran, could bear. Corcoran, cramped into his tiny transparent ball, whipped the turret up with a whine of gears and commenced firing. The Messerschmitt flipped up a wing, peeled off, and under fire of Corcoran and the deck turret above Joe made a flashing attack at 300 knots. In the excitement the fighter pilot apparently forgot to open fire, carried the attack almost into the water, leveled off, and flew away. Neither he nor his friend was seen again. The gunners were jubilant: they were sure from their tracers that their patterns were on. Joe who had refused or forgotten to jettison his depth charges during the attack, continued on his patrol.

2

Antisubmarine warfare by the time Joe's squadron moved to Dunkeswell had achieved most of the basic techniques that survive with equally frustrating results today. Planes flew low, at 1,500 feet or so, for best visual results. Search patterns consisted of long, parallel legs. Radar swept continually for the almost indistinguishable pip on the screen that would mean a periscope or the new German "schnorkel" breathing device. If contact was made on a surfaced sub, the next step was a full-throttle, ear-splitting dive to attack with bombs, punctuated by the crazy yammering of the bow guns, a few hysterical last-minute banks by the pilot as he lost sight of the target beneath the nose, and devout prayers by the crew that the sub would not try to fire back but submerge. If the sub did submerge, there were the traditional depth charges and more recent developments too: "Proctor," a secret and so-far unproved torpedo which homed on the sounds of a churning propeller, friendly or enemy, and so was dropped only if there seemed to be no Allied vessels nearby. On one patrol Joe lost one—it simply dropped from his bomb bay—and he sweated for days reports of Allied shipping mysteriously torpedoed. If contact with a submerged sub was lost, a wide pattern of the equally new sonobuoys was sown. Cylindrical and bright yellow, they dropped with a splash, bobbed to the surface, and automatically lowered hydrophones to dangle below, listen, and broadcast on radio the sound of the prey to the plane circling above. Each buoy had its own frequency; by shifting between them a sharp radioman with a plotting board might estimate after a few minutes the course, speed, and location of his victim. More frequently over the Bay of Biscay he found himself listening to the untranslatable anti-American comments of curious Spanish fishermen who had picked up his buoys.

Sonobuoys were fine in the theory but had never worked. The way you caught subs was with the "Mark One Eyeball," installed by nature in a patient crewman and used to scan the glittering waters hour after weary hour. With good eyes and luck, it was sometimes possible to score. The day after Joe drove off his attacker, Lieutenant W. W.

Parish caught a U-boat on the surface. In the face of AA fire, he attacked, dropping a half-dozen 250-pound Torpex depth charges; the nearest exploded thirty feet from the U-boat and rolled her onto her side. She continued with reduced speed and apparent loss of rudder control; an R.A.F. Coastal Command Liberator joined him with rockets, while Parish feinted to draw fire and strafed. The U-boat crew abandoned her and was rescued by a Spanish fishing vessel; Lieutenant Parish got only ten-percent credit from the R.A.F., but the U.S. Navy gave him and his copilot the DFC and their crew all got Air Medals. Parish would run out of luck next month, but the next day Lieutenant Joe Buchanan was jumped by eight JU-88's; he drove them off long enough to reach cloud cover and escaped. VB-110, shaken after Grumbles, began to consider itself a lucky squadron after all.

By the end of their second week the lonely planes of Joe's squadron had contacted a score of enemy aircraft and beaten off three fighter attacks. Commander Hamilton in Plymouth was proud of them and promised them to the R.A.F. for three daytime patrols and one at night—although they were not equipped with searchlights, they could always use flares. At that triumphant point a front moved in and an aircraft shortage developed. Joe studied the forecast, the mud, and his drunken and self-satisfied fellows at the O-Club. He put in for leave for himself and his crew. Reedy gave it to him and went along himself. They went to London.

3

Kick gave a party for them. Joe could not help but superintend her arrangements, leading her to complain that "you talk to me like I was a member of your crew!" But he wrote home to their parents that the party was "a tremendous success and everyone raved about it. Kick handled herself to perfection as usual and made a terrific hit all around. The girls looked very pretty and made quite an impression on the love-wan sailors whom I brought." Irving Berlin was there and got him tickets to his new show, a sellout in London. Joe talked to fiery, chipmunk-faced Alfred Duff Cooper, rebel First Lord of the Admiralty under Chamberlain. Now he was His Majesty's representative to the Free French, and Cooper thought that there was too much pro-German feeling in England and that people were becoming too softhearted now that the tide had turned. Joe and Kick dined the next day with Ambassador Tony Biddle, U.S. representative to half the governments-in-exile in London. He called on the Argentine Carcano girls and this time took out Chiquita, who would later marry Jacob Astor; he was acting, he wrote home, with Jack's interests at heart. "He certainly is in there solid right now, right after me. That ranch in the Argentine with all those cattle looks better all the time." He dated one of the prettiest girls in London, too, Lord Minto's daughter Bridget. He stayed in the Dorchester Hotel opposite Hyde Park until he had to leave temporarily due to a shortage of rooms. "On Tuesday, Wednesday, and Thursday it is practically impossible to get a room in London. Everything is terribly expensive, far above New York." Homeless, he moved into Bob Sweeny's digs on Mount Street, sleeping on a couch in the living room.

He returned to the mud of Dunkeswell with a cold. If he had run into the girl with the sky-blue eyes again, he told no one. Everything in Mudville Heights was as he had left it, only worse. It was even chillier, and fuel was just as short. His notes home turned dour: he wrote Jean that "the sum total of your letters seems to be a request for prayers for your exams. Your brother is now sporting a moustache. . . . There is some talk of looking like Gable. I am getting awfully sick of looking at the inside of this hut and the mudflats without. We now have a batman who takes care of us. . . . He has his hands full with me. I trust by now your figure is thin and sleek, and if it isn't, have it so by the time I get home. This will probably give you some time."

English dogs, preferring American garbage to British austerity, were all over Mudville Heights. Staring out at the mud in the endless drizzle, Joe saw one of them with mange. He whistled at it, treated its mange, and for a while they were friends, but in a few days the dog left. He bought a tiny black cocker-spaniel pup from a passing crew and christened him Dunkeswell—Dunkes for short. When he wearied of seeing that Dunkes had enough to eat, he sold a half interest to Lou Papas, his trading partner in the candy-whiskey commerce, and Papas soon discovered that he had bought the front end, requiring feeding.

The schedule was relentless: one day in flight, the next day off, the following day spent in the air operations office being briefed by a succession of American and R.A.F. specialists, and then the next daylong patrol. To sweat out fighters one day out of four and return to English weather, barrage balloons, and a snarled wartime control system was almost too much for pilots' nerves. Dunkeswell had been built on a plateau to avoid the morning ground fog, thus placing it just high enough to scrape the evening clouds which scudded in from the Devon coast; no one who took off from there on those December mornings really expected to get back in that night. Joe began to carry a "diversion kit": shaving gear and a toothbrush and, like a true Harvard man, pajamas. Diverted one night into Chivenor Airfield for the third time in succession after a daylong patrol and a brush with an FW-190, he discovered that he had left the kit in the plane. As he signed into the transient BOQ, he asked the Army NCO in charge to send back for it; the noncom looked at him incredulously. "Sailor, get it yourself." There was a moment of shock. Joe exploded and began to talk of a court-martial, but he was too tired to argue long and finally decided to do in Rome as the Romans did. He went to get the kit himself, but he never wrote home again in praise of the Army.

By the week before Christmas the flying weather was ludicrous—the field and Mudville were buried in snow—but the patrols seemed to be keeping the U-boats down through the Bay of Biscay, and when the weather was good enough at dawn for takeoff, the planes went out regardless of the evening forecast, to return as best they could.

At 4 A.M. one morning a week before Christmas Joe and George Charno, who had made PPC, stood with their copilots Kellog and Sleepy Wissman and three other crews in the freezing aerology hut and heard the weatherman predict a front from the west that would close the field by the time they returned at 5:30 P.M. No one scrubbed the hop, though, and finally the two ex-law students and their crews filed into the flight mess for the gigantic preflight breakfast of steak and eggs. They then took off and started their individual patrols. Joe found himself forced to wave-top altitude: the ceiling was only six hundred feet. Peering down at the gale-whipped scud of the Bay of Biscay, he estimated the wind at fifty knots.

At 10 A.M. he got a radio message informing him that the expected front was early: he should return to base by five. He receipted and continued on patrol. Approaching the coast of southern England at the end of his shortened flight, he noticed a change for the better over the Scilly Isles and Land's End. Having received no orders from Dunkeswell to land elsewhere, he assumed that it was still open. Skimming through clouds between his landfall at Hartland Point on the Bristol Channel and his field, he spotted a large fighter airport with good runways. The ceiling was a good 3,000 feet and he considered landing, but his trust was still in Dunkeswell and he decided to pass up the big airdrome and continue home. It was his last chance. The ceiling wedged lower as he flew and he went on instruments, since the wind was so strong at low altitudes that he did not care to try to stay beneath the clouds. Soon he was lost and he asked for a fix from the ground. He got it and arrived over Dunkeswell after dark and completely in the soup. He called Dunkeswell tower and asked for permission to land. No, said Dunkeswell, all planes were to divert east to Beaulieu Airdrome near Southampton. Joe headed east. Radio conditions were terrible, with static punctuating frantic calls from other aircraft. Before his radioman could get a navigational fix from the ground an hour had passed and Joe was sure that he had overflown Beaulieu, a small field used mostly for emergencies. A sudden loud whistle on his earphones galvanized him: he was in the vast cable forest of the Southampton barrage balloons, picking up their warning signal. The cockpit became very small and steamy. He was completely lost again, and not alone: there were half a dozen other aircraft crying for help in the soup. Among the voices he could hear George Charno's copilot Sleepy Wissman: Charno had been out over twelve hours and was running low on fuel, and so was Joe.

"I could hear the Southampton balloon warnings clearly," Joe reported later, "and I knew I was in their area. ... At one point I attempted to make contact with the ground and let down to a thousand feet and gradually worked lower, but had to pull up sharply when I saw a large hill. . . . I kept calling Darky [a control system] on the way in to try to ascertain my position so that I would know when to let down. Flying control then gave me an altimeter setting and told me to let down to five hundred feet. But as the setting was in millibars, it wasn't much help."

U.S. planes set their altimeters in inches, not millibars, and in the red glow of the cockpit, with driving rain smearing the windshield, the rattle of hail on the fuselage, and the smell of fear and sweat and overheated radios, there was no time for impromptu mathematics. But wisely he had dived on his first landfall at Hartland Point and set his altimeter there to sea level, and he knew that it was fairly accurate, so he took his life in his hands and eased down, groping for lights in the void, knowing that with each foot of altitude he gave up he was putting more trust in blind luck and less in carefully learned skills. At seven hundred feet he could stand it no longer. He leveled off and stared suddenly through his window.

"At that point I noticed a hazy light in the clouds so I knew we must be near the airport so I pushed over to 500 feet and saw the perimeter lights about a mile to port. At that time the ceiling was 500 feet, it was raining, but the visibility was good. I lost the field a couple of times circling, but flares which were sent up were most helpful. The wind at the time made it doubly hazardous and trying to watch the field and make a two-needle-width turn at 500 feet in the rain made it quite difficult. I made a short circle and came in."

He landed as the final flares went up for Charno. Joe was the only pilot in the mess aloft to even try to get in; everyone else had fled the area by the time he landed. Charno, with lookouts peering from the after hatches and the imperturbable little Wissman watching to starboard, was making passes at what turned out to be not a lighted field but a truck convoy. This did it. Spiraling above the convoy, he climbed to 5,000 feet, destroyed his radar, turned north, and ordered his crew to bail out. One crew member, perhaps in panic, pulled his chute early and filled the after station with silk. His buddies gathered up his chute, stuffed it into his arms, shoved him out, and followed him through the hatch. Wissman went next, and then Charno detonated the secret IFF identification transponder in his radar gear, turned the plane westward toward America, and hit the silk himself. He landed in Lincolnshire. He was 150 miles north of the field he had been looking for. Neither Charno, Wissman, nor any of their crew was hurt, but the plane must have crashed at sea, for no one ever heard of it again.

Joe was sufficiently exercised at the evening's fiasco to write a three-page report, classified "Secret" and suggesting, among other things, that if the control system had warned him that the weather was too bad to land at Dunkeswell before he arrived instead of after, he could have landed at the fighter field he passed en route. He submitted that six planes should not be diverted to the same airport at the same time—"it was just an act of God that the other planes sat down at other airports, as it would have been impossible to bring them all in"—and that some sort of navigational aid be installed at Beaulieu if it was necessary to divert aircraft there, or that in view of its proximity to the Southampton barrage balloons, at least the balloons be pulled down first. Ten days later, returning from an unsuccessful search led by Commander Reedy for five enemy destroyers, Lieutenant Parish's luck ran out in the same foul weather and he crashed into high ground forty miles west of Dunkeswell, precisely on the flight path Joe had taken from Hartland Point. Parish and all his men were killed.

As Joe's crew saw others die, its own bonds tightened. Corcoran, Jones, Dunning, Dodge, Butler, Guseman, and Cook, manning his guns and glued to his radar, grew used to his perfectionism in the air: everything had to be right, engines, turrets, and radio. Reedy, impatient with Joe's habit of ignoring paperwork on the ground, liked his meticulous attention in the air, where it counted; he considered him to be one of his best pilots and his crew a good example for the rest. Joe was so confident of his own ability to handle men in the air that he began to accept black-sheep crewmen turned down by other pilots. In flight he insisted on standards of discipline unusual in the rag-tag informality of a squadron of reserves: he asked for and got the "aye-aye, sir" that the book demanded. His men accepted it: they seemed to be surviving and that was worth more than the fifty-mission informality they saw in other crews. Their lives were at stake as much as his, and when once he refused to take off in an aircraft he considered a "dog," they supported him, although he was ordered to go anyway and finally did.

If he thought it really necessary he would fly anything: during the mad Invasion days he accepted a plane with a foot-long rip in the elevator: his new copilot Kellog had such confidence in Joe's ability that he did not even protest. The crew grew clannish when others laughed at

their formality in the air, and Joe's roommate Soden saw
Joe draw closer to his own men than to the other officers.
By Christmas Day when Reedy decreed that the squadron
would follow an old R.A.F. custom and that he himself
and his officers would serve Christmas dinner to the enlisted men, Joe had so far unbent that he made one of the
better waiters.

Kick and her friends visited the tiny Dunkeswell O-Club
frequently that Christmas season. The hard-drinking pilots
of VB-110 found her companions too rich for their blood—
one was the Marquess of Hartington—and except for
Reedy and Lou Papas and Mark Soden, drew away; as
always, the one they remembered and liked was Kick.

"Often she would grace our officers' club when she
would visit Joe," ex-navigator Martin says. "Before dinner
the chosen few would huddle with their drinks in a se-
cluded corner, and afterward they would repair to parts
unknown where the elite meet to practice caucusing, and
condition their eyes to cigar smoke." His guess as to the
political nature of the subject matter was close. Billy
Cavendish, Marquess of Hartington, had survived Dunkirk.
He was a professional soldier, a captain in the Coldstream
Guards, but he was running for the West Derbyshire seat
in a by-election. Under British law, professional officers
were ineligible. He was allowed to resign his regular commission, reverting to lieutenant in the reserve; it was, he
explained, the only way that he could become a candidate
and remain available for service when the invasion of
Europe began.

His opponent was a socialist named Charlie White,
whose father had defeated Billy's in the same constituency
years before. White saw his chance when the young lord
resigned his commission: "Another example of preferen-
tial treatment for certain classes. My opponent can give
up his position as a serving officer while men in the ranks
enjoy no such privilege. . . . Lord Hartington will have to
explain to the parents and relatives of serving men and
women in West Derbyshire how he can more or less please
himself so far as military service is concerned while men
and women in the ranks must comply with the rigid
military requirements and discipline."

Billy Hartington went to the hustings in uniform. His
butler Edward manned the loudspeakers. "When demobili-
zation comes," promised Hartington, "I am determined to
see to it that no effort shall be spared to insure that these

good men and women of ours will get jobs at decent wages and good homes and fair opportunities to start again in civilian life." He supported social security and a vast rebuilding and educational program. His mother, the dignified Duchess of Devonshire, "appealed for her lad as the mother of a serving soldier." Kathleen Kennedy, a true granddaughter of Honeyfitz of the Old North End, mailed brochures: "A vote for Hartington is a vote for Churchill."

It was a brave little effort, but it failed. Hartington was defeated by 5,000 votes out of 28,000. He thanked the voters without bitterness and announced quietly that he was going back to the Guards "to fight, perhaps die, for my country." The election brought a special disappointment for Kathleen, who had perhaps pictured him safe in Parliament while the war went on: if he had won, he would have had to give up his peerage to sit in the House of Commons and perhaps one of the family barriers between them would have fallen. But he had lost the excuse to give up his title and the prospect of Catholic peers in the House of Cavendish was still as unthinkable to the Duke and Duchess of Devonshire as Protestant grandchildren were to Rose and the ex-ambassador. Kathleen asked Joe for his advice.

Joe Kennedy, Jr., was as stoutly Catholic as ever: when he was not flying on Sundays he served Mass for Father Gallery, the Catholic chaplain at Dunkeswell. But the war was changing values and they would never be the same: besides, he had seen the girl with the sky-blue eyes again and perhaps he was learning himself how sad love can be when there is no hope. With considerable reluctance and with many warnings to Kick that she must be absolutely sure, he promised that whatever decision she and Billy Hartington made he would support at home.

4

A touch of spring filtered through the air of Dunkeswell, which reeked always of gasoline. Mudville Heights began to dry. A crew had thirty-five missions to fly before being sent home and suddenly everyone discovered that the end was in sight: for some there were only a dozen patrols to go. Nothing else changed, though, and neither hope nor

springtime was protection against flak, fifty-caliber fighter
fire, and the dreary fronts which still marched in from off
the stern Atlantic. George Charno attacked two large
enemy surface vessels before dawn on February 6 and was
driven off by intense flak before it was light enough to
assess the damage, but Admiral "Betty" Stark arrived on
Washington's Birthday to give him and Sleepy Wissman
the DFC and their crew Air Medals. Joe, sensing that he
was ending his combat tour without a decoration, became
more aggressive than ever. He and Reedy discussed the
notion of using the PB4Y as a low-level bomber against
German surface craft along the coast; Joe, who had a
patrol the next day, volunteered the newly decorated Charno to test the theory. If Joe was too busy to check out his
inspirations, he was never reluctant to offer his friends as
volunteers.

The war was not over, nor was the bad weather. Lieutenant John L. Williams, returning from patrol, missed
England in the fog and crashed into Great Skellig Rock
off Ireland. Jim Reedy flew a British Beaufighter to Ireland to investigate but all he found was his own great-uncle
in Boyle. Then "Paddy" Ryan, an experienced ex-enlisted
pilot, possibly enticed over German-occupied Guernsey by
a false navigational signal, called from ten miles off the
Cherbourg Peninsula with engine trouble and was not heard
from again. For a while Joe had hopes that he and his
crew were POW's or even safe in the hands of the Underground. Someone spotted a wrecked aircraft on the coast
and it was rumored that Reedy flew an unauthorized
fighter-recon hop to check it out, but nothing came of it
and Reedy denies it today.

Joe had worked four submarine contacts that winter,
with notable lack of success. On a patrol in March he
spotted his first real evidence of a submarine in a moving
oil slick. He dropped four sonobuoys and circled the yellow
dots below. His radioman heard the sound of a cavitating
propeller, or thought he did. Joe dropped a homing
torpedo with no sign of luck and finally the contact was
lost and he flew home.

The squadron took more losses in March than it had in
any other month. Lieutenant (j.g.) Bob Meihaus lost an
engine on patrol near the Spanish coast. He struggled
home in bad weather to find Dunkeswell socked in: he
was diverted to Chivenor Airdrome, where he struck a
house on his final leg and caught telephone wires and

lost two more engines. He staggered the last 2½ miles on one engine. No one was injured in his crash landing, but four days later Lieutenant Harold Barton was attacked by ten JU-88's and shot down in the Atlantic, far from the Bay of Biscay; perhaps he had turned to sea as instructed and been unable to fight off his attackers. A U.S. Army meteorological plane sighted his aircraft's burning carcass with the Germans still circling it. No survivors were seen. Then Lieutenant Orville Moore called that he was being attacked in the same area by a dozen fighters, and planes were sent to his aid. When they arrived they found wreckage and two empty dinghies but no sign of survivors. The squadron decided that he had intercepted Barton's call, lumbered west to help, and flown into a trap. With these last two crews gone, the squadron had lost thirty-five percent of its flight personnel, but replacements were en route from the States and they began to arrive in April.

Unless his luck improved, Joe had no intention of going home. He had not sunk his sub nor had his crew shot down a plane. Jack's PT-109 adventure in the South Pacific had been reported in the British press, lending their father's tarnished image some of its former luster in the streets and clubs of London, but Joe, Jr., himself, had done nothing, here in England where it counted. Jack had a combat decoration. He had none and time was running out.

D-Day was bound to be in June or July. No one knew the date, but Joe was not about to miss the greatest show on earth. For his thirty-fifth patrol, the last on his official tour, he volunteered for a special mission between Brest and Land's End, looking for surface craft. Nothing happened, and when he returned, he volunteered to stay for another tour. Squadron records indicate that his crew volunteered to stay with him, but the records err: no one asked them and, much as they liked Joe as a pilot, most think now that, had they really been asked, they would have laughed. They had had enough.

5

"Crash-bang" was of course not the farm's real name, but close to it, and so Joe and Mark Soden and the girl called it that. It was a little estate placed, fortunately, far enough

south of London to be safe from bombing for the children, which is why the girl moved to it, and geographical-
ly central for her friends scattered throughout southern
England. The house was a tile-roofed cottage: "a gardener's cottage," Lorelle Hearst calls it, "but charming beyond belief. It was very gay." It was much smaller than
what its hostess was used to; she was wealthy in her own
right and had been so all her life. She had and still has a
certain candor that sometimes comes with lifelong security
and sometimes does not.

"They would all sort of meet at my house. Billy Hartington was stationed at Alton. Joe was stationed in Devon
and Kick was stationed on the other side in London. I was
working part-time in a factory and bringing up the children. We had chickens on the tennis court and even had a
cow. I had a chauffeur who could milk her."

It was a very busy time for the girl, which is one reason
that she grew to like Kathleen so much; she would arrive
and without ceremony simply disappear upstairs. "Ex-
uberant . . . very pretty," she remembers. "Kathleen would
say, 'Don't bother, I'll go upstairs and wash my hair!' "
With rationing gripping the country, everyone brought
something to eat: a fish, a lamb chop, an egg. Joe and
Mark Soden would arrive with canned fruit juice for the
children conned from Dunkeswell cooks. Mark Soden
remembers squabbles between Joe and Kick as to the proper ownership of an Underwood portable typewriter, impossible to replace in wartime Britain: Joe won and kept
it. But the strains were minor, everyone was relaxed: Billy
Hartington left his political and regimental cares outside
the door; William Randolph Hearst, Jr. (and later Lorelle,
who would arrive to cover the war for the Hearst chain
herself) visited here often. Joe's friend Frank Moore
O'Ferrall, the dark-haired horse breeder serving in the
Irish Guards, came too. All were compatible. Everyone
played gin rummy and poker for stakes: O'Ferrall remembers Joe as one of the best card players he ever met. They
would play cards in the garden when the weather was
good. All the wrath that Joe could not let loose at other
card partners fell on Kick's head. "Kick just doesn't have
any card sense," he would say. "I don't want to be her
partner and I feel sorry for any sucker that has her."

Billy Hartington wanted to be her partner, obviously,
and for life. Lorelle Hearst found him very firm and very
good for Kick, who would have scorned a weakling. Kath-

leen, product of the Convent of the Sacred Heart, could not bring herself to agree absolutely that their children would be brought up as Protestants; Billy promised that if the British aristocracy was so weakened by socialism after the war that tradition didn't matter, then they would be brought up as Catholics; otherwise they would have to be Protestant peers of the realm.

It was good enough for Kick and presumably for Brother Joe. They wrote home. The storm broke as predicted. Rose, in Boston's Baptist Hospital after an operation, was "too ill to discuss the marriage" with the press, but the ex-ambassador presumably discussed it privately, heatedly, and by phone, mail, and cable, with Kick and Joe. There were even minor explosions from Bobby, who was considering the priesthood, and Eunice, a deeply religious girl. Two years later, when John Kennedy was running for Congress, Grandpa Fitzgerald was still trying to explain to Boston voters why Kathleen had married a Protestant lord. At the time, caught by surprise in an interview, he simply backpedaled. "Although Kathleen and the young man have been friends for some time the announcement has come in a rush. Quite apart from her family training she is by choice and conviction a Catholic."

Kathleen was shaken enough to see Archbishop Godfrey, the apostolic delegate to Great Britain. "But never," she wrote later, "did anyone have such a pillar of strength as I had in Joe in those difficult days. . . . From the beginning he gave me wise, helpful advice. When he felt that I had made up my mind, he stood by me always. He constantly reassured me and gave me renewed confidence in my own decision. Moral courage he had in abundance, and once he felt that the step was right for me, he never faltered, although he might be held largely responsible for my decision. He could not have been more helpful in every way as the perfect brother doing, according to his own light, the best for a sister with the hope that in the end it would be best for the family. How right he was!"

Ex-Ambassador Kennedy threw in the sponge. He softened so far as to send his favorite daughter word with Lorelle Hearst, enplaning for London, that he was setting aside a fund in her name so that she would not be overwhelmed by the Cavendish millions and so that she would feel beholden to no one. It was hardly a parental blessing, but it was better than nothing at all.

In better times, condoned by the Church or not, the wedding might have been an Anglo-American extravaganza. Now it could hardly even be scheduled properly: military leave for Hartington on the brink of the invasion could not be accurately anticipated, nor could Joe's patrols. Finally, on a May Saturday, in the narrow brick building housing the "Superintendent Registrar of Birth and Deaths of the Royal Borough of Kensington and Chelsea—Hours 9:30 A.M. to 12:45 P.M.," Joe stood in a stuffy reception room before a polished table covered with vases of pink carnations and gave his sister away. A deferential civil servant in a shiny black suit performed the marriage; he, the bride, and Joe were practically the only untitled persons in the room. There was no music. The red double-deckers rumbled unheedingly by outside. Captain Billy Cavendish the Marquess of Hartington, taller even than Joe and much more professional in the trim field dress of his regiment, had chosen a fellow Guards officer, the Duke of Rutland, as best man. His father and mother, the Duke and Dutchess of Devonshire, were there, and Ladies Cavendish and Salisbury and Astor. Kathleen wore a pink dress and a short mink jacket. Joe ran interference for the couple through the crowd of photographers and well-wishers outside: they were showered with flower petals as they left the tiny building and there were two hundred at the reception in one of the family homes on Eaton Square. Then the couple left for Compton Place, one of Billy's father's residences. Hartington had only a little leave, and within a few days Kathleen was living in a small country hotel near his camp at Alton. She wrote Mark Soden, thanking him for a wedding gift entrusted to Joe but characteristically not yet delivered. "A rumor, as yet unfilled, has reached my ears that you very kindly donated some clothing coupons to the cause of my marriage. May I say that I'm very, very grateful. I'm seeing Brother Joe in London tomorrow evening and I hope to get him to produce the coupons as well." She describes the wedding to Mark, who had not been able to go. "I can't tell you what Joe was like. I guess you could probably judge by the fact that his smiling face appeared everywhere. At the moment I am a camp follower. . . . I spend my days listening to all the old ladies talking about what a hard war they are having. It's rather a change from G.I. conversation to say the least."

To spend a springtime honeymoon with the man she loved in a country inn in southern England must have been a dream come true, but there must have been, too, a gnawing dread. He was again a regular infantry officer in an elite regiment. As a "camp follower" she knew the odds he faced when the landings began. And the whole world knew that the landings were very close.

6

For over two years U.S. and Royal Navy planners had been haunted by a hellish vision: U-boats loose in the invasion fleet. Such an event was hard to discuss rationally: it would make Pearl Harbor look like a minor naval embarrassment. Suppose, as Eisenhower's vast armada approached the coast of France, crammed with men and laden to the gunnels with equipment, Doenitz *did* get his subs into the mass? The bulk of the German undersea fleet was still concentrated in Bay of Biscay bases, up to Brest at the mouth of the Channel. It was not far, only 250 miles, from Brest to the Normandy beaches: less than thirty-six hours' run submerged, less than twelve on the surface. If they were successfully sneaked around the tip of Brittany into Channel waters, it would be Drake-in-reverse; the Germans would not even bother, probably, to sink small craft, leaving the troops to be chewed up by coastal defenses while they blasted their supplies to the bottom behind them. It was an awful nightmare, especially for Admiral Stark, who needed no more after Pearl.

The three squadrons at Dunkeswell, along with the R.A.F. Coastal Command, would simply have to prevent it. R.A.F. Group Headquarters and the U.S. Navy wing at Plymouth came up with a concept: "Cork." The cork was to be placed between Plymouth and Brest in the southern end of the English Channel, but it was a misnomer: the concept was less static than that of a cork. It was actually that of a savage in a canoe armed with a paddle trying to kill a swimming enemy: whenever the swimmer arose for air, he was to be batted on the head until finally his lungs failed and he drowned or went home.

Naval intelligence knew that a U-boat in a crash dive

used up as much energy from its batteries as it could charge during thirty minutes on the surface. If a U-boat trying to charge its batteries was forced to dive every half hour, it would show no net gain. Sooner or later its batteries would go dead from the power it spent merely to live. If planes were dispatched from Devon to Brest every thirty minutes, day and night, flying gridiron patterns back and forth to the French coast—if the gridiron was wide enough and the legs within sight of each other—then there would be a PB4Y over every portion of the "cork" every thirty minutes. A "Rover" plane would be held in reserve to attack.

Joe and his fellow pilots sat in the operations hut at Dunkeswell and listened to an R.A.F. Coastal Command officer from Group explain Cork in his terse, English accent; then they listened to Munson, their own flight officer, as he traced out their part in it. The wing's patrols were rectangular and parallel, fifteen miles wide, running north and south across the Channel, which runs almost east and west. The westernmost patrol area for their own squadron was a skinny rectangle from Land's End on Britain's southern tip to the Brest Peninsula on the westernmost point of France. The easternmost rectangle lay from Portland Bill near Dunkeswell to the Cherbourg Peninsula; at its southern end it came within five miles of the enemy coast. Navigation in bad weather would have to be precise, or wave-hopping pilots might find themselves suddenly gazing at a German flak tower at eye level.

Two aircraft were to plow the legs of each rectangle at thirty-minute intervals. Flight duration was 11½ hours, which allowed each plane to make a dozen circuits during a working day. It was an ambitious plan and would have horrified a U-boat commander who knew of it; it was horrifying enough in terms of fatigue to Joe Kennedy and the rest of the men who must fly it, but it seemed to make sense and on June 6, as D-Day dawned under lowering skies, they began.

Joe took off. As he climbed to 1,500 feet and banked toward Cherbourg, he must have stared at his cockpit radarscope in disbelief. His patrol was northwest of the invasion beaches, but Eisenhower's force was so incredibly huge that it spilled over the horizon and he could actually see some of the outlying ships. On the radarscope the mass of the Allied fleet was simply incredible, and it seemed to awe the Luftwaffe. That first day Joe saw more FW-190's, JU-88's, and FW-120's than he had since the bad days of December, but the German pilots evaded battle, and now it was surface ships and subs that everyone was looking for anyway. The day after the invasion they were everywhere in every disguise: Lieutenant R. F. Duffy, a lean, tanned Irishman, still atabrine-yellow from the Pacific, sank two Spanish fishing vessels and left another two burning: he regrets it today, but nerves were taut, the ships were in a prohibited area, and they shot at him first. The next day Joe sighted five German E-boats—fast, eighty-six-ton torpedo boats like Jack's PT-109—and called in aircraft to attack them, but held against all instinct to his patrol pattern as he had been instructed. A force of U-boats tried to penetrate the "cork" and suddenly there were contacts everywhere: fifty-four in seven days and thirty-seven of those caught on the surface trying to charge their batteries. If any subs got through, they were apparently exhausted. The invasion fleet lost not a single ship to a U-boat in the entire month of June. "Cork" had worked; it would continue to work until the Germans perfected schnorkel and could charge their batteries below.

Two days after D-Day Chief Radioman Dee Vilan, who had volunteered for a second tour and had studied Joe from afar since the squadron was formed, talked to him outside the squadron offices. He found him unhappy with his new crew and offered to fly with him as radioman if the skipper approved. Reedy okayed the change and Vilan wrote in his diary that night that Joe was a "no-nonsense guy when on the job and expects the same of his crew. Yet his manner is at all times democratic and engaging. Some of his crew find him a slavedriver but their loyalty and respect is unwavering." It was Vilan's forty-eighth patrol and he still had twelve more to go for sixty, which had been established as enough to complete a second tour. But when Joe landed, Lieutenant C. Horton Smith, the administrative officer, asked Vilan if he had had enough. "Just about all I can take at this point," said Vilan. Whether or not he had finished the sixty missions, they decided together that Vilan would go home August 1.

The squadron, with sixteen crews, averaged seven twelve-hour sorties a day for three weeks. There was a cost, in weary aircraft, sloppy maintenance, and exhausted fliers. Those who had been with the outfit from the beginning

were the first to suffer, and strange maladies and minor
discomforts began to appear. Frank Borden, youngest
officer in the squadron, had turned into sick bay with
combat fatigue. Like Joe, he did not drink much, and
perhaps the drinking was necessary to untie the knots. The
O-Club · became Rabelaisian at night. "Incredible," says
Borden. "Everybody blind drunk, and they had this game,
bombs away, where we'd push a guy on a table and he'd
bomb a target with beer cans." British R.A.F. girls who
had come finally to Dunkeswell to wait on tables in the
mess—because the wing was reluctant to introduce Negro
Navy stewards into the local community—were lawful and
usually willing prey, and the games grew rougher: someone, surprised with a WAF girl unfaithful to her high-
ranking lover, earned his niche in squadron mythology
when he dived under her bed and spent a whole miserable
night cringing there under squeaking springs as her
paramour took his place.

Joe Kennedy seemed relatively restrained. Perhaps it
was the influence of the more stable crowd at Crash-Bang.
Lou Papas recalls that when Joe had a date with a WAF
it was a staid affair: "A perfect gentleman, maybe because
he felt he had obligations to his family." But Joe's nerves
were straining too: he had not seen the action he wanted
and his fatigue on the long boring flights was increasing. As
a second-tour man he thought he had certain privileges.
He was seldom around except to fly. Reedy became air-
group commander at Dunkeswell, the "Senior Officer
Present"; Commander Page Knight, a tall, thin Annapolis man from Idaho, took over as skipper and caught Joe
breaking into a shower off-hours to clean up for a liberty.
He was an easygoing captain, without Reedy's toughness,
but he had a squadron of flight-weary combat veterans to
control. He restricted Joe to his quarters for a day or so.
When Joe was sprung he rented a room and bath in
Exeter: he was damned if he was going to arrive at
Crash-Bang or in London dirty, shower hours or not.

On June 13, a week after D-Day, the first V-1 "buzz
bomb" slammed into a railroad bridge in the center of
London. Three more followed that night. As they passed
overhead, Londoners heard a popping "like the sound of a
lorry on a downgrade and then this frightful silence"
before the gut-squeezing explosion as the missile struck.
By the evening of the 15th the buzz-bomb attack was fully
mounted: in twenty-four hours the Germans fired three

hundred V-1's from their steam-propelled carriages: 144 crossed the coast and 73 struck the city. One hit so close to Crash-Bang on that weekend that Joe and Bill Hearst talked the girl into using her precious gas coupons to take them to the vast smoking site of impact. Joe looked at the damage, poked around in the ruins searching for souvenirs or a clue to the buzz-bomb guidance system, and said nothing. Hearst made a flight with polo-playing Tommy Hitchcock from Elliott Roosevelt's group, which was diving from high altitude on the strange unpiloted craft that traveled at 350 miles per hour; he found the fliers trying to tumble the buzz-bomb control gyros by nudging the tiny wings with their own, it having become instantly apparent that to shoot one down from behind was to die in the explosion. There was talk of evacuating London. A mad quality to this last thrashing of the Reich truly angered Britons and the Americans who saw the damage. A new Battle of Britain was starting, but Joe was out of this one too: fighter pilots would win or lose it: the U.S. Navy would obviously have no part.

When he had volunteered for another tour, he had thought that D-Day would give him the submarine or E-boat he wanted; D-Day passed, the submarine menace in the Channel seemed licked, and nothing had happened. He became wilder and even less cautious. He found a German E-boat grounded on the Brest Peninsula and was only driven off by heavy antiaircraft fire; on his next hop, on the day Cherbourg was opened to Allied shipping, he flew against orders so close to the German-held island of Guernsey off Brest that he drew flak from the enemy, bringing back a partly perforated plane, a copilot—Kellog —who complained half seriously that Joe under fire always turned the copilot's side to the ground batteries, and catching more flak at home from Sunshine Reedy and his new skipper.

It was Joe's last patrol. He was going home. He had been offered a job in London as an assistant naval attaché, but he told Sweeny that his father had left under such a diplomatic cloud that he didn't think he could operate effectively in the Embassy. There may have been a more personal reason: if his attachment to the girl became much stronger, he might be courting a real emotional trap. A rumor had already grown in the squadron that they were engaged. He had let it grow, perhaps in amusement, or to save explanations, or to throw sand in the eyes of the gossips, or perhaps because he so wished it were possible that he could not bring himself to deny it. It didn't matter anyway. The same "tomorrow-we-die" gaiety that England had known in the Battle of Britain had returned as the war on the Continent consumed England's best and the strange new weapons wobbled into London. If he left the girl now, before it was too late, by the time he was instructing in the States or flying over the Pacific, everyone would have forgotten.

He went to Plymouth with Jim Reedy. While he was there Paul Brabazon docked his refrigerator ship *Tarazan*. Joe and Reedy met him by accident on the street and the three had a rollicking shore leave in the fleet officers' club and the ancient waterfront pubs: they were celebrating Joe's promotion to full lieutenant—he had caught up with Jack again, at least in rank. When they sobered up, great plans had been made. Joe would sail back with Brabazon as an honored guest, eating steak and eggs for breakfast on clean linen and sleeping between snow-white sheets.

Back at Dunkeswell, he packed part of his gear and sent it down to the ship. He intended perhaps when his orders were cut to go to London to see Kick and to make a last visit to Crash-Bang too. His war, at least in Europe, seemed over. But wheels had been grinding in London and Washington, and there had been great and secret activity at an Army air field in Florida; three weeks before, on the first of July, a strange little group of naval aviation specialists had enplaned at Traverse City, Michigan, on the first step of a protracted flight, via Norfolk, to England. Their officer-in-charge had arrived that day at Dunkeswell in a Douglas transport and the rest were due in a day or two. Arriving too was a PB4Y like those Joe had been flying—and yet somehow different—and they would need an experienced combat pilot to fly it.

The skipper of the little unit explained to Reedy in general terms the mission, which was quite fantastic, and suggested that the pilot be a volunteer. Reedy offered himself, and was turned down as too senior in rank. So Sunshine talked to Page Knight and the other two squadron commanders at Dunkeswell, intending to ask for volunteer crews from all and to pick the best. Knight began to call in his most experienced PPC's. One of those he called was Joe Kennedy, who volunteered immediately, demandingly, and with great enthusiasm. There were crews from the other squadrons to consider, so Knight told him to wait.

Joe spent that Sunday at Crash-Bang. Billy Hartington had landed in France and Kick planned to fly back to Hyannis until her husband returned. Their hostess planned to spend a part of August with her friend Virginia Sykes at Virginia's home in Yorkshire. Joe had been invited too, for the second weekend in August; if he were selected for the mission and stayed in England, they would meet there then.

Joe's flight was top secret, but he knew so little about it himself that talking of it hardly entailed a security risk. He mentioned to Lorelle Hearst and the rest that he had finally found the mission he was looking for, treating it so lightly that Lorelle did not take him seriously at all.

He walked to Mass in Woking that Sunday with Frank Moore O'Ferrall, his horse-breeding friend. From their old railbird days when Joe was in the Embassy they had always sparked each other to bet. They would gamble together on anything: cards, horses, cockroaches crawling up a wall. Joe, returning from Biscay patrols, would call O'Ferrall long-distance in his London digs to wake him and ask how a horse that Frank had touted had run. Once, at the Salisbury Races, he had ignored O'Ferrall's professional advice and won ten to one on a horse called "Clever Joe." Walking back from Mass this last Sunday at Crash-Bang, he stopped in his tracks and asked O'Ferrall how far he estimated it was to the house. O'Ferrall guessed half a mile; Joe bet him a pound that it was at least a mile. They continued, and as they walked, Joe seemed strangely talkative: he spoke of his family life and what he intended to do after the war. He even let fall a hint that he had volunteered for a special mission: he would not say what it was. O'Ferrall asked him if he thought there was much risk. Joe estimated that he had a fifty-fifty chance. It is likely that he was kidding, because he added: "and that's a darned sight better than most of those horses you gave me."

He lost the bet on the distance to Crash-Bang, and in an hour it was time to catch the train to Dunkeswell. O'Ferrall never saw him again.

4

IN 1939 British intelligence had received from the Continent an anonymous letter. It had warned that the Germans were working on gyro-stabilized rockets as weapons of war. When France fell, a French civilian engineer named Joseph Becker made contact with the British. As his country collapsed, he had successfully passed himself off as a homegrown Nazi. For a year, working for the Germans, he had access to top-secret information giving the location of odd-looking launching sites being constructed along the French coast. The German Air Force was in deadly competition with the Army for the honor of saving Germany; liquid-powered Army rockets were almost ready; the Luftwaffe's V-1 flying buzz bomb was its smaller, less sophisticated, hurried, but ultimately more practical bid for Hitler's favor. In December, 1943, Becker was taken prisoner. While being transported to Germany, he incredibly escaped and continued somehow to send information to the Allies. In May, 1942, while Joe was still flying Mariners out of Norfolk, Flight Officer Lady Constance Babington-Smith of the WAF's, poring over aerial recon prints in her office at Medenham, noted a small, curving black shadow on a high-altitude reconnaissance photo of Peenemünde. A tiny T-shaped object sat at the end of the shadow. Under magnification and with considerable imagination the shadow turned into an elevated ramp and the T at the end of it into an airplane with no cockpit and stubby wings. Simultaneously from Becker and other sources came news of a huge complex near Watten, twenty miles inland from Calais.

All summer long, as Lady Babington-Smith studied her photos, new sites began to appear. Construction work apparently proceeded only at night and was stopped and camouflaged by dawn, but she discovered footprints in the dew on early-morning photos and spotted launching rails, too. The design of the strange pads began to emerge as the photos poured in. The sites were giant bunkers of concrete, with twelve-foot-thick walls and narrow steel doors opening west, thirty feet high. From the doors the short railroad tracks of the Pas de Calais sites aligned ominously on London only a hundred miles away, while those on the Cherbourg Peninsula were pointed at Bristol.

Neither she nor anyone else liked what she saw, but the Prime Minister, with Churchillian scorn, named whatever it was "Crossbow," denoting somewhat prematurely an "obsolete, clumsy and inaccurate weapon." Other Allied sources gave the sites the code word "No Ball," and the launching pads "Ski Sites." As the purpose of the sites became more clear, something close to panic in Allied intelligence grew. Certain secret parliamentary committees began to stir restlessly, demanding action against the emplacements. From the hour of Lady Babington-Smith's initial discovery until D-Day nearly forty percent of Allied reconnaissance flights over occupied France were devoted to Crossbow; over one million negatives were shot and more than four million prints made. Ultimately every foot of the three hundred mile coastal area from Oostende on the north to Le Havre on the south was photographed, with the Cherbourg Peninsula thrown in for good measure. Almost a year before the first buzz bomb was launched, six hundred R.A.F. bombers slammed Peenemünde, the apparent nest of the birds, killing seven hundred men, including a prominent German rocket specialist. This attack, along with a famous dream of Hitler's which told him that none of his large rocket-powered weapons would ever hit England, conceivably slowed up the German Army's ambitious rocket program but seems to have done little to hinder the cruder but more feasible Luftwaffe V-1 "Flying Bomb," which would turn out to be simply an unmanned jet aircraft, gyro-controlled, loaded with dynamite. The "Flying Bomb" was Goering's last bid to save the prestige he had lost by his failure to break the British will in the Battle of Britain.

All through the winter of 1943, while Joe flew Biscay patrols, the R.A.F and U.S. Air Force had been pounding at the odd, threatening sites, some of which now were modified to resemble farm structures or small manufacturing plants and which seemed invulnerable and to grow in number every week. On December 15, 1943, 1,300 aircraft dropped 1,700 bombs on twenty-three of them. Long before D-Day, when U.S. bombers were supposed to be knocking out the railheads of northwest France and softening up the Continent, the *New York Times* caught a hint of the Crossbow problem. "The Germans have now created a diversion. They have at least won a breathing-spell for themselves and temporarily diverted a part of the Anglo-American airpower. The threat alone has succeeded in lightening the wave of the attack on Germany."

Results of the bombing shown by postflight reconnaissance were ambiguous, but seemed to indicate that Allied attacks on the ski sites might be having no effect at all. The Allies even considered using poison gas, but the idea was vetoed by Eisenhower, who did not want to complicate invasion plans with the threat of German retaliation.

A note of desperation entered U.S. efforts to knock out the mysterious bunkers. General Hap Arnold in Washington telephoned Eglin Field, Florida, and suddenly the remote pine barrens of the Florida panhandle swarmed with thousands of troops and civilians assembling, in concrete, steel, lumber, and brick, duplicate complexes of ski sites. For realism, camouflage units and a full antiaircraft battalion were set up and every variety of aircraft and bomb that the U.S. Air Corps could muster was tested. Minimum-altitude attacks seemed the only answer: at least at low altitude the bombing could be pinpointed. Then they tried it in action: six P-47 fighter pilots sneaked in low to score on sites near Calais, showing the effectiveness of low-level bombing, but though they escaped, everyone believed that continued pilot survival would be impossible as the Germans grew accustomed to the attacks, and the Air Corps disliked the low-altitude concept anyway. Other Allied friction developed: Doolittle wanted to leave the ski sites to concentrate on the German industrial targets; Air Vice-Marshal Tedder, understandably, wanted priority assigned to whatever strange weapon was pointed at the heart of his homeland.

Tedder won. U.S. and British forces dropped 100,000 tons of bombs on ski sites and their supporting complexes. In the six months before D-Day alone, thirty-six thousand tons were dropped in twenty-five thousand sorties against the launching pads: 771 airmen and 154 aircraft were lost to flak and fighters. Results were at last evaluated: negligible. Because the first robot plane had not yet flown, doubts began to arise. Suppose the whole thing were a deadly hoax on the Allies? When Allied troops scrambled ashore in Normandy the morning of June 6 and still the pads were silent, everyone heaved a sigh of relief. The strange emplacements were finally abandoned as targets: if the Germans had not rolled out their new weapons in retaliation for the actual invasion, then there must be no weapons at all: the sites were dummies and it had all been an expensive and successful bluff.

Crossbow had been no bluff at all, and London learned it a week after D-Day. The Luftwaffe had been trying to get its new weapons into place and ready to hit the city on the morning of the invasion; Goering was simply seven days late. The attack from the strange bunkers began at midnight June 13, but the first ones launched were, as Churchill had predicted, clumsy and inaccurate; so much so that the whole terror campaign almost ended four days later, when a maverick buzz bomb launched from Saint-Omer turned on its master. Its control gyroscope tumbled 180 degrees and it streaked away in precisely the opposite direction from London for precisely its programmed flight time. Hitler was at Margival near Soissons, lecturing Rommel and von Rundstedt on tactics. At V-1 speed—350 miles per hour—Margival is seventeen minutes southeast of Saint-Omer, as London is seventeen minutes northwest. As the V-1 circled and began its mad flight inland, an Allied air-raid forced the Fuehrer and his field marshals into the *Fuehrerbunker*, built for the leader in happier days to oversee the invasion of Britain. Hitler continued his harangue below: the V-1 *Vergeltungswaffen* "revenge weapons," he assured his listeners, would be "decisive against Great Britain and make the British ready to make peace." The marshals departed, leaving their leader. They had been gone for only a few minutes when the errant buzz bomb streaked blindly in from the northwest, cut its engine at seventeen minutes, and crashed, incredibly, dead center on the bunker. Hitler, unscratched, fled to

Berchtesgaden and never returned to France, but the rain of death on London—its direction corrected—continued.

2

As the first V-1's slammed home, Eisenhower quickly reassigned top priority to the bombing of the Crossbow sites from which they seemed to issue, giving them precedence over all but the most urgent tactical requirements of the troops fighting south from the beaches. No one had yet decided how to knock them out. It seems in retrospect that last winter's successful low-level six-plane P-47 attack by untrained Air Corps pilots should have provided a key. Why not borrow from the U.S. Navy or Marines a squadron of trained dive-bomber pilots, flying the deadly, rock-steady Dauntlesses? Combined with low-level diversionary skip bombing, dive-bombing had already in the face of concentrated fire from Japanese task forces reduced the Imperial fleet to a shadow. No one seems to have thought of that, though; the Army Air Corps had never accepted this naval art; dive-bombing was sweaty work, incompatible with the dream of airborne armadas sailing majestically to glory over an enemy brought to its knees by airpower alone. Anyway, Air Corps minds were running in more esoteric channels: if the Germans could develop robot aircraft, why could not the United States? BELIEF EXISTS HERE, General Carl Spaatz, commanding the 8th Air Force in England, dispatched secretly to Hap Arnold in Washington, THAT THE LARGE ROCKET SITES ARE PRACTICALLY INVULNERABLE TO NORMAL BOMBING ATTACKS. Spaatz suggested a plan thought to have struck a young second lieutenant in his headquarters: that unmanned, radio-controlled, war-weary P-47's or P-38 fighters, packed with explosives and guided by FAST AND NIMBLE mother ships, be tested in Florida with a view toward flying them into the buzz-bomb sites hurling death at London. He suggested using the "television principle" for the final run. So "Aphrodite," named not for the goddess but for a species of butterfly, was brought from its cocoon. Fighters could not pack the necessary wallop, so less than a month after the Germans had proved their openers, forty tired B-17 Flying Fortresses were stripped, gutted, and equipped with primitive radio control, to be loaded with explosives and taken off by a volunteer pilot and technician who would then bail out. The empty Flying Fortress "babies" under remote control from "mother" ships, if rammed into the hitherto invulnerable sites, might do it. The Air Corps found seventeen volunteer pilots and technicians, and would augment the number later. The aircraft were based at Woodbridge Airdrome, north of London. But Woodbridge was a giant emergency field with new fog-dispersal apparatus; there was nothing the base would not do to get a plane down in bad weather. One night it burned away its fog and brought down a JU-88 by mistake. So tight was the secrecy surrounding Aphrodite that when Woodbridge found that it had a live German fighter pilot on its hands the entire Aphrodite operation was flown to Winfarthing-Fersfield Airdrome in East Anglia in fear that the captured German had somehow observed and radioed home its existence. Fersfield was logical anyway: there already were Army units working there with "Batty" and "Glomb," primitive radio-controlled glide bombs to be launched from aircraft.

As Aphrodite, assigned top priority and under tremendous pressure, began to flutter its wings, General Doolittle, new 8th Air Force Commander, made a discovery. The U.S. Navy had for ten years been using radio-controlled "drones" for antiaircraft target practice; it had even with considerable optimism lately dispatched, unmanned and under radio control, seven tired 160-knot TBM "Torpeckers" loaded with explosive against the Japanese fortress-island of Truk, where each was shot down in stately dignity in order of its arrival.

This alone should have provided a hint of the proper use of unpiloted aircraft against pinpoint targets, given the state of the art in 1944. They should have been used as low-level decoys, loaded and fused in case they got through, but primarily as sacrificial targets to divert ground gunners while dive-bombers peeled off above for a pinpoint attack. No such inspiration seems to have struck either the Navy or the desperate Air Corps, which at this point actually asked for naval help.

Admiral King was delighted. On July 1, 1944, two weeks after the first V-1 struck London, the tiny secret group at the naval air station in Traverse City, Michigan, was alerted. A wiry lieutenant with a moustache and a crooked grin took a call in his BOQ just before midnight.

He had been waiting for it for three frustrating years. He was an ex-CPO and had been with radio-controlled aircraft since they had existed merely as targets for fleet antiaircraft gunners. Suddenly he discovered that he was going to England as executive officer of a "special attack unit," whatever that was, on an unspecified mission, for an unknown length of time. It was all so secret that he could not even call his wife, Edna, who was just moving into their new house in Fort Worth.

His name was Wilford Willy. To avoid Willy-Willy he preferred the nickname Bud and he pronounced his last name "Wiley." His skipper, James A Smith, a taciturn, hawk-nosed commander from Missouri, considered him one of his best pilots and an expert on radio control; Bud, known as energetic, enthusiastic, and a "real tiger" by the younger pilots in his outfit, would have agreed, excess modesty not being among his burdens. Both he and Smith, though regulars, had been in a backwater of the war since Pearl Harbor: Willy because he was mustang, ex-enlisted, and could expect no better; Smith perhaps because he had graduated so low in his Academy class during the Depression that he had originally had to join the Air Corps until such time as the Navy had the funds to rescue him.

Quickly the two selected pilots and technicians from the restive officers of their command: the outfit had been "on call" for over two years, and the young Navy pilots, longing for Pacific combat, had for months been writing the Navy Department for assignment at sea, not because they particularly disliked Smith or the science-fiction atmosphere of their work but because they felt that they were missing the war. Smith and Willy chose a pilot and copilot for each of the two mother-ship twin-engine Ventura control aircraft, already equipped with transmitters for drones, and two "control-pilots," qualified Naval aviators who had been trained to fly pilotless "babies" by remote control. They selected pilot replacements and technicians and gunners and radiomen for the mother ships. There would be no crew at all in the drone, except the experienced volunteer they expected to pick up in England at Dunkeswell and whomever he chose to fly with him. For a drone they intended to go the Air Corps one better and use a PB4Y rather than a B-17 Fortress. The Navy owned no Flying Fortresses anyway, and besides the PB4Y could carry a heavier load of explosive.

That night while 161 V-1's fell on London and while

Smith and Willy were choosing their men, a slim, blue-eyed Navy lieutenant in the Main Navy Building in Washington was ordered by Admiral Jack P. Monroe of the Navy's Bureau of Aeronautics to work on a top-secret project. The lieutenant was an armament engineer, a pilot himself and an ordnance and electronic expert. He was a Virginian named Thomas D. Martin, and the admiral wanted him to design a fail-safe system to remotely arm a plane crammed from deck to overhead with explosives. It must be safe on takeoff, safe in the air, if possible even safe should the plane inadvertently crash before arming, but once armed it must be certain to explode on impact. It occurred to Martin that his "arming panel," cleverly contrived and carefully installed, was a useless item: such a load as the Navy contemplated would have detonated on impact anyway, and to install any device to lessen its destruction from a premature crash on friendly soil was the height of optimism. But he had his orders and he went to work.

The sacrificial PB4Y was new—only five months off the Consolidated assembly line in San Diego. Its number was 32271 and on its side was painted T-11. By the time it was fitted out in Philadelphia with the control system and radio receiver which would guide it, Martin was ready with the radio circuit, solenoids, and impact fuses that would arm it. He left for England with Smith and Willy to supervise the loading. He had done it, as ordered, in fourteen days.

3

Smith, Willy, and the technicians who had flown in by transport to Dunkeswell arrived excited: most of them had never been on a wartime airfield. The two Ventura control planes and their crews were weathered in on Iceland, but the PB4Y ferry pilot made it the same night Smith arrived. The plane was put immediately under guard in a hangar, while Smith and Willy met Joe Kennedy in Reedy's office with Commander Page Knight of VB-110. Willy had never met Joe before or even heard of him, but that night when he wrote his wife he described him with the highest praise he ever gave: "Pure vanilla."

In Knight's office they told Joe that the PB4Y now

being gutted in a guarded hanger could carry twelve times the load of a V-1: a dozen tons of Torpex in crates, if properly stowed and stacked and tied down. They told him how it was intended to be fused. They explained what it could probably do successfully in unpiloted flight: climb, glide, bank, lower its flaps, dive. And they told him what it could not do unmanned: take off or land.

Reedy still did not promise him the mission; something, perhaps fear of the political consequences should anything go wrong or a feeling that Joe had done enough, perhaps reluctance to risk the life of so close a friend, seems to have delayed his decision. But Reedy and Knight asked Joe if he wanted to pick a skeleton flight crew and he said he did and to Knight he named some men he would prefer. He wanted to see the plane, so Smith and Willy took him to the guarded hangar. Knight called for the first man on Joe's list. It was Demetrios Vilan.

Dee Vilan, having flown his last mission as a combat radioman, was planning his thirty-day leave in the States. He had decided to go to New York. Chief Jack Degman, who had been given a sailing date to return too, wanted to celebrate and asked him to get a five-day leave and go to Plymouth with him to visit a girl they knew. Vilan wasn't really in the mood, but the movie on the base was dull so he went to the squadron office with a blank leave chit for Skipper Knight's signature. There was considerable activity in the offices for so late at night: Vilan, though he had been sent for and didn't know it, had to wait. Finally he was told to enter: inside he found Lieutenant C. Horton Smith and a wing administrative officer from Plymouth, Lieutenant (j.g.) Thomas Tobey. All Vilan wanted was a signature on his pass, but Knight asked him to take a seat.

"Something has come up," said the skipper, "and we need some men. We have to make up a special skeleton crew of pilot, mechanic, and radioman and I want to ask you if you are interested in volunteering." Knight told him that it would mean staying in England for another month or perhaps longer; but he added pressure, too: "You are just the type of man for the job and I am asking you first."

Vilan was startled. In two combat tours he had had his fill of antisub patrols and he told the skipper this, but Knight promised that this would have nothing to do with antisub patrols.

"Will it be interesting?" Vilan wanted to know.

"Very interesting. And dangerous, you must know that."

Vilan looked at Smith and the officer from the wing. They were staring at the floor. He decided that it sounded intriguing. "I'll take it."

Knight smiled. "Good. You might be interested to know Lieutenant Kennedy will be the PPC." Vilan inquired whether Kennedy knew that he was being asked as radioman, and Knight told him that Kennedy had requested him specifically. Two crews from other squadrons had also volunteered and there would be a meeting tomorrow to decide on the final crew selections. "Now I'll sign your leave papers." But Knight noted that the leave address Vilan had put down, a Red Cross Club, had been placed out of bounds due to the buzz bombs, and Vilan decided to stay in Dunkeswell until after the final selection. He told the squadron's chief yeoman, Reynolds, that he had volunteered for one more sortie: Reynolds thought he was foolish. He told Clyde Zappa, the squadron's leading chief; Zappa congratulated him.

Then he turned in. He decided that the mission was to bomb a submarine pen at Saint-Nazaire, or to fly to Spain to pick up some unknown crew that had been shot down. He couldn't sleep all night. The next morning he loitered near the squadron offices nervously, waiting for the meeting. He did not know it, but Joe Kennedy was inside, arguing for selection so stubbornly that Reedy actually began to suspect that for the first time since he had known him Joe was considering political pressure to get his way. Vilan saw Joe emerge suddenly, his face, "wreathed in smiles."

"When will we know?" he asked.

Whatever had gone on inside had apparently precluded further deliberations. Joe grabbed his hand and shook it: "It's all set. I was just going to send word for you." A meeting was scheduled for Commander Reedy's office in half an hour. When Vilan reported, he found squadron mate Red Bradfield, a tense and conscientious little mechanic, already there. Everyone else concerned was present too; Joe, Vilan, and Bradfield were to be transferred to the "special attack unit" now called "SAU-1" and would be stationed with the Air Corps Aphrodite project at Winfarthing-Fersfield, north of London.

The code name for the naval mission was "Anvil," no one in the planning stage having apparently been highly enough placed to realize that Anvil had been preempted as a title for the landings in southern France discussed by Churchill, Roosevelt, and Stalin at Tehran. Finally Vilan learned the plan: the mysterious PB4Y in the guarded hangar was to be loaded with Torpex and taken off; it had been rigged for remote control; once a mother plane had achieved mastery of it, its own crew would squeeze past the nose wheel—its regular exit through the after hatch having been blocked by explosives—and bail out before the aircraft reached the Channel. The rest of the drone's unpiloted flight was to be controlled by the mother planes, which would herd it across the water to a V-1 site, line it up by means of a television camera in the nose, and simply fly it into the V-1 bunker. As the meeting terminated, the men were actually sworn to secrecy.

There seemed no reason to doubt that the V-1 sites would remain long enough for the mission to take place: Eisenhower, six weeks after the landings, was still neatly pocketed in an area no farther than 120 miles from the beaches between Cherbourg and Le Havre. The Air Corps Aphrodite project might be further along, or might not: knowing the Air Corps, everyone felt confident that the Navy would be first to score. Joe took Vilan and Bradfield to look at the plane. Sure enough, she was roped off behind a twenty-four-hour-a-day sentry. While mechanics pulled a regular 120-hour check on her engines, gun turrets were being removed and replaced with broomsticks, painted black, to fool attacking fighters. Oxygen tanks, radarscope and antenna, bomb racks, even the copilot seat were lying on the hangar floor. Oak-framed plywood decks were being installed to bear the weight of the Torpex boxes. The fuselage and wings were white for better visibility from the mother plane, and a flashing-light beacon was installed at her tail. Inside was a radar beacon to show up on the control pilot's scope. A baffle to protect the crew from slipstream when they jumped was being installed forward of the nose-wheel compartment: Joe checked to see if he was too big to crawl past the nose wheel: he seemed to fit all right.

Vilan asked Joe if both he and Bradfield would be with him for takeoff and bailout. Joe grinned. "You getting frightened already?"

"No," Bradfield said, seriously. "We just want to know."

"They haven't decided," said Joe. "I may go alone, or

.they may decide another pilot is necessary, or it may be one or both of you."

"I just have to take that ride," said Vilan. He remembered the rumor that one of Charno's crewmen had panicked and pulled his rip cord prematurely and filled the compartment with silk; he was curious to see if he could bail out without losing his nerve.

In six days, by July 30, T-11 was stripped and ready for an engineering test hop. In Normandy Patton's new Third Army stormed Avranches but the drive was south, away from V-1 sites on the Channel coast; it seemed suddenly certain that no matter how the Army fared ashore, targets for T-11 would exist until she was ready. Joe picked up his two crewmen for a half-hour check flight. The aircraft, stripped to the bare fuselage, took off like a scalded tomcat; everything seemed so good that Joe decided to leave for the Army field at Fersfield that day. They picked up what personal gear they thought they would need, Joe not forgetting to bring the treasure chest of eggs he had somehow filled again, or his Raleigh English racing bike. They planned on a couple of weeks away from Dunkeswell. At two thousand feet Joe frisked the unburdened plane two hundred miles north over the Salisbury Plain and across the Thames to the gentle East Anglian hills, buzzing Oxford and Cambridge en route. Below, the fields were green and blazed with harvest gold; when they spotted the giant Army air base at Fersfield it looked sterile and ominous in contrast to the soft English countryside.

The base was enormous, vibrant. The Navy's twenty officers, sixteen men, two Venturas, and the PB4Y were lost in the flock of forty Aphrodite B-17's, their Liberator mother ships, and the men who would handle them. There were a thousand Air Corps men there and another thousand R.A.F., Czech, Pole, and Free French. Perhaps because the Allies were themselves still officially aghast at the barbarity of robot flying bombs, the place was under the tightest security that anyone had ever seen, though Italian POW's were working on a railroad track near the gate. Farmers a hundred yards from the fence today swear that a smoke screen covered every landing and takeoff: what they saw, probably, were smoke pots being tested for the visual markers on the radio-controlled glide bombs the Army was trying out. Guard dogs were everywhere with sentries. The field was zipped up tight; Vilan sensed that no one would ever get a liberty pass and wished aloud that he had brought more than three books from Dunkeswell. Joe, who had come well stocked with literature, offered to lend him some if he ran out.

Joe left the plane for more checks on the radio-control gear and moved into a Quonset in the Navy area with Ensign Jim Simpson, an owlish ex-enlisted radio-control technician. Simpson, a hard-rock Baptist, was immediately impressed with Joe's habit of kneeling to pray. It was his first exposure to a practicing Papist and really devout Catholicism. It took perhaps ten minutes for Joe's charm to break down Simpson's religious prejudices: suddenly, more than anything in the world, the careful, diminutive young ensign wanted to make the flight with him. He was not a pilot, but he knew the control gear, and he set to work to make himself even more indispensable to the mission than he already was.

CPO Vilan found that there were no CPO quarters and that he would be billeted with the Navy gunners and radiomen of the Ventura crews in a nine-man Quonset. The Navy had already generated jealousy from the surrounding Air Corps troops when the first naval outriders arrived in trucks from Dunkeswell stuffed with good soft Navy mattresses and blankets, far superior to the Army issue, apparently made of concrete and woven horsehair. To Vilan the outlook for the next few weeks seemed grim. Beer could only be had in the mess hall after dinner. It was very hot, and they had to leave the windows and doors open for ventilation, and thus they could use no lights or even smoke in the Quonset after dark, so strict was the blackout.

Joe had a tour through one of the two PV-1 Venturas that would act as his mother ships. His primary control pilot would be Lieutenant (j.g.) John Anderson, a tall, gangling naval aviator with an intense interest in radio control and electronics. Anderson would squeeze himself behind a console aft of the pilot, facing a radarscope and a television screen which would show the picture of the terrain directly ahead of Joe's plane. On Anderson's console was an odd array of space-age switches and phone dials centered around a chrome lever that looked like an oversized pen with a button on top stuck into a desk-set socket. This was the "peter-stick"; control pilots were "peter-pilots" and the essence of their skill was in flying another plane while sitting in this one. The peter-stick acted like a joystick; to bank to the right you tapped gentle right aileron into it, and when the drone had finished its turn, you pushed the button on top and its wings returned to level flight. Using it was not easy, for there was of course no feel to the stick and none of the seat-of-the-pants pressure that a pilot learns to trust. Next to the peter-stick were two phone dials; instead of numbers you dialed the operations you wanted the drone to perform in unmanned flight: "flaps down," "cowl flaps open," "carburetor heat on." Beneath the dials were ominous red toggle switches, safetied with wire: "Destruct" and "Arm." Forward, for visual control by the copilot, was a similar setup. The whole thing was fascinating. Joe had never seen a television screen except at the New York World's Fair, and that one was only a few inches on a side: this was a full eight inches wide. The idea of radio control still smacked of model airplanes and owlish teen-agers in public parks; here it was, full-sized and sophisticated, the subject of attention of perfectly serious adults who had advanced it so far that, once the problems of takeoff and landing were solved, it seemed that there would be no need for a pilot in the drone at all.

On August 2, three days after its arrival at Dunkeswell, T-11 had its radio-control gear checked out and was ready for her first test flight with a full load. She had already been static-tested in her chocks to see that her landing gear would not collapse under a load half again as large as that she intended to carry; now 25,000 pounds of sandbags were stowed in the same position that the boxes of Torpex would occupy. Simpson, Willy, and four other experts checked out the radio-control gear on the ground: then all squeezed in to make the flight. Joe found that with twelve tons of sand aboard T-11 had suddenly lost her friskiness: she wallowed into the air like an engorged pelican and landed like a freight train.

Six weeks after the first V-1 had streaked across the Straits of Dover, T-11 began flights under radio control to accustom Joe to the jerky robot motion of an airplane flown by someone outside the craft. First Joe trimmed the plane, and then with Simpson's help went through the involved procedure of "putting in the gear." When autopilot and radio were warmed up and the plane trimmed to fly "hands-off," Joe passed the code word "Spade Flush" to Anderson, took his hands from the control yoke and his feet from the rudders. All at once he was not flying the plane anymore, Anderson was, and T-11 began to act like a spastic sea gull. Joe's temptation time and again must have been to grab the yoke and take over himself: turns were hesitant, incremental, more mechanical than the poorest student on his first flight. But Simpson assured him that it was all normal and that he would get used to it. An exception to the jerkiness came when Anderson shifted altitude control to the radio altimeter and eased Joe down to three hundred feet: then the plane wallowed smoothly, following the rolling East Anglian hills below; the only trouble was that it reacted to a slope ahead much more slowly than Joe would have. It took a steady man and deep faith in his equipment, approaching a towering rise, not to take over manually and jerk the nose over the peak.

They flew for hours every day, engaging and disengaging the radio-control gear; Joe and his Dunkeswell crew began to get the impression that the technicians were more interested in testing the radio-control and altitude-sensing features than they were in blasting the final target. Jim Simpson, who flew every time he could with the idea of making himself a permanent fixture, spent eleven flight hours in the drone; when it was decided that the final attack would be made at low level, the two roller-coastered with a load of sand all one morning over the countryside and offshore waters on the radio altimeter: three hundred feet over land and fifty feet over the waves.

Despite the delay that had ensued when the control planes were weathered in Iceland, they were still trying to beat the Air Force to the first flight. On August 3, with the PB4Y ready and the weather foggy, there was little to do. An Army company of Negro soldiers arrived to handle the Air Corps dynamite and Navy Torpex and load it into the planes. Joe Kennedy wandered restlessly around the office spaces assigned the little Navy unit, and when Dee Vilan lent him Santayana's *People and Things,* he told Vilan that he had met Santayana at Harvard. Vilan, who had finished *Appointment in Samara* and even a travel book, complained to Joe that he was out of reading material and Joe drove him to his quarters and gave him Belleman's *Floods of Spring.*

They took another practice hop later that day when the weather turned hot and sunny; everything worked perfectly. Vilan had been nicked lightly on his face when a small battery wire in the radio gear had snapped back and flicked him a few days before; for some reason the scratch started a skin irritation that spread rapidly; shaving became difficult in the cold water at the latrine and the Air Corps doctor at the base hospital told him that he had lead poisoning and gave him a salve. He also told him that his resistance was low from too much flying: "As tensions build up resistance lowers and even a simple scratch can trigger off a series of complications."

Tension had built up with Joe, too. Patton's Third Army seemed headed safely south, but there was ominous activity at the Air Corps line: Aphrodite seemed as ready as they and a rumor began that they were loading. The next day his practice hop was canceled for no reason that he knew; Vilan and Bradfield were already at the plane, and when he drove out to tell them, he seemed to Vilan to be angry and edgy. Vilan had decided that it wasn't easy to know what was going on in his pilot's mind, that Joe was impulsive and a little erratic. He was sure that he had a temper, but felt that he kept it admirably under control. He knew that Joe was an impatient man: he had once lost his poise when his plane wasn't ready for a hop. "If I hadn't known him I would have thought he was a petulant, spoiled brat. He refused to accept any excuses . . . and then it was over. One of his commendable qualities is his capacity to dismiss an incident once he has made his point. He holds no grudges. Relationships resume as though nothing has happened."

The next day, Friday, August 4, the pace picked up. A hurried meeting called by Commander Smith was suddenly canceled, and there was a great gathering of jeeps and brass around the B-17 tie-down area. The Army base commander, a handsome Texan colonel named Roy Forrest, had punctured the Navy's dream of being first by loading four B-17 Aphrodite "baby ships" during the night. As the whole field watched, the battle-scarred veterans rumbled down the runway and lurched aloft: it seemed to Joe and Vilan that they took the whole length of the strip to make it, and the rumor was that if any one of them crashed the explosion would devastate the countryside. The lethal range was estimated to be seven miles. They were followed on takeoff by their B-24 mother planes and a squadron of P-38's for fighter cover.

Joe retired to the unit's office to await the results. There is no way of guessing what he expected to hear, but they must have exceeded his wildest pessimism.

5

FOUR B-17 Flying Forts, nicknamed "Snowbirds" because their upper wings and fuselage were painted white
to be better visible to their controllers, staggered into the
air that afternoon, their load so great that their undercar-
riages had had to be strengthened. Each was assigned a
V-1 target near Calais: at Siracourt, Watten, Wizernes,
and Mimoyecques. Each was packed with ten tons of
RDX, not as heavy a load as the Navy contemplated nor
as potent a charge, but powerful enough if properly
placed to knock out a V-1 site or any other weapon
emplaced by man. Each Snowbird was flown by a first
lieutenant with an enlisted "automatic-flight-control" engineer as crew. The radio-control system of each was roughly similar to Joe's, but the first one carried no TV in the
nose and all used manual arming rather than the Navy's
last-minute, remote-controlled radio signal that was to
arm Joe's plane once it was safely over the Channel. The
Army's system was simple. In order to arm his flying
bomb the pilot, once control had been passed to the
mother ship and his technician had bailed out, would set an
ordinary darkroom timer on his panel to be sure that he
didn't dawdle. He would crawl to a tumbler switch from
which he would remove a pin. Then he would pull a cable
which yanked other pins from fourteen spring-loaded impact fuses. Now any sudden jolt would detonate the plane.
Finally, he would attach a static line from his back chute

to a ringbolt near the hatch and bail out. He wore a chest pack for emergencies.

Lieutenant Fain Pool, the first to take off, transferred control to his mother ship, sent his technician out the hatch, set his timer for one minute, braced a foot on a bulkhead, yanked his arming cable, clipped his static line to the ring, and jumped. Forty-five seconds later, having missed a high-tension tower by ten feet, he was on the ground under the power lines. As he was struggling out of his harness, he heard a monumental explosion nearby; it was Lieutenant J. W. Fisher, who had taken off behind him. Fisher, unable to transfer control, had got his crewman safely out and then rolled and crashed before he could leave the plane. The British picked up Pool, who lied and told them that he had bailed out because his plane had caught fire. Frank Houston, next in line, took off with Sergeant Smith, a big man whose static line so weakened the ringbolt that when Houston followed him the ring tore loose and his chute failed to open. Houston, tumbling end over end, glimpsed the static line following him, suddenly knew, yanked at his chest chute and found himself hanging from a tree. "I was stiff and sore, a little black and blue. The ends of my fingers on my right hand had been cut with something very sharp and I had what appeared to be a rope burn along the right side of my neck. But outside of needing clean underwear I was in pretty good shape." The last pilot to go that day was C. A. Engel. His backpack failed; he popped his chest chute, took one swing, and struck the ground so hard that he broke his back and knocked four teeth down his throat. All the aircraft were lost: Pool's when it exploded off the coast of France, Fisher's of course when it crashed, and Houston's and Engel's when they were shot down short of their target.

The next night German planes circled Fersfield and finally bombed it, missing it by six miles. At the officers' club Frank Houston, celebrating his escape reward—a whole mission's credit without even being shot at— massaged his stiff fingers, glanced at his bandaged hand, and said to Joe Kennedy thoughtfully, "If my Old Man was an ambassador, I'd get my ass transferred out of this outfit." Joe only smiled but the next day he and Ensign John Demlein, the control pilot of the secondary mother plane, got a special pass and along with Lieutenant (j.g.) Harry Fitzpatrick, copilot of Demlein's control plane, cycled to Mass. It was a hot August day and on the way back to the base they lay down to rest in the shade of a hedgerow.

"Jeez," Joe said suddenly, "I just wonder about this damn mission—"

Demlein, a feisty Long Islander, believed that trailing Joe's empty drone over a hostile coastline was just as risky as Joe's part in the mission. He also believed, like everyone else in the special attack unit, that Joe was planning to marry a titled English girl when the job was over.

"What the hell," he said, to raise Joe's spirits, "there's nothing to it. I'd rather have *your* place than ours. You're going to bail out and in a couple of weeks you're going to get married and be off on your honeymoon. Everything's going to be great guns for you and *we* got to go over there—"

"Yeah," Joe said quickly, "I guess you're right."

Joe and Vilan flew another three-hour practice hop that Sunday afternoon, with Lieutenant Willy, Ensign Simpson, and four officer specialists along. Competition for the honor of acting as Joe's crewman was getting hotter. As they landed, Bud Willy said to Joe, "Well, this should do. We're ready when they are."

Willy and Commander Smith had decided, after conferences with Tom Martin, the ordnance expert, to put one more safety device into the arming circuit. It was to be a metal pin, inserted into a plywood panel behind the pilot. It would mechanically prevent runway vibration from cocking the arming solenoid on takeoff, but there was another, more esoteric reason for the pin. In test flights over Philadelphia, the arming system had three times mistakenly cocked itself, triggered by stray radio signals or static. It had not happened here in England, but it seemed wise at this last moment to provide a positive safety device. The receiver had been designed to react to a signal on one of two FM frequencies, for more positive arming, and might inadvertently pick up the proper key from a plane, tank, or one of the British jamming stations trying twenty-four hours a day to confuse German radar or the dreaded V-2 rockets, due any night and thought to be radio-controlled. Stray signals had seemed such a threat to Anvil that an electronic search for them had been conducted only today at Commander Smith's insistence; sure enough, they were there, and though none was closer than

.5 megacycle to the arming frequency, it would do no harm to put in the pin to be sure.

No one gave much thought to the fact that the contemplated safety pin would also restrain a switch intended to open immediately after the radio signal sent battery current to cock the arming solenoid. The switch was to make certain that the flow, having cocked the system, would be cut off almost instantly, before the solenoid could overheat. Martin, who wanted to make the flight too, saw no objection to the pin as an additional safety factor and agreed. Joe's roommate Simpson had reservations about last-minute field modifications but drilled the hole for the pin as instructed. To the pin was attached an ordinary rip cord and parachute handle; it would be yanked by the copilot prior to bailout.

Who the copilot would be was still in issue. Bud Willy had come to the logical conclusion that the greatest safety device he could offer was his own long experience in the air as a pilot and control technician. Martin was a pilot too, but he was an outsider and no one expected trouble with his arming circuit anyway; it seemed after all the *control* of the aircraft that had killed Fisher and given problems to the other three Army planes. The brotherhood of the golden-winged made it easy to believe that Bud Willy as a rated flier would be of more assistance in an emergency than Simpson, Vilan, or Bradfield. Besides, he was senior to any of them and it is doubtful that from the moment he volunteered as copilot that Joe could have picked anyone else if he had wanted to.

Walking in from the plane, Vilan suddenly sensed that he had been outranked by the competition, and asked Joe directly if it had been decided who would fly with him. Joe broke the news: "Lieutenant Willy." When Vilan reacted angrily, Joe sympathized but said there was nothing he could do but follow instructions. By the time Reedy, up from Dunkeswell, asked Vilan whether he was getting a kick out of the project, he was able to swallow his disappointment and say yes.

The Army sent its fifth and sixth Snowbirds aloft that evening against the V-1 sites near Calais. The first pilot, Lieutenant John Sollars, got out of his drone but his arm was so badly torn that it was going to have to be amputated: his plane was dumped into the Channel as unmanageable. Lieutenant Joe Andrecheck, who took off after him, escaped unscathed, but his plane flipped to its back and exploded.

The Army bailout technique was to rush: the idea was to get out quickly, before anything happened, often in sight of the field. There had been so many parachutists drifting down on the nearby meadows that Cyril Hoskins, who had seen three land near his house on Fersfield Road, quit counting them.

If all went as the Navy planned, he would apparently not see Joe Kennedy's or Bud Willy's. At a briefing that night it was decided that they would stay with their drone on a long pattern, first north and then south, and not bail out until the plane had almost reached Dover. The north-ward legs were presumably to make sure that control of T-11 was firmly established, checked, and double-checked before the group turned south, but the long delay as the plane flew south remains an enigma. Lieutenant Rosy Lyon, the ruddy-faced commander of Anderson's primary control plane, protested: he saw no reason why Joe and Bud Willy should ride a plane full of Torpex across Nor-folk, Suffolk, Essex, and the North Downes for forty-five minutes when they could bail out in ten near Fersfield itself. He was overruled. Willy himself had apparently planned the long delay to give Anderson and Demlein plenty of time to achieve control; Commander Smith had approved it. At least the plane would be safely manned when it passed London, fifty miles to starboard off its final overland leg.

A rumor in the unit that Joe planned to parachute to a tryst with his sister Kathleen or the girl he loved in the south was so amusing and dramatic that Joe probably encouraged it, not pointing out that the mission was so secret that he himself did not yet know the name of the ultimate target, that Kathleen was in Hyannis, and that the only girl he cared about was visiting Virginia Sykes in Yorkshire 120 miles in the opposite direction. As they left the briefing, he handed John Demlein the Army parachute knife he had been issued to cut himself free if his shrouds became tangled. "You take this. I won't need it."

"You better keep it," warned Demlein. "Christ, *I* won't need it."

"No," insisted Joe. "If anything happens I've got my own little knife. If I get stuck in the chute I know how to work that better than this knife."

The next day nothing happened: weather. A Catalina

amphibious plane from Dunkeswell brought up mail for Joe, Vilan, and Bradfield. Joe, whose twenty-ninth birthday was only three weeks past, received enough delayed overseas packages to keep him busy all day. Vilan found that most of his own London friends had left the city to get away from the buzz bombs; his London bookstore, though, had sent him *The Razor's Edge.* Joe saw it and said that he was a friend and admirer of Maugham, had read everything he had written, and had been waiting anxiously for his latest book. Vilan offered it to him, but Joe refused it until he himself finished reading it. Joe, who had been scrounging coal from a guarded coal pile to cook eggs on his stove with Simpson, got caught that night by the sentry, and was unpopular for a few hours with Commander Smith, who had to rescue him from the MP's.

The following day he took another practice hop, accompanied by the usual horde of officer technicians; when they landed he seemed to Vilan to be in a "jolly and communicative mood." After landing he turned over the aircraft to the Negro Army armament crew to have the sandbags removed and replaced by Torpex. In the ordnance shack some of the officers began to tease him about bailing out. He took it good-naturedly. Horseplay started between him, Tom Martin, and Anderson, his control pilot, but Vilan sensed that Joe was uneasy and noticed that as he scuffled he kept humming a little tune. When the others left the ordnance shack, Vilan began to follow them; but Joe, who had begun to check the weight and balance of the aircraft with a slide rule, put it down and seemed to want to talk. He said he had heard that Vilan was a writer and asked what he did before the war. Vilan told him his secret: he had acted on the stage and designed theatrical sets. He had left the awful truth off his questionnaires when he joined the Navy, not wishing to be thrown into a USO troop. Joe promised not to tell and told him of his father's investment in Gloria Swanson's career. Vilan, who knew that her Kennedy-backed film, *Queen Kelly,* had never been released, mentioned it mischievously. Joe said, "We don't talk about that one. My father has a million dollars invested in it and all a total loss." Not mentioning the fact that his father had protected the investment by liens on subsequent films, he blamed Eric von Stroheim for the fiasco.

That afternoon and all night long Lieutenant Tom Martin supervised the troops loading the aircraft. He had done some research and discovered that the Army had once exploded five tons of TNT in the ground for test purposes: he was loading more than twice that amount of an explosive almost twice as powerful. He carefully inspected and selected those boxes of Torpex to be used; some which looked battered he rejected on sight. There were 374 boxes, each weighing sixty-three pounds and containing fifty-five pounds of Torpex. There were six 113-pound demolition charges of TNT as well. All were stowed and secured to the frames and bulkheads of the aircraft by quarter-inch steel cable; then they were shored with four-by-four-inch pine timbers. He and the troops worked for ten hours. When nothing could budge, Martin installed the arming circuit. He suspended all electrical leads to the overhead with cord. To prevent grounding, he twisted the wires carefully. When he was through, it was impossible to crawl from one end of the plane to the other.

The next day the fog drifted in and scrubbed the mission. Joe had heard on morning B.B.C. that Patton, having taken Nantes the day before, had left his 7th Corps to handle the Breton ports to the south, then actually wheeled north, and suddenly had a tank column heading toward Le Mans. If he made contact with Bradley, trapping von Kluge with a hundred thousand troops, the German-held channel coast to the north might collapse overnight. The flamboyant American general had a long way to go to any known V-1 site, but suppose the fog persisted, keeping T-11 grounded? Perhaps to keep busy, Joe wrote Mark Soden, bragging about his soft life here. "You will be happy to know that I have volunteered you for the next mission." Then he went to the meteorological hut to keep an eye on the weather.

Vilan strolled out to Lieutenant Martin at the loaded plane and Martin said, "I heard you're a playwright. You should have been out at the plane this morning. You could have written a play about it." He told him that one of the Negro troops had dropped a box of Torpex five feet without its blowing up. He estimated that the plane was already loaded with what was probably the largest explosive charge ever put together. He asked Vilan to help him check the amperage of a fuse needed in the arming system and the two worked until Commander Sunshine Reedy arrived again from Dunkeswell for the launching. They told Sunshine that the mission was canceled; everyone was disconsolate; they wanted to get the mission over with successfully before the Army scored.

That night in the enlisted mess Vilan was seated at a table when a group of the Negro ammo-handlers lined up. "The room immediately became charged with hatred," Vilan wrote in his diary. "A certain element, many southerners and just as many northerners, resented being under the same roof as the black boys. Insults and audible insinuations buzzed in the acoustically perfect mess hall. I was embarrassed and infuriated. One of the boys across from me commented that our 'Nigras' were being spoiled by the English girls. 'Next thing you know,' his companion added, 'they'll be trying to date white girls back home after the war.' "

Vilan, disgusted, left his meal uneaten. Having finished *The Razor's Edge,* he took it to Joe's quarters. Guilty at not having taken a stand in the mess hall, he mentioned the hatred he had sensed. Joe was quiet for a while and then, with a faraway look in his eyes, he said, "There are going to be a lot of changes when this is all over."

Vilan asked if the hop was definitely scheduled for the next day. Joe said that if the fog and overcast burned off over the Channel it was pretty definite and then cycled away to meet Willy for what he hoped would be their last evening weather briefing: the next meeting would be a final one on the target itself.

When the briefing was over he pedaled to his plane, golden in the late summer sun, and talked for a while with Bradfield. He returned to his Quonset, called the girl at Wetwang, and took some eggs from the treasure chest. He scrambled them for Simpson and himself with the coal he had filched from the coal pile. Simpson was still hurt that he had not been picked to make the flight but thanked him for the eggs. They listened to the B.B.C. for a while. Patton's column had left Le Mans and fought its way north toward Alençon, only thirty-three miles from American troops at Falaise. The trap was closing on von Kluge and now, it seemed, there were not a hundred thousand Germans ensnared but perhaps a half million.

It was time to turn in. Simpson noticed as always that before Joe climbed in his bunk, he knelt to pray.

6

DURING August in East Anglia the southeastern horizon begins faintly to brighten by 3:30 A.M. Outside Joe's hut cocks were crowing and the sun was rising by quarter to five. The blackout curtains kept out the light, but neither Kennedy nor Simpson slept much past dawn. At the door they noticed that despite yesterday's forecast low-bellied clouds still lay over the field, slanting to meet the plains to the east and probably kissing the Suffolk coast. There was ankle-high ground fog. A southwesterly breeze was already wafting in the moist pig-smell of the farms beyond the fence, but it was so faint a wind that they knew there would be hardly a ripple on the Channel. They shaved in the latrine and returned to the hut. They noticed the remnants of last night's snack in the frying pan. Although there were still fresh eggs in the famous casket, they went to the officer's mess rather than clean it up.

By breakfast Fersfield Airdrome was well awake. Everyone knew that the Navy was next, and that Joe might go today. The line at the steam table was uneasy and too cheerful. Air Corps pilots would glance furtively at Joe and Willy and then look away, and they were watching the pilots of the Venturas and their control pilots too. While Joe might be said to be a combat veteran, the other Navy fliers were brand new to the theater. Tailing Joe's plane after he had left it, across the Channel to the French coast and over enemy Pas-de-Calais, was no light

240

matter for men who had never seen the flash of an earnest AA gun or felt the jolt of a shellburst ahead; it would be the first combat that Rosy Lyon, husky, blond Lieutenant Harry Wherry, the other mother-ship pilot, or any of their crews had ever seen.

Leaving the mess, Simpson, Willy, and Joe Kennedy heard a distant auxiliary-power unit begin to mutter excitedly, building up a charge. A starter whirred and they heard the early-morning cough of a Pratt & Whitney engine. Red Bradfield, alone in the cockpit of the quarantined drone, was beginning T-11's preflight. The ground fog cleared and they could suddenly see fissures in the base of the marble clouds. The tempo rose. Radioman Dee Vilan, returning to the Navy area after breakfast, was in his hut with the Ventura crewmen when Lieutenant Lyon arrived in a jeep and told them that they were due for a last briefing at 1500. The six radiomen and mechanics who would man the guns began to ready their combat gear, and Vilan noticed great nervousness under a veneer of bravado. He walked a half mile to the drone, nodded at the sentry, ducked his head against the blast from Bradfield's thrashing props, and crawled into the nose-wheel compartment since there was no longer any way through the bomb bay jammed with Torpex. He checked the radio gear while Bradfield switched the number-three engine magneto from "both" to "right" to "left" and tried to get the engine to hold a reasonable rpm. A 150-rpm drop was permissible, but England was damp and magnetos always suffered and some plane captains, impatient with the recurring problem, cheated a little and signed off a plane with a 200-rpm drop or even a little more.

Today was not the day for cheating. Bradfield eased back the mixture controls and the engines coughed and died. In the sudden silence, broken only by the hum of an alternator and the idle headsets keening with Vilan's high pitched test signals, he took a fire extinguisher and crawled out through the overhead cockpit hatch. Straddling number-three engine, he unfastened the cowling and shot a cloud of carbon dioxide at the mag. He buttoned up the cowling and snaked back in. He sat in the sole remaining cockpit seat, started the engines, rotated the mag switch once more. Now the drop was around 100 rpm's. The Air Corps trick had apparently worked again. He filled in the yellow sheet and took it to the line shack.

Vilan finished his radio check, flicked off the plane's

master switch, and walked to the Navy's office. Joe was
there, grinning. "This is it," he announced happily. Something had been bothering Vilan: he had been excluded
from briefings since Willy had been picked, but he knew
that Kennedy and Willy were to bail out near the coast:
What precautions were being taken if they blew into the
Channel? Joe shrugged and changed the subject, "We're
going to get a forty-eight after this is over. How are you
going to spend it?"

Vilan fingered the ugly sores on his face. He told Joe
that he was going back to Dunkeswell after the flight to
check into sick bay and see what could be done with
them. Joe said, "I'll have you and Bradfield flown back in
the Catalina." Vilan thanked him and asked what his own
postflight plans were. Joe, not mentioning the fact that he
was due tomorrow at Lady Sykes' estate, said that he was
going to London to see some friends. Vilan, who months
before had chatted over coffee about Joe with Kathleen at
the Hans Crescent Red Cross Club, asked him to give his
best to his sister, but Joe said she had flown back to the
States.

At 10:30 a new weather forecast was delivered to the
Navy office. It looked promising at the mysterious target
and Commander Smith put the combat crews on four-
hour notice.

Perhaps Joe's support of Kick had strained relations
with his father, or perhaps it was simply an impulse, but
at this last moment he decided to send a message home in
the only way he could. He put in a call to Lorelle Hearst at
her apartment in London's Claridge: "I'm about to go
into my act. If I don't come back, tell my dad—despite
our differences—that I love him very much." At 1400—2
P.M.—the mission was definitely on, and even before the
scheduled briefing at three the crews were straggling into
the briefing shack.

The hut was crowded. Wherry and Lyon's Venturas
each carried a crew of six, including Wherry's drone control pilot Demlein and Lyon's control pilot Anderson.
Most of the navigators and pilots of the accompanying
armada were here, too. A B-17 navigation plane would
guide the task force to the bailout point. Another Fortress
would scout the target area, carrying Joe's roommate, Jim
Simpson; Commander Smith would cram himself into the
forward greenhouse of a modified P-38 Lightning flown
by the base commander, Colonel Roy Forrest, and go too.

One of Colonel Elliott Roosevelt's movie crews would provide coverage of the takeoff from the ground, and the President's son, flying his Mosquito photo plane, proposed to rendezvous on the drone in the air to photograph the bailout. There were sixteen P-51 Mustangs to provide fighter cover above.

The flight plan was minutely explained by Colonel Forrest as Joe took notes on a leg pad clamped to his knee. After takeoff, he would turn and climb to reach 2,000 feet over Framlingham, twenty-three minutes southeast. Meanwhile, Anderson, in Lyon's primary mother plane, would begin to establish control. At Framlingham the drone, with Anderson in control by now and Joe a mere passenger, would proceed northeast away from the target for another twenty minutes to Beccles, checking everything, and then finally turn south for the departure point far down the British coast. Flying over the Thames estuary toward the bailout point, Willy would inspect the arming circuit with a safety lamp. If the circuit was safe, he would make an electrical connection to the arming solenoids; then he would remove the new safety pin behind Joe.

If all went well by the time they passed the Thames Willy would bail out through the nose wheel, at Point X-ray near Manston Field north of Dover, followed by Joe, who would finish the next-to-last arming step by pulling the manual arming wire as he went. He would retain it in his hand as he parachuted, to prove that this part of the arming process had been completed. The plane would not be fully armed yet. After turning it east across the Channel toward France, Anderson in the primary mother plane, using both hands, would flick the "arm" switch, sending out the FM signal which would actuate solenoids in the belly of T-11, finally and completely readying her to explode instantaneously on impact.

The "dumping bill" was explained. If it was impossible during the long triangular flight over East Anglia and Kent to transfer control from Joe to Anderson or alternatively to Demlein, Joe would place the plane on an autopilot heading toward the North Sea and follow Willy out the hatch over dry land. Over water, Anderson could "destruct" if it went wild. Since it would not be armed until after control was established and the pilots had left, the theory was that it was no more dangerous than any other aircraft should it circle and crash in England, although the

experience of poor Fisher's Snowbird, which had practically blasted nude a Suffolk wood, was not encouraging.

But no one expected Anderson to have trouble getting
control. Joe's code word to indicate that Anderson was
now flying the drone was the usual "Spade Flush." After
Joe and Bud Willy parachuted from the drone before
Elliott Roosevelt's cameras, their landings would be
spotted by one of the B-17's, which would set down at
Manston Field to pick them up before anyone asked too
many questions about why they had abandoned a flyable
aircraft so near the London area. Tagging three miles
astern of the drone, navigating it with the copilot's visual
help and by the pip of its radar beacon on his scope,
Anderson would gently dive it to seven hundred feet over
the Channel, keeping below the German radar horizon. At
that point the primary control plane, being closest to the
drone and the coast, would presumably be drawing fire, so
Anderson, having lined up T-11 as a carpenter taps in a
nail to start it, would shift control to Demlein in the
Ventura tagging aft for the final run while Lyon, flying
Anderson's control plane, would turn tail and flee the
coastline.

A map on a stand was uncovered and the target finally
divulged: the V-1 site closest of all to England, at Mimoyecques. It had been assigned an Air Corps plane—
perhaps Fisher's—on that first discouraging day. To look
at it made Demlein wonder if Fisher's controller ever
would have found it anyway. Even on the large-scale
Army artillery map it seemed impossible to spot, especially by its image on a 1944 television screen through a
camera bouncing in coastal thermals and German flak. It
lay seven miles inland, (see map in insert) eight miles
southwest of Calais, and consisted of five farmhouses and
a little tower at the intersection of two dirt roads. It was
completely indistinguishable from the other tiny villages
nestling in the modest hills of Pas-de-Calais. It was so small
a village—less than fifty inhabitants—that its population
was not even shown on the map. It lay just two miles from
the Calais-Boulogne road along which Joe had driven with
Kick five years before.

It looked as if it might be difficult even to find the
town, much less the site that had been spewing out V-1's.
On close study, though, there were clues. Demlein, who
would take control from Anderson as the primary control
plane turned tail and fled, was told to guide the drone

across the shoreline over the resort of Wissant—population 900—halfway between Cap Gris Nez and Cap Blanc Nez. The trouble was that Cap Blanc Nez from the air appeared to be not a cape at all, but simply a curve on a straight beach. If Demlein spotted Wissant and if he and the drone survived coastal flak, he was to steer T-11 on course 120° past a hill named Mont Couple, rising in Gallic grandeur just 489 feet above the surrounding terrain. Dead ahead, three miles past his target, should rest the dark-green mass of the Forêt de Guines; it might make a good landmark to steer for until he could pick up the tiny cluster of stone buildings and two orchards that constituted the whole of Mimoyecques; at least, if he found the drone flying over the woods, he would know that he had guided it too far.

Colonel Roosevelt's photos were passed around. Now the launch site could be seen: a huge concrete bunker sunk in a grassy hill with the turf replanted above it and steel doors thirty feet high opening on short railroad tracks aligned viciously on the precise heading of London. As the drone passed Mont Couple, Demlein would drop her nose toward Mimoyecques, picking up the image of the bunker as T-11 dove and flying her directly at the steel doors growing larger and larger in the lens of her television camera until his TV tube went blank. The prevailing conviction was that he would fly her straight into the doors of the rocket pen, shearing each of her wings between its inboard and outboard engines: the concussion should break windows from Calais to Boulogne and shiver Wehrmacht beer steins in Dunkirk.

The drone would be aloft one hour. It must reach the target at 1900—7 P.M.—when the setting sun would be almost exactly astern, illuminating the bunker for its TV camera and blinding the enemy gunners. Of the one-hour hop, only fifteen minutes would be over the Channel or occupied France. Joe and Willy would be with the plane during three quarters of its flight.

Leaving the briefing room, Demlein did one of the things that people do when they are emotionally stirred—and regret later. Trying to relax the tension, he blurted to Joe, "You got your insurance all paid up?"

Joe flashed his grin. "I've got twice as much as I need. I don't need it and nobody *connected* with me needs it." They shook hands and he said, "I won't say I'll see you, but so long."

Commander Smith, who had taken one of Elliott Roosevelt's prints and squeezed into Colonel Forrest's Lightning for a quick view of the target, returned at 1700, unscathed and jubilant: the target was there, all right, the weather was good, the flak not excessive. Anvil was ready to drop.

2

Neither Project Aphrodite nor its more sophisticated naval cousin Anvil had been at Fersfield more than six weeks, but a tradition had started with the six prior Air Corps flights. When a baby was ready to roll, everyone turned out: not only mechs and armorers and pilots, but clerks and butchers and cooks. By 5 P.M. they were emerging from offices, Quonsets, hangars, and kitchens, some even mingling with the brass on the railed-in roof of the two-story concrete operations tower, others sitting on the tail gates of trucks or the hoods of jeeps. There were aircraft engines starting everywhere as the escort readied itself, and the scent of the nearby fields was drowned in the smell of exhaust.

In T-11, Vilan reset Joe's voice transmitter on the frequencies selected. He left the plane, but Ensign Jim Simpson remained inside, checking the radio-control gear for the last time. Red Bradfield minutely inspected the exterior of the aircraft from bow to stern. All three of the men had expected at one time or another to be chosen to make the flight: each still felt that he had been unfairly outranked by Bud Willy, but they did their best to hide it. Kennedy and Willy arrived by jeep, shook hands with Commander Smith, and awkwardly circled the aircraft, embarrassed by the attention but preflighting it anyway. They carried their emergency chutes: Joe's primary chute was in the drone's seat, and Willy's was stowed in the nose near the last remaining exit. Willy carried a typewritten check-list for the control-shifting procedure.

Vilan and Bradfield shook hands with them and wished them luck. Red Bradfield again mentioned the number-three mag: Joe nodded. With Simpson still in the aircraft, Kennedy and Willy crawled through the nose-wheel compartment. Joe took his seat while Willy stood at his right. Vilan, on the ground, could see Willy reading the pre-start checklist and Joe's shoulders moving as his hands flicked about the cockpit. Crewmen with fire extinguishers stood by outside. Red Bradfield, stationed off the aircraft's port bow where Joe could see him, glanced about to see that the props were clear and finally raised his right thumb. The number-three starter motor began with a growl, rose to a wail, and the starboard inboard prop began slowly to move. Soon it was laboring ponderously and Joe engaged it. The engine coughed once. A frightening tongue of flame and a puff of black smoke flew aft; then the engine settled down into a throaty roar. Number-four engine started, number two, and finally number one. Joe jerked his thumbs to port and starboard and two Navy ground crewmen dashed under the wings, yanked loose the chocks, and dragged them aside. Bradfield held out his right fist and beckoned with his left forefinger. The starboard outboard engine drummed louder, and slowly, brakes squeaking, T-11 turned. Bradfield pointed down the taxiway and flicked a salute, and the huge aircraft, bobbing and squealing, glided along the perimeter to the end of the runway. Here the two Navy Venturas, Colonel Roosevelt's photo Mosquito, the P-38 Lightnings, the two B-17 Fortresses, and the Mustang fighters ticked patiently. The Venturas went first. Airborne, Lyon began to circle the field at 1,000 feet while Anderson, at the console behind him, "put in the gear," checking out the entire radio-control system with Simpson, who was still in the drone on the ground, and Kennedy. Anderson tapped his little stick forward and heard Kennedy on the ground report: "Down elevator." He tapped it to the right and Kennedy said: "Right aileron." When rudder, aileron, and elevator were all shown to be slavishly following the signals from the plane in the air, control was disengaged and returned to Joe.

The final ground test had been necessary: if the drone had not been checked out, Joe and Willy might have risked their lives on takeoff to find themselves in an explosive-laden aircraft which they could not in good conscience leave over friendly soil. Now Jim Simpson's job, after years of preparation and frantic weeks of work, was done. He shook hands with Bud Willy, who was squatting at Joe's right shoulder, and with Joe: "I wish I were going along with you."

Kennedy knew Simpson was disappointed. "You'll make

the next one," he said. "And if I don't come back you can have the rest of my eggs."

Simpson left the plane and went to the B-17 which was to cross the Channel to observe. The Mustangs began to snarl into the sky, in threes. Vilan, in a jeep with Red Bradfield, watched while Joe, brakes locked, eased the throttles forward for the mag check. As each engine tested its strength, the roar would drum at Vilan's ears unbearably; then finally, Joe would throttle that engine back and the next would take over. The props splintered late-afternoon shards of sunlight into his eyes: each prop tip threshed its own ring of moisture from the damp English air.

Number-one engine checked out, and number two. Number three, although it sounded all right to Vilan, seemed to make Bradfield nervous: Vilan thought he was sweating more than normally and noticed that he was squeezing his fingers through his cupped hands. "It's a good thing you're not in that plane," Vilan shouted over the sound. Bradfield looked at him as if hurt and ran toward the aircraft. Joe throttled back and motioned him into the cockpit. Bradfield crawled in and they ran it up again. This time it was all right, and Bradfield nodded and left the plane, which waddled suddenly to the takeoff position at the head of the runway. Colonel Roosevelt's movieman knelt at the side of the concrete strip, shooting everything. Again the engines blasted, each in turn, as Kennedy checked them once more and again once more. Finally, after seven full minutes, he poured on full power but leashed it with the brakes as the aircraft strained to be free. The hood of the jeep shivered and danced in the noise. When it seemed to Vilan that his ears could stand it no longer, T-11 began to move. It started so slowly that it seemed impossible that Joe actually intended to take off on this run, but the plane persisted, ducking its nose doggedly and thundering faster and faster toward the end of the concrete and the rutted meadowland beyond. The nose wheel clung to the ground, until finally at the very last instant it rose, and then the main wheels were off too, spinning in the sunlight until Joe tapped the brakes and stopped them. T-11 tucked them ponderously into her belly and a cheer broke out along the strip.

Vilan was by now soaked with sweat. He watched Colonel Forrest, with Commander Smith crouched forward, take off again in his Lightning, followed by another

P-38. Colonel Roosevelt's Mosquito roared down the runway, gaining fast. Four laggard Mustangs tailed the colonel, and finally the two Fortresses rumbled off, the one with Simpson proceeding directly to the target area to watch what promised to be the greatest explosion ever engineered by man.

Joe Kennedy, rising five miles away into the setting sun, tossed up a wing and banked toward Framlingham. Vilan and Bradfield watched until they lost him in the streaky eastern sky. Then they went to chow.

3

Take-off was at 1752—eight minutes to six. The route lay southeast, north, south, and then southeast across the Channel, and it was 150 miles long, but the PB4Y-1, even loaded to the overheads, could make 150 knots and the 7 P.M. estimate at the target was well within reach. Eighteen minutes after takeoff, at 2,000 feet en route to Framlingham, Joe had the aircraft trimmed and the autopilot warmed up and engaged. He picked up his microphone and called the mother ship lagging off his stern. "Spade Flush," he said to Anderson, and Anderson began to tap the "peter-pilot" on the console before him. He flew Joe's plane by its radar blip on his scope, helped visually by Lyon's copilot, Buser, and glancing occasionally at the TV screen, which should have shown the Suffolk coastline taking shape ahead of Joe's nose bubble but which for some reason looked more like a snowstorm. But since he had control and radar he steered the drone by this to Framlingham, where he turned Kennedy left, approximately toward Beccles, and he and Joe began to check out the individual controls: elevator, aileron, and rudder, just as he had a half hour before while the drone was still on the ground.

Five minutes later T-11 should have been inland on the route from Framlingham to Beccles. Instead it had strayed seaward during the control checks and was twelve miles off its track. One mile south of the River Blythe, approaching Lumphall Walks and Newdelight Wood on the edge of the Westwood Marshes, it was droning northeastward, still roughly toward Beccles. Colonel Roosevelt's photo plane had slid within a few hundred feet for some pictures. Contrails from the Mustangs laced the wispy skies above. Commander Smith, in the nose of Colonel Forrest's plane, had Kennedy's plane in sight ahead and far below.

The Army B-17 which in half an hour, far south near Dover, was to land and pick up the two parachutists, was in a shallow dive trying to catch up. Both Joe and Willy could be seen: Joe in his cockpit and Willy in the Plexiglas nose bubble forward. Anderson's TV picture of the terrain below Kennedy was still poor, but the drone was transmitting a good one to Demlein in the other control plane and it was Demlein who after all would fly it on the final run to the target in forty minutes, so all could be said to be well.

Anderson tapped Joe into a gentle left turn. Just as he did, at 1820 Greenwich Civil Time—6:20 P.M.—T-11 exploded over Newdelight Wood with two high-order blasts one second apart.

4

Commander Smith saw it and thought nothing larger than a basketball had survived. Lyon heard his copilot, Buser, grunt, looked ahead, and saw the photo plane peel off through debris. John Demlein, watching his radar in the secondary mother plane, saw the pip on the scope disappear. Then he felt the Ventura rock under his feet. He slid from his console to Wherry's shoulder, looked ahead, and saw two bright-orange columns, one heading skyward and the other earthward: "The biggest explosion I ever saw until the pictures of the atom bomb." Wherry saw "a terrific flame and many, many pieces." Colonel Roosevelt's photo Mosquito was slammed almost to its back; he remembers barely missing wreckage. In the nearest Army B-17, B. H. de Sandre felt the Fortress thrown off course and had a sensation as if his head had been split down the middle. He tried to bail out but could not buckle his chest chute; by the time he could, the Fort was back in level flight. Today he is president of Isotronics in New Bedford, and his left ear still rings from the concussion.

The explosion had occurred over an area known to the citizens of Blytheburgh, the nearest town, as Newdelight Wood. Three hundred yards northwest of Newdelight was

Shepard's Cottage, a little brick tile-roofed house belonging to Miss Ada Westgate. Miss Westgate, a sturdy, cheerful forty-four-year-old spinster, was outside, facing Newdelight Wood and Lumphall Walks. She was chatting in the summery evening with her neighbor, who stood in her own doorway. She saw a flash like lightning and then flames in the sky, heard a "terrific, quick crack," and wheeled and ran in to "see how my people were." Her cousin, a refugee from London's buzz bombs, had been sitting by the door inside. She found that it had fallen on him and that, besides, the pantry window had dropped out. He was unhurt, but she had an aunt and uncle who lived on the Fen nearby, and it seemed to her that they had been even closer to the explosion than she, so she sent a niece upstairs to get a coat, intending to run to their house. Her niece called down. "Oh, Aunty, the ceiling's all down." While they were cleaning up the mess, her uncle arrived from the Fen: everyone there was safe.

The area became crowded with people looking for debris. Steel-helmeted American airmen of the 3rd Bombardment Division arrived in jeeps the next day, searching. There was no attempt to cordon off the area; wreckage was scattered over a mile-wide circle. There was so much of it that most of it remained where it was. One part too heavy to lift lay on the road seventy-five yards from Miss Westgate's cottage all through next winter and the following spring. Mr. Dick Collitt, of Mill Farmhouse, the forty-four-year-old district manager of the Petroleum Board, cycled past wreckage for a fortnight before he finally trucked a jagged, torn bomb-bay door, six feet by two, home to Southwald, where it remains today. Collitt, had military connections and thought he would have no trouble learning the details of the spectacular display or the origin of his souvenir, but "despite all inquiries I was unable to obtain any definite information."

Mr. Collitt was not alone. Anvil was top-secret and so it remained. The debris was too scattered to effectively remove, so the Army simply left it and the Navy for some misguided reason tried to move the scene of the explosion, possibly ashamed to admit that it had risked so great a charge over so friendly a country. Twelve years after the war, official Navy historian Admiral Samuel Eliot Morison could not obtain the documents on Kennedy's death for his naval history *The Invasion of France and Germany*. When finally he was given access, for an article in

Look, in 1962, he was led to place the explosion near the village of St. Margaret, where Joe Kennedy should have been had the plane not strayed west. Although the official Navy press release a year after Joe's death placed his target incorrectly in Normandy rather than Pas-de-Calais, that had by 1962 apparently moved too, perhaps for reasons of Franco-American amity, from the friendly soil of France to the armed German island of Helgoland. Commander Smith wrote officially two days after the blast that a search team had reported no finding; Admiral Morison, still using Navy records as source material, concluded that the plane had disintegrated completely and that "nothing big enough to pick up was found—not even a button."

There was much more than a button to be found. Sir R. B. M. Blois, a local landlord, reported that three engines fell near his Hinton Lodge; the other lay for years over a *mile* away, near Blytheburgh water tower, itself damaged by concussion alone. It took native-son Christopher Elliott of the local *Halesworth Times* twenty-five years and considerable digging to discover that Joe Kennedy was the pilot of the plane that had disintegrated over his quiet beat with what he quite correctly called "the greatest airborne explosion over England of World War II." His mild, humorous readers in the Westwood Marshes had not known who died in the sky that day, but their recollections of the event itself needed no jogging: not only was Miss Westgate's roof, which still sags, damaged, but fifty-nine other properties as well: the Blytheburgh School lost some of its glass, the Red House Institution of Bulcamp, two miles north, had lost a leaded window eight feet high, and there were three ceilings down in the police station. No one on the ground was hurt.

5

In Project Aphrodite's television-radio shack at Fersfield Airdrome, Lieutenant Colonel Joe Pomykata had for amusement been monitoring the Navy's TV picture. As a technician he was academically interested in the clear image of the Suffolk coastline he, unlike Anderson, saw unfolding beneath T-11's camera. In the next cubicle radarmen followed the drone's flight, similarly intrigued by the fat Navy signal the drone's radar beacon was sending them. Suddenly their scope swam with "grass," as if jammed: they later decided that the biggest jamming station in England had suddenly gone on the air. They reported to the colonel that they had lost the target eighteen miles from the field: then Pomykata's screen went blank itself and he felt the sudden jolt of an explosion. At that point he suspected that something had gone wrong. He had always disliked the Navy's remote-control arming, and he could only hope that whatever it was had happened after the bailout point.

Joe's radioman Dee Vilan and his mech Red Bradfield were lying on their bunks in the hut they shared with the crewmen of the Ventura control planes. At 7 P.M., when Joe's empty plane should have been blasting through the steel doors in Mimoyecques, the men from one of the Venturas walked in and began to strip off their flight gear. They avoided Vilan's eye almost furtively. They said nothing. Vilan sensed bad news and had to make himself ask for it. "How did everything go?"

A Ventura crewman said, "It didn't. The plane blew up."

Vilan hesitated and asked shakily, "*After* Kennedy and Willy bailed out?"

The crewman finally looked him in the eye. "No. They didn't bail out." For a long moment Vilan stared at the other man. Suddenly he heard Red Bradfield groan: "It was number-three engine! I shouldn't have let them take off!"

Obviously, Bradfield was wrong: ignition trouble in one engine of a four-engine plane could hardly cause a problem except on takeoff, and never an explosion. Everyone knew it, but Bradfield seemed inconsolable. Vilan put his arm around his shoulder and led him outside and finally the redheaded mechanic had to admit the magneto could have had nothing to do with it. They picked up their flight jackets against the evening chill and hopped a ride on a passing truck to the squadron office.

Everyone there was standing around in silence. Vilan was near tears; Lieutenant Lyon offered him a cigarette and took him and Bradfield aside. No one had any explanation for what had happened; Lyon thought perhaps that the load had somehow shifted on takeoff. Control pilots Anderson and Demlein had been interrogated on landing; they had not moved their "arm" or "destruct" switches, which were found wired in the "safe" position. Rumors were already starting. The Germans must be somehow to blame: sabotage or enemy jamming was mentioned. The effect of the blast could hardly be exaggerated, but was: a Lightning or Mosquito was supposed to have been so badly damaged that the pilot had been rushed to a hospital; the photo plane had had its windshield blown out.

Commander Smith drove up in a jeep. Vilan thought he looked ten years older. He called everyone into a solemn circle. He seemed to Vilan to have difficulty speaking: "This accident was very unfortunate. In Mr. Kennedy and Mr. Willy we have lost two valiant gentlemen. But we are not beaten. We are not giving up." He kept his eyes on the floor and he was biting his lip. Finally he looked up. "That's all I have to say now." He walked into his private office and closed the door.

Bradfield and Vilan stood around for a while and finally went back to the hut. The Ventura pilots had given their liquor ration to their men; the radiomen and mechs were already drunk and getting more so by the moment. The two combat veterans stretched out on their bunks. They had not been airborne; they were ignored and not even offered a drink. Vilan stood it as long as he could. Then he took his toilet gear and walked to the latrine fifty yards away, intending to clean up. He found a warrant officer, Van Marlin, standing there; Van Marlin had a bottle of Scotch and insisted that he share it. They sat on washbasins in the blackout for a long time, passing the bottle back and forth, unconscious of the urinal smells or the evening chill, discussing the accident and looking for reasons; when Vilan finally returned to the hut, everyone had passed out or fallen asleep. He threw himself on his bunk, emotionally drained, and finally he slept too.

6

Joe Kennedy's roommate, Jim Simpson, braced himself between the pilot and copilot of the Army B-17 off the coast of Calais. At target time, with the drone due, they strayed too close to the shore and drew flak from a battery at Wissant. Bursts appeared off their wings and the fuselage rattled until the plane writhed free and circled further away. No drone or escort appeared, and when finally they got the signal to return, they landed at Fersfield with no notion of what had happened. A lieutenant named Olsen met them at the plane and Simpson asked where the drone was. The lieutenant was shocked: an hour and a half had passed since the explosion and he had thought everyone knew.

He told Simpson, who has no recollection of getting to the room he had shared with Joe over a mile away. Joe's clothes were everywhere, and the casket was still half full of eggs. The eggs Simpson knew he could never eat, the clothes he and Anderson must inventory and send God knew where. He remembered suddenly that SAU had been so sure of Joe's and Willy's safety that it had not, as would be normal on a combat flight, even collected their wallets before takeoff. Tomorrow he would face, with the rest of the technicians of the unit, an investigation into the cause of the explosion.

He went to the club. At the bar he joined a group drinking toasts to Joe and Willy, to such effect that he finally found himself by a slit trench in the dark emptying his service automatic into the air in frustration and anger. Then he had to help everyone look for the source of the shots.

7

Within an hour of the blast, Commander Jim Reedy at the fleet air-wing office in Dunkeswell had the word by telephone. Ninety minutes after the explosion a top-secret dispatch was sent from Fleet Air Wing Headquarters in Plymouth informing ex-ambassador Kennedy's friend Secretary of the Navy Forrestal. Plymouth was excited enough to send Joe's middle name as "Peter" and to call Wilfred Willy "Wallord Willey." Plymouth asked that the commander of Fleet Air Wing Seven be informed when the next of kin were notified.

In Dunkeswell Reedy called in VB-110's Commander Page Knight and Mark Soden. Knight and Reedy decided to put up Joe and Bud Willy posthumously for the Congressional Medal: Soden's first thought was to notifiy Kathleen, but he knew that she was at Hyannis with the family. Now, early Saturday afternoon on the East Coast, would be a reasonable time to get it over with, but he could not make a move until the next of kin had been notified officially. Knight told him to inventory Joe's Dunkeswell effects. Reedy called the wing at Plymouth for permission to fly the next Anvil hop, if there was to be one; again he was turned down. Tomorrow he would fly to Fersfield for remains, if any; in the meanwhile there was nothing anyone could do except to head for the bar, and they did.

The next day in Boston was sultry. Father Francis O'Leary, a rotund, roughhewn Navy chaplain fresh from Pacific duty on U.S.S. *Brooklyn*, had just returned to his apartment after holding Mass and was stripping down when he got a call to report to the First Naval District Headquarters downtown. There he found, on a Sunday, no less than the admiral's chief of staff, who handed him a dispatch from Secretary of the Navy Forrestal asking that the senior Catholic chaplain in the district inform Ambassador Kennedy that his son was missing in action. A staff car waited outside to take him to the naval air station at Squantum; there an amphibious plane squatted on the runway, ready to fly him down the Cape. In half an hour Father O'Leary had landed at a tiny Navy Ordnance depot in Hyannis. The weather had turned muggier; a south wind was making up across Nantucket Sound; the local Navy aerologist informed him that the plane must leave, with or without him, in an hour. He was driven to the big white house at the breakwater. Here, alone, he stood on the wide gray porch and rang. A butler admitted him. In a room off the hallway he met Rose and Joe Kennedy, and the details are his, and theirs, for only the butler and the parents saw him and he saw no one else and assumed the rest of the family was gone. He left the house and made his plane and took off on the nose of the storm.

The house was not as empty as it had seemed to him. Jack was home on weekend leave from Chelsea Naval Hospital and so of course was Kathleen, who intended to spend the rest of the war with her family unless Billy Hartington was for some reason posted back to England. The whole family was there, even Robert, home from Navy R.O.T.C. They were sitting down to dinner when the bell rang and they waited for their parents to return to the table and it was there that Joe Kennedy, Sr., who had never breathed a word even to Rose when Jack was missing in Blackett Strait, told them their brother was gone. Then he went to his room and closed the door.

8

At the Yorkshire estate of Lady Sykes, where Joe was expected that Sunday afternoon, her houseguest had sat down the day before, perhaps while he was taking off, to write a letter to Mark Soden in Dunkeswell. She enclosed his spoils from their last gin-rummy game at Crash-Bang: "I *think* this is what I owe you. Anyway, I bet you were giving up all hope of getting a penny! Here I am, staying with Virginia Sykes plus all my children—just eating and sleeping and lying in the sun. When Kennedy has organized himself back to normal you must come up to Crash-Bang with him. We did have fun, didn't we?" She had posted the letter and this warm Sunday Virginia Sykes, who did not expect Joe for another two hours, went for a walk; when she returned, her chauffeur met her and told her that the RAF was on the phone trying to track down Lady Kathleen Hartington. She could not imagine what the RAF wanted with Kathleen, whom she knew had gone back to the States, and decided to take the call herself.

The RAF told her. So it was she, who had known Joe first and cherished him long ago, who had to tell the girl, and as if that were not enough, two days later the girl's husband was killed in a German ambush in Italy.

On Monday Dee Vilan was flown back to Dunkeswell from Fersfield. He carried Joe's effects. He went to sick bay, where his skin trouble was diagnosed as impetigo. Everyone he saw stared at him as if he were a ghost: they thought he had been killed with Joe. He delivered Joe's things to Mark Soden, who sat all day in the hut in Mudville Flats trying to inventory everything that had not gone back on Brabazon's ship to the States. Someone came in for Joe's extra combat boots—like the infantrymen in *All Quiet on the Western Front*, VB-110 had achieved a certain hardness when it came to survival equipment—and Mark let him have them.

Mark had decided from contact with Joe to study law. Lawyers—even would-be ones—are meticulous. He wrote down everything he found. There was an incredible pile:

Joe had traveled to war more like an admiral of the fleet
than a junior j.g., and he had accumulated more in Britain. There were Wilson matched golf clubs and a Dunlop
tennis racket, four pairs of colored swimming trunks, a
black and silver robe, and seven suits of pajamas. There
were copies of the *New Yorker* and overseas editions of
Time and sixteen books, including *Under Fire*, *So Little
Time*, *War and Peace*, *A Key to Pan American Spanish*,
The Unknown God, *Until the Day Break*, and *Wartime
Prayer Book*. There were address books, two rosaries, and
two St. Christopher medals, leading Mark to wonder if
Joe had had a third with him on Saturday. When Soden
had filled five boxes he knew that he could put off a
transatlantic call to Kathleen no longer: Joe had left him
instructions regarding effects to be sent her if he were
killed—a Victrola, the Underwood portable, a Zeiss
camera, and a Zenith radio. She might want them left in
England for her return rather than shipped to America. He
got through to Hyannis; despite wartime chaos on the
telephone circuits, when you wanted to speak to the ex-
ambassador, there were ways. As censors listened, he
talked to Kick, who wept and finally promised to write
instructions. The letter came in a few days: "Dear Mark—
I'm so sorry I broke down tonight. It never makes things
easier. The things he wanted me to have please send to
Flat 58, 49 Hill Street, London W.1. I don't know whether I'll ever want to use the much-discussed typewriter but
it will make me always think of that hard-talker Joe. I
still can't believe it. It's hard to write. I don't feel sorry
for Joe—just for you . . . and everyone that knew him
'cause no matter how he yelled, argued, etc. he was the
best guy in the world. . . . Affectionately always, Kick."

Two weeks later Billy Hartington, heading his column
of Coldstream Guards up a quiet road in Normandy, fell
dead to a sniper's bullet. Kathleen, in a plane provided by
the British government, flew back to his family in England, to his grave at Chatsworth, to the deserted flat on
Hill Street and the Red Cross Club off Hans Crescent.
Thinking of the resistance of their families and churches
to the marriage, she once said to a friend, "I guess God
has taken care of the matter in his own way, hasn't He?"

She finally bought from a British cabinet minister a
house in Smith Square. One Saturday evening in 1946,
while she was in the country, a man with an American
accent telephoned her home. He talked to the maid and

he asked if Lady Hartington was there. Later that night another man phoned for Lady Hartington, and when the maid left for the evening, they picked a lock and broke in. They took $25,000 in jewels and a pair of Billy Hartington's cuff links. Then they stole a pair of golden Navy wings. On the back was inscribed: "To K from J." In the press next day she pled with the thieves for the wings and the cuff links—they could keep the rest—but they never came.

7

AT Fersfield, Special Attack Unit Number one and Anvil were in trouble, but as Commander Smith had said, they were not finished. There were other PB4Y's at Dunkeswell to use as drones. There was even another pilot volunteer selected in VB-110, a lately arrived lieutenant named Ralph Spalding, son of a Navy captain. With Normandy falling into Eisenhower's hands, V-1 targets would be scarce, but there were always the sub pens at Helgoland: a long way off, but more appropriate for the Navy anyway.

First, it would be wise to discover the cause of Joe Kennedy's death. From what had been written about his father, it might be even wiser to proceed cautiously. If the ambassador was a good friend of Navy Secretary Forrestal's, even the top-secret status of Anvil might not protect anyone guilty of negligence or poor judgment. The day after the explosion Commander Smith was called to Plymouth to explain the accident to Captain Tom Hamilton, Commander of the Fleet Air Wing. Lieutenant Rosy Lyon was left at Fersfield as senior officer of SAU while he was gone, and he filled the vacuum with an informal inquiry, the results of which were inconclusive and got into Army Air Corps channels rather than Navy. His recommendation—and Tom Martin's—was simply that drones no longer be armed remotely but mechanically, as the Army's were. Smith returned to Fersfield, limping and scarred from a jeep accident at Dunkeswell which had put

Reedy, Page Knight, and Captain Hamilton into sick bay. He was not pleased with Lyon's initiative, his report, or the disposition thereof. He began his own, as ordered, to no less than the Judge Advocate General's Office of the Secretary of the Navy himself. He listed possible causes for the explosion: static electricity, sabotage, a single direct hit by "friendly" flak, gas leakage into a bomb bay ignited by an electric spark, instability of Torpex, heating of electric fuses from an unknown source, and finally, "unknown and undetermined."

He knocked them over, one by one: an explosion sparked by static electricity was improbable since the plane was carefully grounded; sabotage unlikely because the sentries had been questioned and could remember no visits by German spies; no flak bursts had been observed by accompanying planes; gasoline leakage into the bomb bay was doubtful as no one had smelled fumes prior to takeoff. Regarding the instability of Torpex and the heating of electrical fuses he reserved judgment.

His last possibility, that the cause of the explosion was "unknown and undetermined" was obviously true, but there were certain weaknesses in that as an explanation and everyone knew it and braced for a storm. Tom Killefer arrived at Dunkeswell from his carrier in the Pacific. He had orders to the British Empire Central Flying School, and he had called Ambassador Kennedy in Hyannis en route and promised to try to find out what he could about Joe's last flight. As an embryo lawyer, he had a nose for facts—now he is a vice president and general counsel for Chrysler Corporation—but as a junior lieutenant in the Navy, in transit and without portfolio, he was restricted in his investigation. He was reduced to questioning a local rector named Kenneth Williams, who swore that Joe's aircraft had exploded coming in for a landing, and Colonel Elliott Roosevelt, who would tell him only that it had exploded before his eyes in flight. He saw Jim Reedy, who was fairly open but seemed to know as little of the possible causes as he and could not discuss the mission at all. Everyone he talked to in Plymouth and Dunkeswell had gone to Annapolis with either Smith, Reedy, Page Knight, or Fleet Air Wing Seven Commander Hamilton; if any of them thought there had been negligence or poor judgment nobody was admitting it: anyway, it was all top-secret. Frustrated, Tom called Kathleen and told her that at least Joe was up for the Congressional Medal. He promised to see her in London, borrowed a weary British Spitfire to go there, had engine failure, and had to ditch in the Thames. He gave up.

Someone more technically knowledgeable than Tom Killefer was coming from Clinton, Oklahoma, headquarters for the Navy drone program. He was an electronic and ordnance expert named Clayton W. Bailey. He too was only a lieutenant, but his mission, unlike Tom's, was at least official. He was to try to solve the mystery of Joe's death before Spalding's flight. He got somehow lost en route to England, in the manner of experts, but he showed up eleven days after Joe's explosion. Fortunately he arrived in Fersfield before Spalding's hop. He had a theory. Had the flight ever reached the coast of France, the FM radio signal from Anderson's "arm" switch in the control plane had been intended to start an electrical sequence which would cock back six solenoids to arm the drone's impact fuses. After the solenoids had cocked, they were intended to be disconnected instantaneously by an automatic switch before further current through them could heat them up. Into this switch the special attack unit at Fersfield had inserted, to prevent arming by vibration or jamming, its extra safety device, the pin which was to be removed by Willy just before he bailed out. If a stray FM or jamming signal, friendly or enemy, had tried to arm the plane and the safety pin restraining the switch from breaking the circuit was still in place, the solenoids would theoretically in two and one half minutes heat up enough to explode the surrounding charge.

First, where had an arming signal come from? Not the control planes, obviously—their switches took a positive, two-handed effort to move and were found still wired on landing. But the electronic search the day before Joe's flight had shown that there *were* stray FM signals in the area. None were on any control frequency contemplated by Anvil, but nevertheless they were present. The air of Britain was in fact full of electronic garbage: even the Army used FM frequencies for tank communication. Further, the FM receiver for the arming device was set up with *two* channels in parallel so that a stray signal on either one of two separate frequencies could accidentally arm it.

No one told Bailey that there was a rumor at Fersfield that the largest jamming station in England had gone on the air just before the explosion, but an electronic search the day after he arrived, while pinpointing nothing, produced "illuminating results." The Air Corp's 3rd Division theoretically had informed jamming stations near Joe's flight route, but perhaps it would be wise to check with the British.

Bailey and Commander Smith visited the Air Ministry Lab at Great Malvern. Here they were given an interesting promise: *if* the Ministry were notified in sufficient time, they might advise the radar countermeasures network next time. The implication was that they had not been *last* time, or claimed not to have been. The Ministry seemed not particularly perturbed about Joe's flight until the two Americans suggested that Spalding's might be dumped on friendly territory should they attempt jamming.

Two days before Spalding's flight, having tried to scare the British into not doing it again if in truth they had done it the first time, Commander Smith sent Lieutenant Leonard Hole of SAU to a special Army P-38 outfit—the 100th Airborne Radio Radar Search Group near Fersfield—to pick up a plane to monitor the frequencies. Hole found to his amazement that though the unit came under the same command as Colonel Roosevelt's outfit, it had never heard of Anvil, had intercepted and misinterpreted Anvil's recent control signals, and that, with German V-2 rockets in mind, it was "working frantically twenty-four hours a day on jamming equipment and would have jammed the mission on 3 September [the next day]." The Air Corps' own communications may have been at fault—Colonel Roosevelt recalls today that the 100th *had* been informed.

So much for a signal, British or U.S., that could have triggered Joe's blast. The Bureau of Aeronautics, noting to Admiral Ernest J. King, CNO, that the controversial safety pin had not been incorporated until after *it* had delivered the plane to Commander Smith, felt safe in conceding that if a stray arming signal were received, the very safety pin that was to have prevented arming on the stray signal would have caused the arming solenoids to overheat, thus effectively pulling the rug out from under its representative Tom Martin, who had designed the whole panel for them on two weeks' notice.

The Bureau of Ordnance, which had designed the actual solenoid and fuses, set out to see if the latter would detonate if the former overheated. Admiral George F.

Hussey, the chief of the bureau, admitted that a test of six
Bureau of Ordnance fuses identical to those used proved
that they would fire in four or five minutes if treated to a
similar rise in temperature, but went on to say that none
had fired when actually *surrounded* by a charge like that
surrounding Joe's. In case the concept of an explosive
charge as a good cooling agent proved confusing, he
added that the fuses used were not intended for this
purpose anyway and suggested, as everyone else had, that
hereafter mechanical fuses be utilized. The advice came
late: Commander Smith had no further intention of letting anyone take off in a drone with remote-control fuses
anyway, and Martin, though he had never believed that
the fuses "cooked off," and does not today, agreed. Concluding, Admiral Hussey suggested again the possibility of
detonation by a single antiaircraft shell from a friendly
battery, not bothering to note that the PB4Y's familiar
Liberator silhouette, in broad daylight at 2,000 feet, with
a British-built Mosquito on one wing, a Flying Fortress on
the other, two P-38's and two Venturas astern, and sixteen
Mustangs above, was an unlikely target for British Coastal
Defense.

There the matter lay, filed under a red top-secret label,
proof apparently even against Ambassador Kennedy's connections until it seemed to matter no longer; the mystery
described as simply insoluble, a puzzle that Joe Kennedy, Sr., would presumably be too busy or weary to
investigate, and that no one bothered to solve for him.

Spalding took off without a copilot and with manual
arming on September 3 and bailed out, sustaining only
sprains. No one jammed the drone. All the rocket-sites
near Calais had been taken or evacuated, so it was flown
over the North Sea to Helgoland, encountering en route a
B-17 with false markings, apparently captured by the
Luftwaffe: the B-17 fled. Ensign Demlein had primary
control this time as the sub pen came into sight after the
long flight up the North Sea. He passed control to Anderson, as had been planned, and Anderson lost it during a
rain squall and passed it back to Demlein. By that time
Demlein had missed the chance for the sub pen, which
was on nearby Dune Island, so he slammed the drone into
a coal yard on Helgoland itself; flames rose three thousand
feet in the air. After a brief ceremony at Dunkeswell,
Spalding started back for the States with his Navy Cross,
via Port Lyautey in North Africa. Taking off from Mar-

rakech, he flew into a mountain in clear weather and was killed with his crew.

Anvil and SAU Number One were finished ignominiously, but Aphrodite and the Air Corps were not. They still had drones to use, and they intended to use them before they ran completely out of targets. A week after Spalding's flight, they sent out another mission. First Lieutenant Richard W. Lindall bailed out, nothing opened, and he was killed. The drone was shot down a thousand yards short of its target on Helgoland. On September 14, another Snowbird left, bound for an oil refinery on the Kiel Peninsula. The pilot broke a leg on landing; the mission was unsuccessful. On October 15 another Aphrodite plane missed the sub pen on Helgoland and crashed into the lower town. It leveled three city blocks, but no military installations were destroyed. The Air Corps shifted its targets to cities on the North German plains. The last two missions were on New Year's Day, 1945, against Oldenberg near Bremen. One drone hit two miles over the target and one five miles short.

Seventeen Army flying bombs and two Navy had taken off from Fersfield. None had accomplished the least military good. By May Germany was finished anyway and everyone flew home.

2

On the afternoon that he was informed of Joe Junior's death, Joe Senior did certain things that he thought he must. He called Bud Willy's young widow, Edna, in the house that Bud, as if by premonition, had made her get in Fort Worth. The ambassador asked her if she would come east to visit; if not, did she need anything? She thanked him and, though she had no idea how she would meet the mortgage on the new home or educate their three tiny children, she said no. Over the years he would become more insistent: he sent her two sons to college and contributed a hundred dollars a month until they were grown. Bucking up Bud Junior, who was flunking at Notre Dame, he said, "I wish I had a nickel for every time I failed at something."

On the weekend of the explosion Red Bradfield's father in Charlotte, North Carolina, heard that the son of the former ambassador to England was missing in action. He knew that Red had expected to fly with Joe, and suddenly he was certain that his own son was dead. He wired Ambassador Kennedy an inquiry; Kennedy was on the phone in minutes, reassuring him.

These things done, grief hit Joe Kennedy full force. Jack, at Chelsea Naval Hospital, started a book, *As We Remember Joe,* and included anecdotes submitted by Reedy, Simpson, O'Ferrall, Reardon, even young Teddy, who wrote that Joe, displeased when he let a jib sheet go in a race, "zized me by the pant and through me in the cold water. I was scared to death practually. I then heard a splash and I felt his hand grab my shirt and he lifted me into the boat. . . . One fault Joe had was he got very easily mad in a race as you had witnessed. But then he always meant well and was a very good sailor and swimmer." In the preface Jack himself, trying to be objective, mentioned Joe's hot temper, "a problem in my childhood." But he credited Joe's example for anything he or his brothers or sisters might later accomplish and his own affection comes through more plainly than any of the panegyrics he selected. He chose the closing lines of Baring's poem on spring as the final tribute:

> Our grief shall grow. For what can Spring renew
> More fiercely for us than the need for you?

The volume was privately printed and forty copies were distributed to the family and Joe's friends. Though another five hundred copies have been printed since, it is a rare book: Parke-Bernet Galleries in New York auctioned two copies for $1,500 each in 1945; in 1964, at another New York auction, a mysterious blonde who would not identify herself and said she was twenty-three but looked like a teen-ager bid $1,100 for another copy and won.

Jack Kennedy had helped blunt his sorrow by work on the book. When it was finished, his father looked at it, opened the cover, tried to start, and closed it again. In the opinion of Arthur Krock, who contributed, Kennedy has never been able to read a line in it. Years later Bob Considine, preparing an article on the family, sat at lunch on the Palm Beach porch. Joe Senior ticked off descriptions of each of his children, omitting Joe: when Considine prompted him, the ex-ambassador dropped his head. "Ask Rose about that one," he said. "She can talk about him, I can't." The columnist realized suddenly that Kennedy was crying. Rose obliged with a short sketch, as she did for the author.

Her own grief had an outlet in religion; the father turned to music. He sat closeted for months in his room listening to symphony records. He wrote Mark Soden thanking him for sending Joe's gear, which he gave away, and the old antiwar bitterness shows in the letter: "It has become such a horrible mess that I can quite understand why the boys who have to fight now wonder more than ever what they are fighting for, but you have our best wishes and our prayers. We haven't heard anything at all about Joe's award, although I got a note from Kick saying that something was going through. . . ."

The Congressional Medal never came, although it was so close that the official squadron diary of VB-110 lists it as having been awarded. Instead, Joe and Bud Willy got the Navy Cross. But that was more than the Navy-Marine Corps Medal that Jack had got for the crewman he had saved in his PT-boat disaster, and Secretary Forrestal ordered that a 2,200-ton destroyer be named the USS *Joseph P. Kennedy Junior* and the ex-ambassador made a speech as she towered on the ways at Bethlehem's Quincy Yard: she would carry Joe's spirit "over the waves as he would wish it." Joe's favorite godchild, Jean, christened her and Robert left Harvard's Naval R.O.T.C. program to serve as a seaman in her gunnery department, and when John Kennedy ordered Russian freighters stopped in the missile crisis seventeen years later, it was she who stopped the first.

The father began to recover. In seven months, as the war drew to a close, he bought Marshall Field Company's Merchandise Mart in Chicago: the "ugliest commercial building in America." He got it for less than thirteen million, because Marshall Field directors feared that when the war offices of the federal government moved out there would be unrentable space. Joe knew better, and his investment—only one million of it in cash—brought the Kennedy family an asset valued today at seventy-five million dollars.

Joe Junior's great dream had died with him, and his father's dream too of a son in the White House. And yet perhaps not: there was Jack. He has said that Jack didn't want to run for Congress but that he told him that Joe was dead and that it was therefore his responsibility. Jack once said of his brother that "if he had lived, I'd have

gone on being a writer." Those who knew John Kennedy
best, including his widow, disagree. But however it happened, Jack ran for Congress in 1946, and Joe Kennedy,
Sr., chatting in Maverick Square not far from his own
birthplace, was startled to see his second son walk up
to a group of grimy East Boston laborers as Joe Junior
would have done, stick out his hand, and ask for their
votes. Jack ran away with the nomination and won the
election.

Joe Kennedy was proud, but the ache remained. The
family worshiped in Hyannis in the neat white frame
church of St. Francis Xavier. He bought it an altar: on a
sky-blue background, a pair of golden Navy wings soars
between St. George of England and St. Joan of France.
Joe had loved Rosemary deeply; his father started the
Joseph P. Kennedy Junior Foundation, which donates a
million and a half annually to research and care of the
retarded.

There was little else he could do. In May, 1948, he was
in Paris. Kathleen would leave London to join him in
France and they would vacation on the Riviera. Her close
friend, the Earl of Fitzwilliam, one of England's richest
peers at thirty-eight, accompanied her to London Airport
and on impulse chartered a plane, pilot, and radio operator to take her. The earl went too. Fog and rain swept the
Continent that night: fifty-five persons in various aircraft
died. Fitzwilliam's plane landed in Paris, took off, and
started south for the Riviera. Buffeted by a thunderstorm,
it slammed into a ravine in the Cevennes Mountains near
Lyons. A farm worker heard the explosion; it took two
hours for local police to locate the site. From her passport, Lady Kathleen Hartington, wartime Britain's "Girl
on a Bicycle," was identified. Congressman John Kennedy
was notified in New York; he called his father in Paris.
Joe Senior flew to Lyon and motored to the little town of
Privas. Passport or not, he refused to give up hope. He
waited in the rain until he saw her body brought down
from the mountains in a peasant's cart. She was buried in
the Cavendish plot at Chatsworth, next to Billy Hartington. If anything remained of the wall that her marriage
had caused between Rose and the Duchess of Devonshire,
it was broken down now in the grief they shared.

Most of those in Britain who had loved Kathleen and
Joe were there: Lady Harlech, Lady Sykes, Frank

Moore O'Ferrall, the girl with the sky-blue eyes. The Protestant ground was perhaps unconsecrated by the Catholic Church, but so was the air over Newdelight Wood, and no one seemed to mind.

EPILOGUE

AFTER St. Patrick's Cathedral in 1968, Robert Kennedy's funeral train rocked under the Hudson River and rumbled south, twenty-one cars filled with those who knew and loved him and those who loved him and had hardly known him at all. It clicked quietly toward Washington, D.C., and Arlington, where he would lie with his next older brother John. In the press of bystanders, the train ran late through Jersey, later through Pennsylvania, later still through Maryland. At some trackside shacks a single mourner might kneel; the edge of a culvert or underpass might be jammed so tightly with bodies that those on the train held their breaths in passing; there were flags and signs hurriedly painted and hymns along the roadbed and a group of white-frocked nuns saying their beads. Two mourners intent on the funeral train were killed by another express.

In the cars it was stuffy and the bar had run out of ice. A big auburn-haired youth of fifteen moved down the aisles, stopping at each seat for a moment. In the next few months he would go to Spain with his surviving uncle to dull their pain and to fight a bull and be gored by it; next fall in prep school he would, like another uncle, tear a knee in football, but now, though his father had been dead for less than seventy-two hours, he was trying to take over the burden from his mother. Although he knew perhaps

270

not one in twenty of those aboard, he missed not one: his blue eyes were steady and his handclasp firm.

"Thank you for coming," he said, over and over. "I'm Joe Kennedy ... the Third."

CHRONOLOGY

JOE KENNEDY, JR.
1915–1944

1848 Great-grandfather, Patrick Kennedy, leaves County Wexford for Boston.
1858 Grandfather, Patrick Joseph Kennedy, born, Boston.
1888 Father, Joseph Kennedy, born, Boston.
1912 Father graduates Harvard.
1914 Father marries Rose Fitzgerald, buys Beals Street house.
1915 Joe Junior born, Hull, Massachusetts.
1917 Jack born, Boston.
1918 Rosemary born, Boston.
1919 Kathleen born, Boston.
1920 Family moves to Naples Road, Joe enters Edward Devotion School.
1921 Eunice born, Boston.
1924 Pat born, Boston.
1925 Robert born, Boston.
1926 Joe and Jack enter Noble and Greenough School (later Dexter).
1928 Jean born, Boston.
     Family moves to Riverdale, New York.
1929 Father establishes Joe's trust fund.
     Family moves to Bronxville estate.
     Family buys Hyannis home.
     Joe enters Choate School.
1931 Jack enters Choate School.
1932 Teddy born, New York.
1933 Family buys Palm Beach winter home.

Joe studies under Laski at London School of Economics. Joe visits Russia.

1934 Joe enters Harvard.
1937 Jack enters Harvard.
1938 Joe graduates Harvard.
      Joe joins London and Paris Embassy staffs, travels Europe.
1939 Joe sees Madrid fall, leaves Berlin on eve of World War II.
1940 Joe enters Harvard Law.
      Joe a delegate to Democratic National Convention in Chicago.
      Jack publishes *Why England Slept*.
1941 Joe enters naval-aviation program as cadet.
      Jack enters Navy as ensign.
      December 7: Pearl Harbor.
1942 Joe commissioned ensign.
      Joe instructs, Jacksonville.
      Jack sent to PT-boat Squadron, Vella Lavella.
      Joe sent to Puerto Rico.
1943 Joe stationed at Norfolk.
      Jack's PT boat sunk. Jack decorated.
      Joe joins Squadron VB-110, goes to England.
      Joe stationed in Cornwall. Meets The Girl in London.
      Joe transferred to Dunkeswell. Bay of Biscay patrol begins.
1944 Joe completes first tour, volunteers for second.
      May 6: Kathleen marries Billy Hartington.
      June 6: D-Day.
      June 13: First German V-1 rocket hits London.
      July 1: Special attack unit departs Traverse City, Michigan, en route Dunkeswell, England, via Norfolk.
      July 25: Dunkeswell: Joe cancels plans to return to the United States, volunteers for special-attack-unit secret mission. Drone T-11 arrives Dunkeswell from the United States.
      July 30: Joe flies T-11 to Fersfield Airdrome.
      August 4: Fersfield: four Army drones crash or downed out of four launched. One pilot killed, one pilot crippled.
      August 6: Fersfield: next two Army missions launched unsuccessfully. One pilot loses arm.
      August 12: Fersfield: Joe's mission. Joe killed.
      August 14: Girl's husband killed, Italy.
      August 26: Billy Hartington killed, France.
1948 Kathleen killed, plane crash, Cevennes Mountains, France.

AUTHOR'S NOTE

The author did not know Joe Kennedy, Jr., but like Joe found himself in the Navy when World War II began, and when his flight training was over he flew the same elephantine PB4Y-I's as Joe. The author flew them for several years over the Atlantic and Newfoundland and Labrador. While this was not combat over the English Channel or the Bay of Biscay, the weather encountered and the plane itself helped in understanding the last year of Joe Kennedy's life.

The references listed below were valuable too, and the people essential, but what helped most of all was a glimpse now and then of a certain innocence, which in the memories of some who knew him—Louella Hennesy, Rose and Robert Kennedy, the Girl—glittered through the fog of twenty-five years, and it was this that kept the task from growing dull.

H.S.

CHAPTER NOTES

Works cited by short title or author's name are cited in full in bibliography. Secret documents now declassified.

INTRODUCTORY QUOTES
"Someday I'll be President": Joe Kennedy, Jr., as quoted in interview with A. H. Whitelaw, Tar Barrel Hill, Connecticut, 2/8/68; also, Mrs. Harold Laski, London, 1/24/68.
"I'm only trying to fill his shoes . . .": John F. Kennedy, quoted in Cutler, *"Honeyfitz,"* p. 302.

PART ONE: SILVER SPOON

Chapter 1:

INTERVIEWS WITH:
James Simpson, JPK Jr.'s roommate, at Fersfield, 2/14/68; "Red" Bradfield, his mechanic, 11/24/68; Captain James A. Smith, USN (then Commander), his last C.O., 2/15/68; Demetrios Vilan, his radioman, 9/20/68; Thomas D. Martin (then Lieutenant), who loaded explosives onto his plane, 3/23/69; John Demlein and John Anderson, SAU control pilots, on 5/12/69 and 3/23/69 respectively; Robert Sweeny, an old friend and RAF pilot who introduced Joe to The Girl, 1/68; Lady Virginia Sykes, 12/3/68; Colonel Elliott Roosevelt, photo pilot for mission, 10/8/68; Marie Greene, friend of Rose Kennedy, 9/68.

OTHER SOURCES:
Author's visits to Fersfield Airdrome, Suffolk, England, January, 1968; to 151 Meridian Street, East Boston, September, 1968; to Hull, Nantasket, September, 1968. JPK Jr. letter to mother November 16, 1930. Squadron VB-110 Diary. Diary of Demetrios Vilan, Joe's radioman. Craven, *Army Air Forces in World War II*, Vol. II. Whalen, *Founding Father*, pp. 3–42. Top-secret Memorandum 14 August 1944, from Commander James A. Smith, O-in-C Special Attack Unit #1, to Secretary of the Navy. Bergan, *Old Nantasket*.

Chapter 2:

INTERVIEWS WITH:
Mrs. Rose Kennedy, 3/8/68; Richard Ludington, Jordan Marsh Co., Boston, who restored Beals Street interior, 9/1/68; Professor W. Barton Leach, who went to Edward Devotion School, 9/4/68; Helen Gallagher, JPK Jr.'s kindergarten teacher, 7/10/68; Dr. Donald Lytle, principal Edward Devotion School, 9/21/67; Senator Robert F. Kennedy, 1/17/68; Myra Fiske, ex-principal Dexter School, 9/9/68; John Clark Jones III, JPK Jr.'s classmate at Dexter, 9/9/68; Richard Flood, his Dexter athletic coach, 9/10/68; Marie Greene, family friend, 9/68; Elizabeth Dunne Anderson, a Kennedy governess, 10/7/68; Alice Cahill Bastien, a Kennedy governess, 9/11/68; Louella Hennesy, a registered nurse who traveled with the Kennedys, 9/7/68.

OTHER SOURCES:
Author's visits to Kennedy Palm Beach mansion, March, 1968; to 83 Beals Street, Brookline, September, 1968; to Edward Devotion School, Brookline, September, 1968; to Dexter School, Brookline, September, 1968. Also school records, Edward Devotion School. Also Whalen, *Founding Father*, pp. 51, 58, 59, 67, 162; Cutler, *"Honeyfitz,"* pp. 243, 244; *Fortune* magazine, September, 1937; Wheeler, *Yankee from the West*, p. 252.

Chapter 3:

INTERVIEWS WITH:
Marie Greene, family friend of Kennedys, 9/68; Eunice Kennedy Shriver, 11/26/68; Harold Klue, Riverdale School principal, 1968; Herb Corirossi, JPK Jr.'s schoolbus driver at Riverdale, 8/27/68; Tom Schriber, JPK Jr.'s Choate classmate, 5/9/69; Elizabeth Dunne Anderson, Kennedy governess, 10/7/68; Whitney Wright, JPK Jr.'s schoolmate and member of BoBeWiJo club, 9/21/68; Alice Cahill Bastien, Kennedy governess, 9/11/68; Eleanor Leavens Smith, JPK Jr.'s first love, 11/7/68.

OTHER SOURCES:
Author's visits to Kennedy Riverdale home and Hyannis, September, 1968.

Chapter 4:

INTERVIEWS WITH:
Tom Schriber, JPK Jr.'s Choate classmate, 5/9/69; Jack Hopwood, JPK Jr.'s Choate roommate, 5/11/69; Eunice Kennedy Shriver, 11/26/69; Marie Greene, family friend of Kennedys, 7/68; Mrs. Rose Kennedy, 3/8/68.

OTHER SOURCES:
Author's visit to Choate School, Wallingford, Connecticut, February, 1968. Also letters from JPK Jr. to Eleanor Leavens dated September 28, 1929, and February 3, 1930; from JPK Jr. to his mother dated December 1, 1929, and November 9, 1932. Letter from John F. Kennedy to his father, quoted in *JFK: As We Remember Him*. Letter from Rose Kennedy to Choate Headmaster St. John quoted in *JFK: As We Remember Him*. JPK Jr.'s Choate marks from Kennedy files, made available to author by Senator Robert F. Kennedy, 1/17/68. Also Whalen, *Founding Father*, pp. 135–137.

Chapter 5:

INTERVIEWS WITH:
Aubrey H. Whitelaw, JPK Jr.'s London roommate, 2/8/68; Mrs. Harold Laski, 1/24/68; Mrs. Rose Kennedy, 3/8/68.

OTHER SOURCES:
Letter from JPK Jr. to his mother dated April 20, 1934. Letter from Harold Laski to Justice Oliver Wendell Holmes dated March 25, 1929, in *Holmes-Laski Letters*. Also Martin, *Laski*, p. 62; John F. Kennedy, *As We Remember Joe*.

Chapter 6:

INTERVIEWS WITH:
Henry Lamar, JPK Jr.'s freshman coach, 5/12/69; Robert Downes and Timothy J. Reardon, his roommates, 2/11/69 and 9/25/67 respectively; Harvard end-coach Wesley Sessler, 5/9/69; backfield coach Howard Odel, 5/69; team mate Tom Bilodeau, 5/23/67; Congressman Torbert MacDonald, 10/6/68, another team mate. Also Arthur Krock, 8/30/68, and John G. F. Speiden, ranch-owner, 2/5/69; ex-police Commissioner Joe Timilty of Boston, JPK Jr.'s friend, 3/22/69; Senator Edward M. Kennedy, 9/18/68; LeMoyne Billings, a team mate of JPK Jr.; Eunice Kennedy Shriver, 11/26/68; Chet

Crosby, Wianno boatyard owner 9/11/68; Gertrude Niesen, 4/68.

OTHER SOURCES:
Author's visits to Harvard, 1967–1968. Letter from JPK Jr. to his father dated April 11, 1936; reply from Joe Kennedy, Sr., dated April 13, 1936. JPK Jr. telegram to Paul Murphy dated February 7, 1936. Arthur Siegel, "Eulogy to Harlow," Boston *Globe*, February 20, 1962. Boston *Herald*, November 21, 1937, and *New York Times*, November 21, 1937, for account of 1937 Harvard-Yale game. *New York Times*, June 22, 23, and 24, 1938, for account of 1938 McMillan Cup sailing races. Also, McCarthy, *The Remarkable Kennedys*, p. 13; Krock, *Memoirs*, p. 340; Cutler *"Honeyfitz"*; JFK, *As We Remember Joe*.

PART TWO: GOLDEN CRUCIBLE

Chapter 1:

INTERVIEWS WITH:
Louella Hennesy, Kennedy registered nurse, 9/7/68; Elizabeth Dunne Anderson, Kennedy governess who lived with family abroad, 10/17/68; Duke of Devonshire, to be Kathleen Kennedy's brother-in-law, 1/68; Terry McCulloch Scott, Embassy receptionist, 7/23/68; Lady Virginia Gilliat Sykes, London debutante and close friend of JPK Jr.'s, 12/3/68; Robert Sweeny, amateur golfer and friend of JPK Jr.'s, 1/68; Air Marshal Slessor, Aide de Camp to King George when Joe met king, 1/68.

OTHER SOURCES:
Author's visit to Princes Gate, London, 1968. Letter from JPK Jr. to a friend in New England, winter, 1938; letter to Tom Schriber, former Choate classmate, November 5, 1938; letter to *Atlantic Monthly*, February 15, 1939; McCarthy, *The Remarkable Kennedys*, pp. 13–15; Whalen, *Founding Father*, pp. 212, 213, 223, 231; Mosley, *On Borrowed Time*, pp. 29, 30; JFK, *As We Remember Joe*; Jackson, *The Spanish Republic and the Civil War*; Baker, *Ernest Hemingway*, p. 319. London *Daily Express*, 6 July 1938, for JPK Jr. in Club 400; London *Daily Express* 16 March 1938, for Kathleen Kennedy and Peter Grace. Martin Paige "Hung on Lord Harlech," *Esquire* magazine, November, 1968, p. 106. *New York Times*, March 31, 1940, for JPK Jr. meeting with Jan Wszelaki; London *Daily Mail*, December 23, 1938, for JPK Jr. and Megan Taylor. New York *Herald Tribune*, February 16, 1939, for JPK Jr.'s Valencia cable to father and latter's reaction.

Chapter 2:

INTERVIEWS WITH:
Sr. Antonio Garrigues, Spanish Ambassador to the Holy See, Rome, 2/3/68; Senator Robert F. Kennedy, who recalled hearing the firing-squad story from JPK Jr., 1/17/68; Mr. Hugh Frazer, M.P., who made trip with Kathleen and JPK Jr. through Spain after war.

OTHER SOURCES:
Author's visit to site of old U.S. Embassy, Madrid, also scene of University City battles, and Calle de Esse, February, 1968. Alumni Supplement, Choate *News*, May 13, 1939, for JPK Jr.'s description of Communist uprising and fall of Madrid. London *Daily Express*, April 1, 1939, for Joe Senior reading JPK Jr.'s letters to Chamberlain. *New York Times*, April 2, 1939, for JPK Jr. at fall of Madrid. *New York Times*, August 1, 1939, for bathing incident on San Sebastián beach. Boston *Herald*, September 19, 1939 for JPK Jr.'s return to U.S. U.S. State Department, *Foreign Relations, 1939*, Volume II, for Embassy damage and Ambassador Kennedy's reaction to threat of war. JFK, *As We Remember Joe*, for sister Kathleen's sketch of their Spanish trip.

Chapter 3:

INTERVIEWS WITH:
Charles Garabedian, JPK Jr.'s law-school classmate, 9/18/68; Tex McCrary, JPK Jr.'s wartime friend, 1968; Tom Bilodeau, JPK Jr.'s law-school roommate, 9/23/67; Lorelle Hearst, William Randolph Hearst Jr.'s ex-wife and a friend of JPK Jr., 5/9/69; Tom Killefer, law-school classmate and roommate, 9/27/68; Robert Downes, law-school classmate who shared Joe's apartment, 2/11/69; Richard Flood, another law-school classmate who lived with JPK Jr., 9/8/68; William H. Burke, 1940 Democratic state committeeman who put JPK Jr. on slate, 9/68; Speaker John McCormack, who served with JPK Jr. on state delegation, 9/1/68; Arthur Krock, who covered convention, 8/30/68; Joe Timilty, ex-Boston police commissioner, who attended convention, 3/22/69; William Randolph Hearst Jr., JPK Jr.'s close friend and host at Wyntoo, 3/17/69; Princess Pignatelli, at Wyntoo while JPK Jr. was there, 3/4/69; Mrs. Wayne Killefer, JPK Jr.'s hostess at Hermosa Beach, 10/7/68.

OTHER SOURCES:
Letter from JPK Jr. to his father in London dated March 17, 1940; JFK, *As We Remember Joe; JFK: As We Remember Him*, for JFK's letter to father regarding Nazi White Book; Donahoe, *Private Plans and Public Dangers*, for description

of behind-the-scenes politics at 1940 Democratic Convention. Whalen, *Founding Father*, pp. 296, 338, 339; Sulzberger, *A Long Row of Candles*. *New York Times*, March 30, 1940, for JPK Jr.'s part in Nazi White Book scandal; Boston *Globe*, March 17, 1940, for JPK Jr.'s name on ballot contested.

Chapter 4:

INTERVIEWS WITH:
Eunice Kennedy Shriver, 11/12/68, and Jean Kennedy Smith, 12/18/68, who both described Kennedy Christmases; Professor Arthur Holcombe, 9/18/68, and Professor W. Barton Leach, 9/4/68, who described JPK Jr.'s speaking style.

OTHER SOURCES:
Time magazine, July 22, 1940, for Ambassador Kennedy's close squeak with falling plane; Boston *Herald*, January 10, 1939, for JPK Jr. versus Townsend Plan. Boston *Herald*, October 24, 1940, for JPK Jr. distributing Roosevelt literature. London *Daily Express*, 7 January 1941, for JPK Jr. and intervention; also *New York Times*, same date. Boston *Herald*, January 26, 1941, for JPK Jr. debate with President of Williams.

PART THREE: THE MISSION

Chapter 1:

INTERVIEWS WITH:
Joe Timilty, ex-Boston police commissioner, 3/22/69; Bill Ash, a flight-school classmate of JPK Jr.'s, 2/23/69; Phil Kind, another flight-school classmate, 3/25/69; James Otis, who instructed JPK Jr., 5/69; Msgr. Maurice Sheehy, then base chaplain at Jacksonville, 8/18/68; Edwin M. Wilson, who ran against JPK Jr. in cadet election, 4/9/69; Captain Lester McDonald, then flight surgeon at Jacksonville, 3/11/69; Harry Lawrence, one of JPK Jr.'s students, 12/3/67; Captain Orville Dean, an instructor, 12/10/67; Captain Vance Dawkins, a flight-school classmate of JPK Jr.'s, 4/19/69; CPO William Sherrill, a crewman in JPK Jr.'s first squadron, 12/16/68; Frank Haines, another crewman, Chief Jack Degman, and ordnance man Bob Wurdack, 8/17/68; Admiral James Reedy, then commander, 5/1/69; Paul Brabazon, a college friend, 9/15/68; Mark Soden, JPK Jr.'s roommate, 5/1/69.

OTHER SOURCES:
"Navy Flight Instruction Record of Joseph P. Kennedy Jr.," procured for author by Senator Edward M. Kennedy, 1968. Undated JPK Jr., letters from Jacksonville and San Juan to

Jean Kennedy Smith. Letter to author from E. J. Martin, VP-203 navigator, dated December 12, 1967.

Chapter 2:

INTERVIEWS WITH:
Reedy, Degman, Timilty, Soden (see above). Also Demetrios Vilan, VB-110 radioman, 9/20/68; C. Horton Smith, squadron administrative officer, 5/10/69; William Randolph Hearst, Jr., then a war correspondent, 3/17/69; Robert Sweeny, RAF pilot and friend of JPK Jr.'s, 1/68.

OTHER SOURCES:
Letter from JPK Jr. to John F. Kennedy, dated October 15, 1943; letter from JPK Jr. to his parents, dated October 27, 1943; "Fleet Air Wing Seven History" dated 11 June 1945; "VB-110 Squadron History."

Chapter 3:

INTERVIEWS WITH:
Mark Soden, JPK Jr.'s roommate, 5/16/69; Robert O. J. Streuber, VB-110 navigator, 1/21/68; Captain Louis Papas (then Ensign), a squadron mate of JPK Jr.'s, 8/17/68; John Kellog, JPK Jr.'s copilot, 5/10/69; George Charno, VB-110 pilot, 5/13/69; interview with hostess of "Crash-Bang," 1/68; Lady Virginia Gilliat Sykes, 12/3/68; William Randolph Hearst, Jr., 3/17/69; Lorelle Hearst, 5/9/69; Frank Moore O'Ferrall, 9/27/68; Frank Borden, VB-110 navigator, 1/15/68; Captain Page Knight, second C.O. of VB-110, 9/21/68; Paul Brabazon, 9/15/68.

OTHER SOURCES:
Author's visit to Dunkeswell Airdrome, January, 1968; to Chelsea Registrar Office, London, 1968. Demetrios Vilan Diary. Squadron VB-110 Diary. JPK Jr.'s action report #1101578, dated 9 November 1943, describing attack off Spanish coast. Letter from JPK Jr. to parents, dated November 23, 1943. USN secret report of JPK Jr. on flight of 18 December 1943, describing landing at Beaulieu; also statement of Lieutenant (j.g.) Charno of flight 18 December 1943. Letter from E. Martin to author, dated December 12, 1967, on Kathleen and her friends at the Dunkeswell O-Club. Letter from Kathleen Kennedy Hartington to Mark Soden, dated May 23, 1944, describes her life as Army wife. JFK, *As We Remember Joe*, for JPK Jr.'s support of Kathleen's marriage; Whalen, *Founding Father*, p. 370, for reaction of Robert and Eunice, and O'Ferrall's description of last walk to Mass. London *Daily Mail*, 17

February 1944, and London *News Chronicle,* 9 February 1944, for Hartington's campaign for parliamentary seat.

Chapter 4:

INTERVIEWS WITH:
Lieutenant Commander James Simpson (then Ensign), radio-control expert who roomed with JPK Jr. at Fersfield, 2/14/68; John Anderson, JPK Jr.'s control pilot, 3/23/69; John Demlein, his back-up control pilot, 5/12/69; Captain Hugh Lyon (then Lieutenant), control-plane pilot, 1/20/69; Harry Wherry, another control plane pilot, 3/22/69; Warren Harrison, a control plane pilot, 2/15/69; Thomas D. Martin (then Lieutenant), who designed arming panel and supervised loading, 3/23/69.

OTHER SOURCES:
Author's visit to Fersfield Airdrome, January, 1968. Also secret documents 1 July and 1 August 1944: "USN Special Designs Branch Radio Controlled Project—Status of." Also top-secret TWX from Alfred R. Maxwell, Colonel U.S. Air Corps, Director of Operations, dated 20 June 1944, to A-3 Ops. Secret weekly progress reports from Commander J. A. Smith, U.S. Navy Special Attack Unit #1, various dates. Also Demetrios Vilan Diary. The story of Hitler's bunker hit by a V-1 is well-known, appearing in Shirer's *Rise and Fall of the Third Reich,* p. 1040; also in Manchester, *The Arms of Krupp.* It is so incredible that it bore checking on a time-distance basis; this was done, and the story is apparently true. Also, for general background on the V-1 and V-2 programs: Craven, *U.S. Air Forces in World War II,* Volume III, and Collier, *The Defense of the United Kingdom.*

Chapter 5:

INTERVIEWS WITH:
Joseph Pomykata, then a Colonel, a Fersfield technical officer with Aphrodite, 5/9/68; Colonel Fain Pool, an Aphrodite pilot, 9/25/68; Frank Houston, another Aphrodite pilot, 9/25/68; James Simpson, T. D. Martin, Captain James Smith (see above).

OTHER SOURCES:
Demetrios Vilan Diary gives chronological sequence of Fersfield events. Top-secret report of 19 September 1944 from Lieutenant C. W. Bailey, USN, to Commander Training Task Force, states Bailey's contention that explosion was caused by extra safety pin installed at Fersfield and a stray radio signal: "During test flights at Philadelphia, sensitivity of the receiver was set so that the arming panel was operated a number of

unsolicited times. This arming panel was constructed so that when the arming circuits were energized, a solenoid release on the actuating arm was energized, which permitted the arm to travel a distance and pull the four arming pins on the impact switches. As this arm reached the armed position, it opened a switch which was in series with the arming lead to the Mark 143 fuse arming solenoid. SAU-1 had inserted a pin in the actuating arm on the arming panel to prevent accidental arming of the impact switches. This in turn kept the series switch to the arming solenoid closed. This solenoid was designed for approximately 8 volts, at which it drew 3.2 amperes. As operated in the PB4Y-1, this solenoid drew 11.2 amperes, which would provide sufficient heat to detonate the fuse in about two and one-half minutes, as proven in a bench test. It is my assumption that noise or a signal on either channel three or four caused the holding relay to close and energize the arming solenoid in the Mark 143 fuse and the release solenoid for the actuating arm on the arming panel, the actuating arm being safetied with the pin prevented the opening of the series switch to the fuse with the result that the load was detonated in approximately two and one-half minutes. It is my opinion (1) that channels three and four should have been in series rather than in parallel (2) holding relays should never be used in such a circuit (3) SAU-1 should have added a master switch to the arming panel in addition to the safety pin in order that the electrical safety would have obtained as well as mechanical safety (4) the same loading and fusing can be made as safe electrically as it can be for standard impact."

Chapter 6:

INTERVIEWS WITH:
Red Bradfield, JPK Jr.'s mechanic, 11/24/68; Lorelle Hearst, who received JPK Jr.'s last phone call, 5/9/69; Elliott Roosevelt, eyewitness to explosion, 10/8/68; Captain Hugh Lyon, John Demlein, Harry Wherry (see above). Ada Westgate, ground witness to explosion, 12/68; Dick Collitt, who found bomb-bay door, 12/68. Joseph Pomykata (see above); Mark Soden and Admiral James Reedy (see above). Lady Virginia Sykes, 12/3/68; Father Francis O'Leary, 9/10/68.

OTHER SOURCES:
Top-secret report from Officer-in-Charge, Special Air Unit One, to the Secretary of the Navy (Office of the Judge Advocate General), dated 14 August 1944 and signed by Commander J. A. Smith, USN, gives flight route and loading as well as possible causes for explosion. Letter from B. H. de Sandre, dated May 15, 1963, to Senator Edward M. Kennedy describes explosion; letter from The Girl to Mark Soden, JPK Jr.'s roommate, from Lady Sykes's estate at Sledmere, is dated

Saturday. Letter from Kathleen Kennedy Hartington to Mark Soden is dated Monday. General Register Officer, Somerset House, London, certifies death of Girl's husband as occurring 8/14/44, in Italy. Whalen, *Founding Father*, p. 374, for death of Billy Hartington. Christopher Elliott, Halesworth *Times*, Suffolk, February 8, 1968, gives report of ground damage. Official inventory JPK Jr.'s effects, dated August 14, 1944, signed by Soden; also inventories signed by Simpson and Anderson. London *Daily Express*, 27 October 1946, for burglary of Kathleen Hartington's town house.

Chapter 7:

INTERVIEWS WITH:
Tom Killefer, 9/27/68; Edna Willy, JPK Jr.'s copilot's widow, 12/16/68; James Fayne, Kennedy associate, regarding father's grief and purchase of Merchandise Mart, 1/17/68.

OTHER SOURCES:
Commander James Smith's Secret Report of 14 August 1944 (see above). Top-secret memorandum, 19 September 1944, to Headquarters Training Task Force from Lieutenant C. W. Bailey (see above). Bureau of Aeronautics Report, dated September 26, 1944, from Chief of Bureau of Aeronautics to Chief of Naval Operations, signed by Admiral D. C. Ramsey, USN, disavows Bureau of Aeronautics responsibility. Bureau of Ordnance also disavows and tries to answer Bailey's report: Top-secret letter of 27 September from Chief of Bureau of Ordnance to Chief of Naval Operations signed for Admiral G. F. Hussey, Jr,. reads: "It is positively concluded that [overheating due to leaving the arming current on too long] will not result in fuse detonation when the fuse is mounted in a Demolition Charge Mark 9 and about 28 volts is applied for a prolonged period." But two weeks later in top-secret letter dated 10 October 1944, Hussey admitted the possibility: "The theory [advanced by Bailey] . . . that prolonged application of over voltage to arming circuit of fuze Mark 143 produced cook-off has been considered. The bench-test referred to [by Bailey] is believed to be one in which a fuze without surrounding charge was fired in 2.5 minutes by a continuous current of 11.2 amperes. This result has been approximately duplicated, with fuze firing in four or five minutes, but when the fuze is assembled in a Demolition Charge Mark 9 its temperature rise is less, and cook-off has not been accomplished in six trials to destruction of the arming solenoid. *It is conceivable, however that such cook-off could occur* . . . [ital. auth.] this Bureau proposes to abandon the use of Fuze Mark 143 in comparable material." Author's visit to Hyannis altar for description of same, September, 1968. Also Krock, *Memoirs;* Whalen, *Founding Fa-*

ther, pp. 372, 374, 392; London *Daily Express*, 23 May 1964, for value of privately printed book on JPK Jr. *New York Times*, July 27, 1945, for launching of USS *Joseph P. Kennedy Junior*. London *Daily Mail*, 15 and 20 May 1948, for Kathleen Hartington's death and funeral.

EPILOGUE

SOURCES:
Joseph Roddy, "The Train," in *Look* magazine Memorial Issue on R. F. Kennedy. Also recollections of those who traveled on it.

BIBLIOGRAPHY

BAKER, CARLOS. *Ernest Hemingway: A Life Story.*
Charles Scribner's Sons, N.Y., 1968
BERGAN, DR. WILLIAM. *Old Nantasket.*
Spaulding-Moss, Boston, 1968
BURNS, JAMES MACGREGOR. *John Kennedy: A Political Profile.*
Harcourt, Brace & Co., N.Y., 1961
CHURCHILL, ALAN. *Remember When.*
Golden Press, Inc., N.Y., 1967
COLLIER, BASIL. *The Defense of the United Kingdom.*
HMSO, London.
CRAVEN, WESLEY FRANK and JAMES LEA CATE. *Army Air Forces in World War II.*
U.S. Government Printing Office.
CUTLER, JOHN HENRY. *"Honeyfitz."*
Bobbs-Merrill, Inc., 1962
DONAHOE, BERNARD F. *Private Plans and Public Dangers.*
University of Notre Dame Press, Notre Dame, Ind., 1955
DONOVAN, ROBERT J. *PT 109: John F. Kennedy in World War II.*
McGraw-Hill Book Co., Inc., N.Y., 1961
FAY, PAUL B., JR. *The Pleasure of His Company.*
Harper & Row, Publishers, Inc., N.Y., 1963.
HOWE, MARK DE WOLFE, ED. *Holmes-Laski Letters.*
Harvard University Press, Cambridge, 1953
JACKSON, GABRIEL. *The Spanish Republic and the Civil War.*
Princeton University Press, Princeton, N.J., 1965
KENNEDY, JOHN F. *As We Remember Joe.*
Published privately, 1945
KROCK, ARTHUR. *Memoirs: Sixty Years on the Firing Line.*
Funk & Wagnalls, N.Y., 1968

MANCHESTER, WILLIAM. *The Arms of Krupp.*
  Little, Brown & Co., Boston, 1964
MARTIN, KINGSLEY. *Harold Laski, 1893–1950.*
  V. Gollancz, London, 1953
MAYER, MARTIN. *The Lawyers.*
  Harper & Row, Publishers, Inc., N.Y., 1966
MCCARTHY, JOE. *The Remarkable Kennedys.*
  Dial Press, N.Y., 1960
MOSLEY, LEONARD. *On Borrowed Time: How World War II
  Began.*
  Random House, N.Y., 1969
SCHAAP, DICK. *R.F.K.*
  New American Library, N.Y., 1968
SHIRER, WILLIAM L. *The Rise and Fall of the Third Reich:
  A History of Nazi Germany.*
  Simon & Schuster, N.Y., 1960
SORENSEN, THEODORE C. *Kennedy.*
  Hodder & Stoughton, Ltd., London, 1965
SULZBERGER, C. L. *A Long Row of Candles.*
  The Macmillan Company, N.Y., 1968
U.S. STATE DEPARTMENT. *Foreign Relations 1938, 1939* (Vol. II).
  U.S. Government Printing Office.
WHALEN, RICHARD J. *The Founding Father: The Story of Joseph
  P. Kennedy.*
  New American Library, N.Y., 1964
WHEELER, BURTON K. *Yankee from the West.*
  Doubleday, Garden City, N.Y., 1962

Index